HANGING BY A THREAD

HANGING BY A THREAD

A Peacebuilder's Quest to End
Zimbabwe's Political Conflict

Edward Chinhanu

To order additional copies of this book, contact:
Xlibris
1-888-795-4274
www.Xlibris.com
Orders@Xlibris.com
803272

Contents

THIS BOOK IS DEDICATED TO THE MEMORY OF MY LATE FATHER;

G.D. CHINHANHU

For planting the seed
Father, you suffered silently under Zanu PF, and died with the hurt and hate. May Your Soul Now Rest in Peace.

AND THE LATE

MAIKURU JESCA

For tending and watering the seed with warm tears. "They were their pumpkins."

ACKNOWLEDGMENTS

The writer wishes to thank the following people, who helped in different ways, unbeknown to them, in the writing of this book:

Batsirai Webster 'Tsano Mbuu', for typical Ghetto style brotherhood

Fay Ballard for typical, top-class Rotary Peace Fellowship, friendship and inspiration.

John Guri, for keeping me company, carrying my bag and taking me off work, during stressful times

My daughter Chiedza Chinhanu for facilitating a lot of things

My brother, David Chinhanu, for being there when needed, as always.

Jeff Mapungwana for probing and encouraging questions

My wife, Julia Chinhanu, for the comfort, meals and gracious company when needed

Doreen Ruwocha, for the cigarettes. They kept me alive and going, but I'm quitting now.

Mai Vangu, My spiritual mother, Mbuya Mukwindidza. Thank you, mum for your blind faith and encouragement. You're a typical Ghetto Style-e Mother.

My 'Other Mother', Mbuya Marjory Nyandoro, you're an inspiration, a shelter and a brimful of love and patience.

Mai Katsande and Mr. Pahla at the Turner Memorial Library, and Lucy Chiduku at the American Corner of the same library.

. Thanks for the help.

Mr. & Mrs. Muchacha and their son, Admire, at the Ministry of Youth, Sport, Arts and Recreation building in the Showgrounds

John Nyamunda for sharing the script on 'How to Eat Sadza'.

Mr. Never Chanza of Carltec Internet Cafe

Hubert Masvikeni

My Maininin Mrs Soneni Marimo Chinhanu

Mr and Mrs Nyamadzawo and Tsverukai Dube at Chikanga Spar market. You win my Best Business Couple of the Year 2019 Award! Keep the fire burning.

Addmore Maningi at Chikanga Spar. Yours is one of the most expressive Zimbabwean names, like Tutsira Stereki, a lady I knew growing up.

All the ghetto crews at Chikanga Spar and Mwamuka. I say, keep your hopes alive. The ghetto never dies!

All of you are safe. The regime will not hurt or even ask you a disturbing question. Get ready for the tasks ahead!

THE FIRST 10-15 YEARS OF INDEPENDENCE (1980-95)

"Darling", said Farai one Sunday morning as he got out of the cold shower, rubbing at his hair with a large towel, "prepare Melissa, I want to go with her to the stadium."

"Ah, really? She's still too young, Fatso. She will worry and bother you."

"That's no problem. I'll manage. Just prepare everything that she'll need."

"You're serious aren't you? But she hasn't slept a wink yet since she woke up. She might fall asleep anytime. That- and the toilet business. I tell you, it's not a wise idea going to that packed stadium with her."

"We will manage, I tell you. Are you taking me for an irresponsible father? I see so many fathers who come to the stadium with their little babies. So proud and fatherly. Some of the kids are even younger than Melissa. One and a half years is old enough to explore and enjoy the open air and colourful crowds."

"Open air in the stadium? She might even pick up the flu or some disease from the coughing drunks who urinate everywhere in there."

"We will find seats in good places. We will sit in the shaded area. Not the Vietnam terraces. Just get her ready."

"OK. if you say so. Her pram is ever ready. Let me see to her toiletry and stuff."

Farai's wife proceeded to make her baby ready for the journey to the stadium. The journey itself was an easy, leisurely walk among the colourful crowds who littered all roads to and from the Munos shopping centre down the road. It was a bright, beautiful Sunday morning, and the local Tanganda Football club was playing Dynamos from Harare.

Farai felt proud as he pushed his beautiful baby ahead of him down the road. She was all pink and red, and sucked fresh milk from a red plastic bottle. He was in a bright red Liverpool jersey, which matched perfectly with his khaki jeans, a latest purchase from GR Leach, finest clothes merchants in town. He knew people admired him from all fences, windows and hedges, and so, proudly he went.

At the shopping centre he stopped, looked around for his gang of friends and noticed one or two at the far end, out on the lawn. He made a beeline for them. They were happy for him, but one of them asked, "Why the baby, Fatso?"

"Haa, I just thought I should bring her. You know, the mother is busy with this and that, and I'm free, so why not?" He could tell that his friends envied him, but were reluctant to admit it.

He accepted a mug from one of them, and brought it to his lips. It was around eleven o'clock, and the game would start at 3. There was still plenty of time yet before the stadium filled up, though people were trickling in and a booming voice reached them from a PA system inside the ground. It was promising to be a jolly good afternoon, just like in the good old days, Farai thought.

A few more of his friends came to join them, and a round of lagers was bought. Farai sat down, watching over his baby. More friends came, and more beer, and the tales and jokes started.

Most of them were in their early or mid-twenties and knew each other very well. They had attended the same primary or secondary school, and most had been classmates, or they were very close neighbours, or had played plastic balls together in the streets as boys.

As usual, when they met like this most of their talk centred on five things: education, girls, beer, music and a little about work. All of them were employed across the town and industries and had money to spend.

Teachers, too, were many and in those days after independence, teaching was a well- paid and respected job, attracting some of the best brains.

The government was also engaged in a huge investment programme to expand the education system, and schools were opening up between less than 5km.

In the urban high density areas, designed by colonialists for urban workers' dwelling, there was little or nothing else to do around the small yards and gardens, except sit around and read, or spend time in the council and private bars and restaurants scattered across town. Very few homes had TV sets. Despite this, life was very good and very few people were very poor.

Uppermost on the boys' minds was their education. During that time, students competed with each other to get a place at the most popular boarding schools, and these included St. Augustine's, Hartzel, Chikore, Goromonzi, Fletcher, St. Mary's, St. Faith's, Gokomere and others. They were so serious with books, and nothing else, to the extent that they made sure that their future was guaranteed.

I remember role models like Oliver Chapeyama, Weston Tawonezvi, Wilson Kakumura, the late Peter Chipunza and others who set trends in education, lifestyle and Ubuntu, and everyone desired to be like them.

They also competed among themselves in the area of social development. Some would buy housing stands, full houses and furniture. They also sought to improve themselves job-wise, and sought to attend as many courses as they could.

The guys also shared and exchanged music by rock bands like AC/DC, Thin Lizzy, Boston, Chicago, the Commodores, Lionel Ritchie, Bob Marley, Jimi Hendrix, Roy C and a variety others. They played and sang wildly along to the music of Crosby, Stills and Nash, especially Suite: Judy Blue Eyes

Bob Marley had come and celebrated independence with them in Rufaro Stadium, and Zimbabwe was on top of the world. Live on stage, Marley had lit a marijuana cigarette, to the joy and celebration of fans. Years later, the police revealed that they'd tried to arrest him, but had been stopped by a higher power. Though the story tells you a lot about implementing the law in Zimbabwe then, most people would swear that nobody would touch Bob Marley that night. Another war for another freedom would have started, and again, won by the people.

But the fact that an individual, one person, would free a guilty Bob Marley points to dictatorship, and a violation of the law by that individual.

Perhaps that is the early signs of the tricky thing about the Zimbabwean people and their dictatorship. It serves certain people, disregarding others.

When Zimbabweans look back to that incident with the benefit of hindsight, Bob Marley should've been arrested, and later freed by a court of law, either that night, or the following morning.

This is because if you make the law supreme, you promote equality among yourselves, equal access, and fairness in all things about life.

Those early years, Thomas Mapfumo was already established, but that was also the time Oliver Mtukudzi (Tuku) rose to fame Leonard Zhakata came onto the music scene later to sing about things gone bad. Locally the guys revelled in and with the RUNN Family, their own local music international export, with popular song commiserating the death of President Samora Machel of Mozambique in 1986.

The boys' meeting place every Saturday was the Stirrup Cup Bar, where John Dhliwayo and his band made live performances of John Denver's Leaving on a Jet Plane", Tracy Chapman's 'Talking About the Revolution', and many, many other popular songs of the day.

The bar itself was so small, but they all fitted in there. It was always full, but never too full. People kept pouring into the smoke-filled happiness hole, right into the wee hours.

That was the most popular drinking day across town, and on other days during the week, they did not meet much, and there were no cell phones then.

Even years later, as late as 2018, radio DJs and television presenters continued to talk about the 80s as the period of the best music in living memory. There was no satellite TV yet, and so music was the biggest pastime as they competed on who had bought the latest Rock, Reggae, Country, and so forth.

That time, music was mostly in the form of LPs and cassettes, and the guys criss- crossed streets carrying these.

They also paraded their latest jeans and bell bottoms from CT Stores, GR Leach, CW, Barnard and Hodges, and other shops in the city. As a result, they were always smart. But they drank too much, especially in the Stirrup Cup.

It was the time of the Harare Mambos, Safirio Madzikatire, Lovemore Majaivhana, Mai Rwizi, George Shaya at Dynamos, and Hulk Hogan in the wrestling ring and Big League Soccer on television.

On Sunday, they had a similar pattern. They would leave home early for the local bottle store, under the pretext of 'buying the Sunday Mail' newspaper. However, they would often end up as far away as Fiesta Park, Inn On The Vumba, Tukuza, Matimba, Dangamvura, Madziro, White Horse Inn, or even Harare, without breakfast.

Those who liked church would go, often visiting friends' churches as guests. There were more established churches than indigenous ones, and people either belonged to those ones or did not go at all. It was real freedom, at last.

Of course, they always came back for work the following Monday. They had a strong work ethic, because they knew their life depended on it, even though the boss was black or white. They regarded their jobs as their second identity, and no one messed with that. It was the joys and adventures they sought.

The guys lived the life of their work and music. They matched it, and spoke of it so knowingly you'd feel blended with it. They were on top of the world. They felt safe to do anything with anyone in the world.

And why not? Because they were educated, knew things, and were hardworking.

Money was pouring into the country from all corners of the world, and there was expansion everywhere, schools, clinics and hospitals, roads, agriculture and every facet. A project called ZIMCORD had been started by the then Minister of Finance, Bernard Chidzero, to pool international resources for a new Zimbabwe.

Everyone supported the same ruling ZANU PF party, and there were no differences. No one worried about politics, neither was it a taboo subject for public discussion, as it later became. Things appeared good and showed great signs of improvement. Zimbabwe was headed for heady days. The days of milk and honey as was said by their liberators over the radio and newspapers.

It was also a time women and girls' rights were being enforced, a time for equal rights between men and women. Many feminists and child rights groups rose. Women and girls could also freely put on trousers without any shame, embarrassment or second thought, for the first time.

The wearing of pants by women revolutionized sex in men, especially the traditional minded, most of who regarded the perfect woman as one with large buttocks and full fleshed body.

There were a lot of interesting discussions over women's rights in courts of law, universities and other institutions. The country was poised for development in all spheres of life, and everybody was equal before the law. Zimbabwe was in sync with the world.

During that time, there were also some interesting communities of interesting fat white folks, and their pencil slim and quick footed ladies who gathered at social clubs and dam sites for fishing, water games, as well as camping and mountain climbing in Nyanga and Chimanimani. The town was full of white folks from different parts of the world; Germany, Greece, Ireland, Portugal, Sweden, Denmark, you name it.

The fat white guys remained aloof. But the ghetto guys knew it was to keep them far from their wives. The guys knew that once you caught a white lady, you were in for both love and money. It was the sweetest love.

A love affair with a white lady was fierce, furious and intense, and the boys made the best of it, even though it could be very dangerous.

But they were sure to keep their skills sharpened.

By the way, nobody had ever heard the word AIDS, and a very small group of people knew a condom, or talked about it.

And those were the days the younger, growing up guys paraded their private parts to all and sundry, especially when they'd contracted syphilis or gonorrhoea, or any other visible clap, to show that they were men. They would do so proudly, with a dozen pairs of keen eyes glued. They were quick to visit Dr. Obonyo's the next Monday, to get the clap fixed. And it was sure to get fixed.

In the sprouting secondary schools known as 'upper tops', some scholars changed their names and assumed fancy names like Fairfax, Denver, Pride and so forth. This was in order to move with the times. This was before names like Nigel, Spencer, Brenda and other popular ones took hold. And of course, among the Gweja Generation, the most common and popular name today is Tawanda, or T1 for short. There're very few places you can go in Zimbabwe without finding a T1, be it at a market, growth point, combi rank, church, bar or anywhere.

To these guys at that time, falling sick and being admitted in hospital was a welcome relief for detoxicating and recuperating from life's abundant joys, because the General Hospital was well staffed with well-trained, equipped and immaculate professionals. Usually, they came back changed, with rosy cheeks and a healthy body. They would stop drinking for a while, only to start again with a vengeance, after a month or two.

There was also a thriving coloured community in Florida. Most of these guys were into motor and diesel mechanics, and drove around in the fanciest home engineered cars and bikes. On most weekends they would fly warm air balloons across the sky, and drink all day.

Often, there were a few fights between blacks and coloureds. And these were mainly over girlfriends or a shoddy business deal.

Otherwise all communities had friends in other communities, and the guys would mix and mingle all day and night, and the atmosphere had a peaceful and relaxed aroma.

Just like the word 'condom', 'corruption' was an unknown and unused word. Today, however, kids learn the word in school and the streets, and every one of them secretly love it, because they know it means 'money', which is so hard and painful to come by.

The first and only sign that things might not go well for Zimbabwe was the Willowgate Motor Scandal in 1988. In it, some government ministers and other high ranking officials were discovered to be buying luxury cars from the Willowvale Mazda Motor Industries at very low prices.

Names were publicly named in newspapers and other media. Although Mugabe was embarrassed by the publicity and spoke strongly against the practice, he did not take any action against the mentioned ministers and officials, and only one of them, Maurice Nyagumbo, committed suicide over the scandal.

Life soon returned to normal for the rest of them, and it appeared all they had to do was be a bit more discreet. Unbeknown to the public, stealing, looting and other corrupt activities would go on in Zimbabwe. The Willowgate Scandal was only a tip of the iceberg.

Now, thinking retrospectively, the guys knew that Mugabe that his ministers looted, but ignored it. He would use their corruption crime to do his bidding. And they did, on their knees, begging and giving presents.

This was how he felt; a natural, perpetual King, with everybody begging favours.

That was also the time many lives were lost, especially through HIV/AIDS.

The country was full of love. For why not? Independence and freedom was here, at last. Freedom to do what they wanted, how they wanted it, and when. Dreams had come true, it was a time to show happiness and extend it to all and sundry. At one time, people who kept records said between six and nine people were buried at St Josephs and Yeovil Cemeteries each day.

There was a strong similarity between Zimbabweans and South Africans on that score. When freedom came with the release of Nelson Mandela in 1994, South Africans perished as they succumbed to HIV/AIDS. It was estimated that as many as 6 million died. Zimbabwe was not far off.

Many favourite friends lost each other, and one lived in perpetual fear that they might be next. It seemed there was no escape, for as long as one continued to have intercourse. Indeed, it was by the Grace of God, or luck, and certainly not intelligence, for those who survived.

Otherwise they were all prone to the disease, curtesy of a husband, wife, girl friend or boyfriend. Unless one totally abstained, which many found a hard road to travel. It was not as easy to break from sex as it was at the time of writing, and many innocent people were killed, with their eyes wide open.

It was that period which wiped away the myths about death and dead people in the minds of many Zimbabweans. And today, kids can play soccer with plastic balls, raising dust and shouting at each other, while across the road, or next door, people are mourning a death. Cars too speed past, wild music blaring.

To these guys, life was gone to the dogs.

As Farai drank with his friends, he began to question the wisdom of taking his daughter into the full stadium. Then he remembered 'Queen Latifa', his high school girl friend who lived with her own 2 year old son in the same suburb. As others got into the stadium, he pushed the pram up towards Mazhambe suburb. Luckily, Queen was there. "No problem", she said at once. "She can play with Tawanda here. And I will be here all day. But what about nappies and stuff?"

"Use Tawanda's. Here's a dollar for more milk and things, just in case." And he turned and directed his feet to the stadium.

War Vets

Still in those days of plenty, the country's liberation war heroes, otherwise known as war veterans, were loved and respected. To be honest, though, it was a love mixed with fear and awe. They moved around in threes and fours, drank together, mixed with the crowds, who never got tired of listening to the tales of war. Everywhere they went, they were held in awe. They were especially known for discipline and cultural respect. Their respect for culture and the elderly was second to none. This however was in spite of their heavy drinking and concomitant unruly behavior.

While some of them joined the army, others opted for civilian life. These had the option of going back to school, form agricultural cooperatives, seek other jobs or anything they wanted. They were highly privileged and received priority over all other groups of people on anything.

They also received money from various sources, besides the pensions, monthly Bush Allowances and grants to start up projects. Such preferential treatment made them view themselves as one and the same with the country they had liberated, and some of them knew no law binding them.

Many fights broke up in bars and public places between a war veteran and policemen or their groups, or between war veterans and soldiers. The war veterans always made sure that they won, no matter how or the circumstances, just as they had won the country.

A fistfight victory over a war veteran was taboo, and no matter how much they were thrashed and left for dead, they would gang up days, weeks or months later and do anything to revenge. The bulk of their behavior made people doubt their sincerity in respect, and whether it was not a way of demanding that respect themselves.

As it turned out, the majority of the war vets had not been well prepared and trained for integration into civilian life. They were not told that civilians were people with special rights. Instead, the war vets continued to use and abuse civilians as they did during the war; commanding them, bullying them, and mistreating them. There was no change from the war. This time around, with more freedom, the war vets dominated society. They became the crème de la crème of society.

The idea of free money flowed easily among them and affected war vets negatively, such that many of them did not invest in income-generating projects, nor did they put the money to much good use, such as building homes. The bulk of the money was spent at bottle stores, bars and restaurants. They threw parties everywhere, where they were the centre of attraction and bragged about defeating the British army.

"Where else have you heard it?" some of them would seriously ask, "that a mere guerrilla army, untrained in modern warfare, can defeat one of the best armies in the world?" and they would pause briefly for effect, then continue, "We are unique, I tell you! And we were guided by the spirit of Nehanda. We are not ordinary!" and they would dance their feet off.

Needless to say, this sense of invincibility made them do anything they wanted. They would claim any girl or woman, no matter they did not match the class or standard.

To demonstrate that they had a lot of money, stories were abound of them buying alcohol for all patrons in a bar. They would feed starving, teetering cattle with cabbage at the growth point shops, or would sponsor a soccer or netball competition for a day, for money. Their money was for spending, and spend they did.

However, the money did not come from government, but had been donated by the international community as part of the demobilization, disarmament and reintegration programme. Consequently, it ran out, and the veterans became destitute. Most, if not all the self-help projects that some had started folded up.

Between 1995 and 1997 the war veterans ganged up and threatened to withdraw their support from the government unless their role in the liberation struggle was recognized. "This is the case in every country," they argued, "War veterans are entitled to a life pension. Go to America right now, and you will find that those who fought in the Vietnam War, more than 50 years ago, are still getting money from their government. It is the same in Britain. Soldiers of the British army, which we fought and defeated, are receiving allowances and pensions, right now as we speak. What about us, the victors and owners of the money and country? No. That's impossible! If necessary, we will go back into the bush to fight for what belongs to us! We died for this country!"

That became a very common statement, "I /We died for this country." It entitled the speaker to everything in that country, without any question.

At this point the economy was showing signs of slowing down, but had stabilized, with the Zimbabwean Dollar pegged at ten per cent against the US $. Though many (white) investors and industrialists had left for South Africa at independence, the 20 000 that had remained were committed to the country. Most of these did not have anywhere else to go. The only home they knew was Zimbabwe, and they were determined to make the best of it.

Because of pressure, the government gave in to the war veterans' demand. Each of them was given 50 000 Zimbabwean Dollars. So began the culture of 'free access to everything', in the country. This was a very huge sum, and which had not been budgeted for. Again, there had not been prudent research by the government to establish how many war veterans were still alive, or what impact would such a huge sum of money have on the economy.

There was an interesting guy that period, Chenjerai Hunzvi, a trained medical practitioner and a war veteran of some sort. He carried out medical examinations on war veterans to determine what percentage, and how much they would get.

Some people with 99% disability could walk, drive, laugh, and make love and everything else. This became popularly known in the vernacular as Mari Yezvironda, or, literally, money for wounds/damages.

That was another looting, separate and besides the $50 000 gratuity to each war veteran.

As it turned out, the number of living war veterans had actually increased since the days of the war. While at independence the figure had been less than 40 000, this time it had risen to 50 000. This day in November, on which the pay-outs were made, was known as Black November and signalled the collapse of the country's economy.

Again there was squander and jubilation.

AN OVERVIEW OF ZIMBABWE'S POLITICAL MINEFIELD

A sustainable resolution to Zimbabwe's political conflict lies in a good understanding of the country's brief political history, since independence. It also allows us to design the right tools and consult key people.

The country was colonized by the British in 1890.

As the years went by and the demand for independence and freedom from the black nationalists heated up in the 1960s, the British relented and demanded talks between the Rhodesia Front Government, led by Ian Smith, and the nationalists. Smith, however, could not listen to that, and declared what became known as the **Unilateral Declaration of Independence (UDI)** in 1965.

So, it is not correct to say that Zanu and its guerrillas fought and defeated the British army over Zimbabwe. They fought the Rhodesia Front, under Ian Smith. During that war, Smith's government had global sanctions imposed on it, and the guerrillas received a lot of international support in their 30-year struggle.

By then, ZANU had been formed in 1963, under the presidency of **Ndabaningi Sithole**.

There was infighting within ZANU, and other leaders came. Herbert Chitepo came in briefly as Chairman. Mugabe assumed presidency of ZANU in 1975, after Ndabaningi Sithole. Soon, ZANU overtook ZAPU, an older political party with a longer history of the struggle, under Joshua Nkomo, a Ndebele, otherwise known as 'Father Zimbabwe'.

There were always infights within ZANU, but it commanded widespread support from the masses, because it was Shona-led, and the latter are larger in population than the Ndebele.

When elections were finally held in 1979, after the **Lancaster House Conference**, ZANU won with a clear 51% majority. By then, it had assumed the PF, to differentiate it with Sithole's ZANU. It is important to note here that none defeated the other in the war. Smith took heed to calls against massive civilian killings and agreed to the talks.

Allegations of a tiff between Mugabe and his general, **Josiah Tongogara** and which led to the latter's death just before freedom and independence, were also rife.

Mugabe was very popular in Zimbabwe and abroad. **Bob Marley** came to sing at his inauguration. Mugabe adopted the socialist ideology as a guide to his administration and the nation. However, he could not tolerate any opposition. He parried off opposition from the losing parties and their candidates: **Ian Smith**, Sithole, **Bishop Muzorewa, Joshua Nkomo** and others. He said nasty things about them, rallying the nation to see them as against development of the Zimbabweans he had liberated. He also went on a hunt for his opponents, killing and incarcerating them.

Finally, Joshua Nkomo saw reason and decided to stop the fights and unite the nation. He signed the **Unity Accord** with Mugabe's Zanu in 1987. The majority of Nkomo's ZAPU members, however, were not included in the talks, and did not agree with what Nkomo had done. They remained silent, however, with some of them being delegated ministerial positions, especially that of Home Affairs, and a guaranteed vice presidency.

That was Mugabe's dream; a one party state, with him as supreme leader. He could not imagine any opposition party ever rising in Zimbabwe.

Some observers say this Unity Accord was the start of the road to failure by the party. With the Accord, the party took within its fold different people with different agendas. Some hated the party for one reason or the other during the long, bitter struggle, wanted to settle scores, and pursued their own personal or previous party agendas.

Zanu P.F. continued to run the country with little but insignificant opposition until Mugabe's own Secretary General during the war and after, **Edgar Tekere** formed the **Zimbabwe Unity Movement (ZUM),** The party fought hard and provided a possible alternative, but Tekere dropped off midway towards elections, and re-joined ZANU PF, leaving the people hanging.

When the **Movement for Democratic Change (MDC)** was formed in 1999, the environment was tense. People slowly turned to it at first, out of fear, but later came in numbers. Sensing danger, Mugabe adopted all sorts of strategies, techniques and tactics to put it down. However, the harder he tried, the more determined became the people. Events during the first campaign of the MDC are well documented by national and international organisations. In the face of armed soldiers and secrete police operatives, the people continued to support the MDC. In the first election in 2000, the MDC won most of the parliamentary seats. That became a wakeup call for Mugabe. He ranted and unleashed terror on the nation.

Living standards began to fall, as money ran out due to unbudgeted pay-outs, such as to war veterans, and others, including Mugabe's globetrotting with large entourages. Mugabe sustained his hold on power by using the war veterans, and food, and other things necessary for survival.

This became his trend at every election time. He would use Lorries and busses to ferry people to rallies in their thousands, as if to say to the world, "See? Do you see how popular I am?" Using those people filling up stadiums and grounds, with people he forced to come to rallies, he would rig the election. He knew that he did not have support, but used crowds as support, then rig elections. He also had widespread use of the army and secret services. In all cases, he used tokens such as farms, business licenses and other much needed perks that people desperately wanted.

The biggest and hottest elections came in 2008. Mugabe clearly and resoundingly lost. There were countrywide beatings of people, in what was termed 'Operation Who did You Vote For (wavhotera papi?)/ It later came out that Mugabe had conceded defeat in that election, but was told to stay put by his Deputy, now President Emmerson Mnangagwa.

After a spell of beatings, somebody suggested and offered the money for a re-run. Fearing that his supporters would go through another painful experience, Tsvanagirai withdrew from the re-run, and of course, Mugabe ran alone, and won.

Things remained tense, until Mugabe called for a **Government of National Unity (GNU)** with Tsvangirai's MDC, and the other split MDC led by Welshman Ncube. The GNU was signed in 2009.

Soon after its formation, things began to change for the nation. Empty shop shelves filled up, and in three weeks banks had money. Life returned to normal for Zimbabweans. This was a period of bliss.

However, it appeared the MDC slept on duty while in government, because the GNU was for five years only, and in the next election in 2013, they lost to Zanu PF and were booted out. Soldiers were also involved, threatening and beating up opposition supporters. Mugabe was back firmly in the driving seat now, as he had always been.

There followed another period of campaigning. Tsvangirai had become sick with cancer, under heavy Zanu PF food poisoning suspicions. He died before elections, and his two deputies assumed power at the helm of the MDC.

There was a fallout between the two deputies, with Nelson Chamisa emerging the legitimate heir to Tsvangirai.

After much infighting over who should succeed Mugabe (at 94) in Zanu PF, there was a coup on 14 November, 2017. The coup was by Mugabe's General, Constantino Chiwenga, on behalf of Mnangagwa. In an operation code-named **'Restoration of the Historical Legacy'** Chiwenga and his colonels wanted Mugabe out, and Mnangagwa in.

Millions of Zimbabweans participated in that coup, hoping at least for another GNU. It never came, and right now the country is under military rule, with Chiwenga as Vice President.

Thokozani Khupe, the other MDC president, continued using the name for her own party and supporters, while Nelson **Chamisa** teamed up with other earlier MDC splits of **Welshman Ncube, Tendai Biti** and others, to form the MDC Alliance. They contested the 2018 elections under that banner, won, but lost to Mnangagwa's shenanigans. Chamisa launched a **Constitutional Court** application challenging the results, but even as he did so, the nation knew he had no chance. In a case presided over **by Justice Luke Malaba,** Chamisa lost. There were many allegations, including over the mismanagement of the election and its results by **Justice Priscilla Chigumba**, Chairperson of the Zimbabwe Elections Commission.

Now, as the nation waits for **the 2023 elections**, life is gloomy for the majority of Zimbabweans. Prices are skyrocketing every day, there is no electricity, fuel, jobs and other amenities. That year is too far ahead for many Zimbabweans and, when it comes, it will bring another bloody election filled with irregularities, forced disappearances, torture, beatings, rape and all other forms of human ill-treatment.

Celebrating the Gun.

Though independence came as a result of the Lancaster House Conference in London in late 1979, which opened way to elections in 1980, Zanu PF insist that it was the gun that brought independence and freedom to Zimbabwe. The song 'Zimbabwe ndeyeropa (is about blood) is very popular in the party, and many Zanu PF members died tragic deaths after independence, for their work in the party and government, talk **of Border Gezi, Eliot Manyika, Moven Mahachi, Edward Chindori Chininga** and others. All these Zanu PF patriots met their deaths under suspicious, unclear circumstances. The art and skill of politics was determined by who held the gun. Even the people must shut up. Up to now, nobody has managed to point a finger at the chief suspect in the killings.

The people of Zimbabwe are traditionally peaceful, so Zanu PF uses the gun, a symbol of violence, to keep and maintain them that way. Violence was spewed everywhere, with threats of arrest, deprivations, torture, forced disappearances, beatings and other forms.

Another major stumbling block to any aspiring president for the country is the cry by Mugabe and his Zanu PF stewards that no person who does not have liberation war credentials can ever be president of the country. This mantra shuts out a lot of capable Zimbabweans from the race, and should be changed, in order for people whose hands are not tainted with blood, to lead the nation.

The Death of Robert Mugabe at 95

The news came on the morning of 06 September 2019. As he broke the news, the guy who came with it faced a barrage of questions, which he could not answer.

Some asked if it was really true this time because the guy had been declared dead several times in the past, only to see him jogging up plane stairs the next week.

The most common comment was, "He died too late, after destroying a beautiful country beyond repair, and without being held accountable".

A general comment was made about his recent announcement, that he didn't want to be buried at the National Heroes Acre. Instead, he'd said, he would rather be buried beside his mother Bona in Zvimba, his rural home.

Mnangagwa was said to have sent a delegation to Singapore, to try and persuade Mugabe (in hospital) to accept Heroes' Acre. The result of the talks was not known at the time of his death.

But why was Mnangagwa so desperate to have Mugabe's consent to be buried at the Heroes' Acre?

Part of the answer lies in the fact that it was a place for Zimbabwean liberation war heroes, and everybody knew and acknowledged the job that Mugabe had done, so without him, the national shrine was nothing but a confirmation of what it actually was, a burial place for the biggest thieves and murderers in the country!

Some guys said it was Mugabe's right to choose where to be buried. After all, he'd been deposed by those who would bury him there and speechifying over his body. No one would like that!

Others however felt that it was him who had built the Heroes' Acre, selected who should go there, and speechified over them, why shouldn't he be buried at his own shrine?

So, nothing much of significance on Mugabe's death, except a wild shout here and there, and a very cloudy, cold and wet day later on. People could not believe the cold, in September of all months, when we should be sweating hot!

Anyway, as per African tradition, they attributed the inclement weather to the death of a big man, Robert Mugabe.

Some Zimbabweans went further to suggest that he didn't want to be buried at the Heroes' Acre because he was scared of meeting the spirits of those he'd murdered and buried there, and would know no peace.

Whatever comments are given about Mugabe, the glaring truth was that he ruled in his death. Even in his death the dictator's orders were obeyed. After the 2017 coup that ousted him, he made it clear that he did not want to be buried at the national Heroes' Acre. To make sure he was understood, towards the 2018 election he publicly denounced Zanu PF, his party, and even hinted that he would vote the MDC. That was a sure way to get fired from the party. In the end they had to respect his will, to bury him beside his mother in rural Zvimba, leaving the shrine to others, most of whom did not deserve to be there.

His burning desire was to die in office, but his colleagues betrayed his wish.

So, in a way, Grace Mugabe had been right: Mugabe could stand an election in Zimbabwe in a coffin, and still win. Very few Zimbabweans doubted that anymore. But for the coup.

Politically, the death of Robert Mugabe, with his sixteen farms, has cast a long, dark shadow over Zimbabwe. As said elsewhere in this book, some people were calling for his return to the presidency. They compared his performance to Mnangagwa's and felt that it was far better.

Now we hear that instead of burying his body at the national Heroes Acre, they are building a mausoleum in his honour. They may put an effigy there, or carved portrait of him, but not Mugabe himself. He's decided to run away to his mother in rural Zvimba, where he was born and grew up. By the way, this will take 30 days, and that is the nation will stay and wait for a dead body to be buried.

Remember, though he also used the military to an extent, Mugabe was largely a legalistic dictator, while Mnangagwa is a military bully, and is surrounded by the military. So, with Chiwenga in hospital and all that, people were wondering who would come after Mnangagwa. From many people's observations, it would be Valerio Sibanda, now commander of the Zimbabwe National Army (ZNA). Many people didn't think the army would release power to civilians in the near future. It was going to be a long, tough time of hustling for the majority of Zimbabweans.

Above all, Mugabe threw books and education into the dust bin. While he could talk eloquent sense and you could listen to him for hours, his performance as an educated man betrayed his high education. Yet he was born under colonial power, grew up in it, and lived under the Smith regime. Couldn't he have learnt at least something else besides his expensive suits and buffets?

Mugabe loved higher education only for himself, so that he could manipulate and control people, instil awe and wonder in them and cow them. When other people got a higher education, he despised them.

And Mnangagwa is taking us backwards, further than where Mugabe left us. We should not allow that to happen, Remember, everybody supported Mugabe in the beginning, and gave him chance. As it turned out, it was a chance to destroy a beautiful country. Mnangagwa must never get this chance. He was with Mugabe all these years, ruling with him. What more does he want, except to fill up his personal coffers? His hatred and disinterest has already caused enough damage in Zimbabwe, as it is. Remember, unlike Mugabe, Mnangagwa rules by a gun in one hand (to crush and threaten dissenters), and a gun in the other (to destroy every facet of ordinary human life, be it economically, socially, academically and other spheres),

A lot of fear and horror was expressed at what would happen if Mnangagwa fell dead. People had no doubt that there would be killings at the senior political levels. To most Zimbabweans, it was taking too long, and the sooner it happened, the better.

So, can we say Mugabe's death has closed a chapter on Zimbabwe's political history? To many ordinary Zimbabweans, the answer is no. Their suffering continues under his party, Zanu PF. There's no difference between Mnangagwa and Mugabe. Same fanana. The killings continue, but more specifically, abductions.

To Zanu PF supporters, Mugabe's death does close a chapter. To them, no one can ever take his place, either from Zanu PF or the MDC. He was an irreplaceable icon. They also miss Mugabe's affordable prices for basics like maize meal, rice, cooking oil, bread, transport, electricity, candles and stuff. As one of them said during Mnangagwa's hard reign, "Imagine, on that day of the coup, I woke up early as usual, had a shower with a $1, 50 bar of soap, bought a loaf of bread for 80c, a crate of eggs at $3, 00, boarded a combi to work at 50c, lunch for a Dollar, and my day was done. These days, transport to town on a combi costs $3, 00, one egg costs $1, 20, which is an unaffordable $36,00 per crate, bread is $8 per loaf. A 5kg of mealie meal, which cost $3 during Mugabe's times, now sells at $27. If I think about these things, I feel like killing E.D. and eating his ass like crocodile tail."

In this, they share with the MDC supporters and rest of country. What to do about it though, remains a mystery. While a few are still hopeful, many are slowly but surely giving up.

Still, as they bemoaned their hard life and meagre existence, Mugabe's body remained unburied, 20 days after his death, with some people saying he would be buried after 30, and others declaring that he'd already been buried. Nobody, except those very close to him, knew.

People also made interesting observations about Robert Mugabe and Nelson Mandela's lives. For example, they couldn't help noticing that both had died on a Thursday, 5 September, at the same age of 95. Both their first names have six different letters of the alphabet. Both surnames start with 'M'.

Mandela left a widow named Graca, and Mugabe's widow is Grace. Both Graca and Grace were second wives to the leaders. In addition, the two leaders went to the same university.

May be this had to do with fate, the stars or mere coincidence? For a practical example of that, I refer you to **A Way of Life.**

Mnangwgwa's Politics of the Gun

The present President of Zimbabwe, Emmerson Mnangagwa, rules by the gun. Besides employing a lot more military guys who staged a coup on his behalf, Mnangagwa's history in the politics of Zimbabwe is littered with violence. He is finger-pointed in the death of many ZANLA combatants, including Herbert Chitepo and General Tongogara, among many others. He was also heavily involved in the Gukurahundi massacres between 1983 and 1987. And he staged a coup against his long-time ally and leader, Robert Mugabe.

Since the coup and establishment of Mnangagwa's government, there has been a sharp increase of private citizen abductions. As at 19 September 2019, 50 people had been officially abducted. Even the abductors of Itai Dzamara are known and walking scot-free, while Itai remains unaccounted for.

As recently as September 2019, the president of the **Zimbabwe Hospital Doctors' Association, Peter Magombeyi**, was abducted, and presumed killed. He was found days later, abandoned in a forest, 35 kilometres away from his home. The entire incident caused nationwide strikes by medical staff, which affected health delivery systems in the country.

Now the Zanu PF factions are blaming each other for the abductions. Mnangagwa's Lacoste faction is blaming Mugabe's G40 faction for the abductions. For how long shall Zimbabweans stand this? As things stand at present, anyone can be abducted for anything, including drinking water or saying a word. Can the world watch us perish like this?

We are scared.

ZIMBABWE'S GENERATIONS AS A FACTOR IN THE POLITICAL MATRIX

While on one hand, a generation is defined as a collective group of people born and living at the same time, and on the other, a period it takes to bring up a child until he/she gets married. Which is roughly 30 years; there have been four distinct groups of people who have emerged in Zimbabwe between independence in 1980 and the present era, to whom I conveniently and purposefully ascribe the term 'generations'.

The Last Rhodesian Generation.

This is a group of people between 65 and 80 years old, or over, at the time of writing. These people worked for whites during the colonial period. Though they are not that many, the few who remain are easily recognized by their age

Most of them have houses of their own, their children are long gone, and they can afford to let in their houses, for income. Because they can no longer afford to work, they depend on their offspring, and investments.

They also tend to stick to tastes of days gone by, for example, they might not like today's coke and fanta drinks, preferring different ones like sugar-free Pepsi, a certain type of coffee, and a special way of preparing food.

These are the guys who popularized various music such as by the Beetles, Hurricanes, Rolling Stones, Otis Redding and Percy Sledge, among others. They also wore bell bottom trousers and high heel shoes.

Though they celebrated independence when it came in 1980, most fun and life-loving people of this generation look down on modern standards, trends and habits, be they in food, dress, drink and life style. They try to exude quality, and a better standard of living than what they experience. However, they can only do so when given the chance and right environment. They also talk fondly of the whites, and how they encouraged high standards, education, style and hard work. To them, the most important thing is working hard and reaping from your sweat. Quality was of importance, not just doing things for the sake of it. To this group, Zimbabwean life was being wasted on undeserving crooks and cheats.

It is important to note that among this generation are also whites, and blacks with ID cards marked 'A', indicating they're foreigners. These whites and 'foreigners' have no other home but Zimbabwe. They should be persuaded to take part in all national activities as full citizens.

The Independence Generation

This is the generation of Zimbabweans who were alive and grown up during the liberation struggle. Many of them crossed over into Mozambique to join Zanu and its guerrillas, but others could or did not. The majority of them were war collaborators, and assisted the guerrillas in their fight. As a result of their participation, many of this generation were caught in crossfire and died. Their survivors constitute the Independence Generation in Zimbabwe.

This generation can say without doubt that they brought independence to the country. They celebrated and enjoyed it. Since they'd had a taste of the Rhodesian life from their parents and brothers, it is safe to say that they had an experience of the Rhodesian way of life, too. They lived through the Mugabe era, the inclusive government, and Mnangagwa's military government.

Most of them managed to get an education (during the colonial period), had jobs, and managed to build or buy houses. Since they were educated, they made investments, though in things of little value; insurance policies, bank accounts, education and so forth. However, the majority of them lost these investments with time, and as inflation set in.

Though they still miss their music on LPs, to the present Independence generation, the major problem is that after experiencing the good life in the old days, they cannot cope with the modern. They see a wide difference between the Zimbabwe they knew, and the current one in which there are no rules and standards. Their struggle is to adjust and fit in, or perish in an insignificant, undeserved death.

One interesting thing about them is that despite their changed circumstance, they still have hopes and dreams, and love to make progress in their socio-economic lives. Most of their talk is around people they grew up knowing, but who have climbed up the social ladder. They boast to each other when they receive a call from such guys, or when they get some money, or get an invitation for a beer binge.

The Independence Generation like Fatso and Tindo jumped over raw sewerage as they crossed streets, while others of their age flew to their children's school visits in a helicopter, in the same country. Opportunities were shut, closed to them. They would leave nothing to their children, except maybe a house, education, and nothing more, while others left millions, even in US Dollars.

The question, which they didn't have to ponder much, was: which was better, Mugabe's Zanu PF or Ian Smith's Rhodesia Front? They had lived through both, and knew the evils and sweet side of each.

That, to the guys, was the million dollar question. But who would they ask? The new generations didn't care. All they cared about was money, and good living.

In fact, it was rather curious that this new generation of born frees, gwejas, hwindis and computer and other technical gadgets expected them to liberate them, after liberating the country for them, with the guerrillas.

The Born-Free Generation

This is the generation of Zimbabweans born after independence in 1980. Especially between May 1980 and 1989. A peculiar thing to note about this generation is that though they have a beautiful name for their generation, the majority of them have never been employed in their lives. They grew up at a time Mugabe was killing and destroying industry, and so by the time they finished school, industry was closed, and the majority of whites had left. Many tales are told on social media of members of this generation asking for everything, from toilet tissue, bread, airtime, underwear, a drink, etc, from their parents, especially the mother.

Very few of them have houses of their own, or can dream of having one, even a car or any property. They only get married when they impregnate their girlfriends, and even then, getting them to accept the girl and the pregnancy will be a tall order. They prefer living their lives as it is, under the care of their mothers, with the hope that one day, she will drop dead and they inherit the house and furniture. Then, they become bosses, and begin to live like that, on the fast lane, like they watch on videos all day. Except from some unproven bits and pieces, they have no idea how Zanu PF destroyed their country, or how they came to be what they are. Zanu PF fills their minds with sanctions and western vitriol.

This generation is also very eager about academic qualifications, though not the education process itself. They are desperate to have a degree. They don't care the field or area, as long as they have a degree. To them, it is a status. A quick thing to observe about them, however, is that though their degree might be in a different field, they can learn so fast at their current condition and even excel in that, too.

The Gweja Generation

Also called 'Makorokoza', the Gweja Generation emerged during a period of countrywide strikes by the main government sectors of the country, particularly education and health. Also called the Lost Generation, this generation, born after 1990, was in school or growing up at that time. As a result, most of them did not complete high school, mainly because of the strikes and shortage of money. Some of the Gweja generation, however, managed to overcome the odds. These had working parents with good salaries, or a diaspora sponsor. While those without sponsors had their education suffer, these latter ones thrived and became computer technicians, lawyers, engineers and other professions.

Those who could not continue with their education as described above, became illegal miners, diamond dealers and scrap iron merchants. The word 'gweja' itself is associated with illegal mining more than anything else.

Besides illegal mining, gwejas also became public transport conductors, or hwindis.

So, these are basically the same, the young emerging lawyers and hwindis and gwejas. This generation is associated with money more than anything else. They are also the biggest group at church congregations, because they are praying for money and success. They don't care much about anything else, so long they have money.

This is the same generation that brought the 'zvangu zvaita' culture. As long as their mission in anything is accomplished, they don't worry about anyone else or anything. They fight for themselves, just as they have since dropping out of school, or going through thick and thin to be what they are at that time.

An Interesting observation about the Born Free and Gweja generations is made by the Last Rhodesian and Independence generations. They say that the quality of their ZIMSEC 'O' and 'A' Level qualifications, with a chain of distinctions, plus a first degree, is equivalent to the Standard 6 (modern day Grade 7) qualification of the 60s and70s.

This, they say is because they have learned nothing from their school system. They have problems constructing a grammatically correct sentence, and gold is still on mountains, as it was in all the last centuries.

One funny thing about this generation is that the females do not like to be associated with the name. There are no female gwejas or hwindis. Yes, there are females in the mining sector, but they don't like to be called gwejas or gwejelinas. This causes a lot of fights between the two groups.

Apparently females do not have any generation, but belong to that of their males. Females have cultures within a generation. For example, we have the 'Salad' or 'Salala' culture among the women. These are free women who are not tied down to traditions. In fact, they do not like traditional food that much, neither do they like traditional dress, means of transport or anything else. They move with the times. In particular their name comes from the fact that 'salad' is not a traditional, but western or foreign food, and they like it.

The other culture among females is the 'Nose Brigade', This belongs to women who speak English through the nose, so that they sound like indigenous speakers of the language. It is very easy to confuse a 'Salala' with a 'Nose Brigade'. A Nose Brigade is not as worried about dress and food, or even transport, as a 'Salala'. A Salala does not just tolerate anything; she goes for class and style.

It is important to note that these two cultures do not belong to the Gweja Generation only, but across generations, that is why they are cultures.

There is also the 'bling' culture. This one is all about being on a thrill and having no worries. You want to show the world that you've no problems in your life and everything is sweet and shiny. You're in control.

It is also important to note that these generations are not exclusive. It is common to find a member of the Independence or Born Free Generation associating with the Gweja Generation in mining, or any other business, and agree to be called a Gweja.

The Intergenerational Conflict

While the political conflict in Zimbabwe has brought many people to their knees, deaths through massacres, dubious state operations and political violence, and has destroyed the lives of many people to the extent that they could kill or die for it, the surprising thing is that to the Born Free and Gweja generations, everything is normal and perfect.

First, they say that it's the two elder generations that freed us all. They brought great things like independence and freedom, and now people can do what they want.

So here's the party that brought independence and freedom. Why should they not support it, especially the party is like Zanu PF, and uses the means of freedom (the gun) to suppress sellouts and their followers?

Except to a wizened and experienced mind, that argument wouldn't make sense to anybody else.

Also called the Lost generations, they found themselves locked in a violent and vicious cycle of freedom between Zanu PF and the opposition MDC. While the former proclaimed that they brought freedom and independence, the latter denied this, and sought to establish a new, more democratic and peaceful political order, but which the latter generations could not understand.

Thus members of these younger generations found themselves caught in a spiral of confusion. Some of them seek to establish patriotism, freedom and independence by supporting Zanu, while others found themselves nowhere, confused and at a loss. This drives the majority of them to church, instead of confronting their problem head-on.

As things stand in Zimbabwe, with uncleansed men and women leading us, real freedom comes to these latter generations with the death of their parents, instead of dethroning Zanu PF, which is much easier to do, instead of waiting for their parents' house, car and furniture.

The fathers, however know this, and try to live as long as they can. But Mnangagwa is threatening that, and is tying a rope around their necks.

The solution to Zimbabwe's political conflict thus can be found when the first stone is laid, and that's when the generations begin to talk. It is important for the Independence Generation to sit down and talk to the young men and women, educate them kindly, understand them, and tell them life is a cycle. Zimbabwe could be a much better country than this. These younger generations see it as the responsibility of that generation to remove Zanu PF, and not theirs. Some of them, however, have formed pressure groups, such as Tajamuka, in a bid to free themselves, but these groups have been embroiled in conflict.

Time for a New Generation

If things remain like this and there is no resolution found to the Zimbabwean political conflict, the country will go to ruins and another form of recolonization will happen to it. This is because as things stand, there is no nation to talk about in Zimbabwe.

The presidential position in the country is vacant at the moment. Zanu PF was rejected by the people years ago, and it is still being rejected at every election.

The MDC, on the other hand, have failed now for 20 years to remove Zanu PF. Their history is of failure, though we know it was through Zanu PF rigging machinery.

I step in to cool the high temperatures caused by the political conflict. We've been against each other and divided for too long as a nation. My position is to show us that yes, we can live together peacefully, despite our differences. We can develop our communities and nation. A better life is possible in Zimbabwe and for Zimbabweans.

I step in to introduce a new generation, the Freedom Generation, where people are free to talk, mix, travel, save money and use it to develop themselves and their communities.

It is the responsibility of the living to form a nation that has the same values, mindset and vision. This way, we leave a legacy to our children

The Freedom Generation will build a new democratic, independent and peaceful Zimbabwe, from the moment I step in.

There was one youth dialogue organized by Ibbo Mandaza and his SAPES Trust in 2018, and posted on the internet. In that, the young generations had a most fruitful and honest discussion. The dialogue should also be extended to the Independence Generation, who have experienced a better life in Zimbabwe and know that it is possible.

OPEN LETTER TO NELSON CHAMISA

Dear Nelson Chamisa, President of the MDC Alliance

Although I've never had the opportunity, let me take this one to congratulate you for fighting for freedom and democracy in Zimbabwe. I've watched you navigate the bumpy road and its curves with admiration.

I have noticed that we share a common passion: for change for our country, although our methods may differ.

Having said this, I would like you to allow me to make my own personal contribution to your and indeed every other Zimbabwean's.

My name is Edward Chinhanu (or Chinhanhu), and I'm a professional peace builder, peace maker, Transitional Justice Fellow and conflict resolution practitioner. I was born and bred in Zimbabwe.

My contribution lies in my suggestion, that is; let's find someone or allow me to stand in for transitional justice president, for our country until Zanu PF is dead and buried.

I will find ways to kill and bury Zanu PF, without help from you or your supporters, although I know many would love to help.

The person or I will be President for only two (2) years, mainly to achieve two objectives

1.   to facilitate the national healing and reconciliation exercise.
2.   to set the cultural code for the presidency in Zimbabwe.

The national healing and reconciliation exercise will be in full swing and running by the end of the second year

I would use my term to demonstrate to Zimbabweans that they're a loving, peaceful people, and that their president doesn't have to live in barricaded mansions surrounded with soldiers, or travel in armoured motorcades, but lives with and for the people.

That was what we expected at independence, but got guns and sjamboeks instead. Yet Mandela demonstrated it was possible. Give me a chance to be the Mandela of Zimbabwe. I can do it.

In June 2018 I facilitated a national peace building conference for all peace organizations in Zimbabwe. I co-facilitated it with Peace Direct, a UK-based NGO with international links. We did it for 3 days at the Holiday Inn. Some of my work with and for them can be found on www.peaceinsight.org/conflicts/zimbabwe, or www.peaceinsight.org/blog2016/07

The promise should be to give you the presidency to complete the remaining 3 years, after which there will be a general election between you and other interested political parties depending on the will of the people.

Like me, the person should not be a politician, and promise not to contest that election after the two-year stint. My suggestion here would be Father Fidelis Mukonori.

Incidentally the door will be open for you and your close, trustworthy associates with relevant experience, into the transitional cabinet.

I have made this letter public because I want to be held accountable for what I say. I do not expect or want any changes to that. It is my offer, and I will not change it.

The real task is removing Zanu PF, but as I said, leave that to me. I won't even need the services of our bored, unused but abused ZNA.

Incidentally with the current splits and divisions in the army, there would be a bloodbath. Now, we all know that is Zanu PF stuff, and Zimbabweans are sick and tired of it!

I won't spill their blood, as they would mine, but I want them to leave the country on their own accord, at peace and without interruption.

I have my own support base, but I've written this letter to ask that you render your political support to my vision and plans. I am a qualified Transitional Justice Fellow, with the Institute for Justice and Reconciliation (IJR) in Cape Town, South Africa, as well as a Rotary Peace Fellow. Part of my Rotary Fellowship took me to Cambodia, where I visited the Killing Fields and saw first-hand the atrocities Pol Pot committed on his people in the 70s, and learned about their transitional justice mechanisms.

Remember, Nelson, This was the 70s, the same time Zanu guys were wedging their war. It is very highly likely these guys (Pol Pot and Zanu PF) had the same kind of thinking, treating people, you know.

This, and numerous other experiences I've got in Zimbabwe, from Rwanda, South Africa and Argentina and elsewhere, and the international networks I have created give me full confidence to do what I need to do for our people.

You can read the transitional justice process I want to set up, and how I intend to go through National Healing and reconciliation in this book's section of Queen Latifa, in the chapter, **Queen Latifa Picks Herself Up.** The chapter also contains the names of Zimbabweans I will approach and work with, if they're willing and available. Of course, the door remains open to others, and all Zimbos.

I shall be ready to talk any time. Meantime, as our people continue to suffer, I say

Aluta continua

If you want to know more about me, and probably yourself, too, I refer you to **Zimbabwe's Generations as a Factor in the Political Matrix.**

Your fellow patriot

Edward Chinhanu. (I.D.N: 42-081007Z-42)
Email" edwardchinhanu@gmail.com

MESSAGE TO THE INTERNATIONAL COMMUNITY

I, Edward Chinhanu, a member of the human race and nationality of Zimbabwe, Southern Africa, send this message to you on behalf of my fellow citizens who have gone through horrific experiences under their government in the last 40+ years. To be exact, this has happened since 1976 when our liberation war intensified, and continued after independence in 1980

My message is simple, that you focus your eyes and ears on Zimbabwe in the next few days. I ask you to pray, fast, think and look at its location on the world map. This way, you keep us on your mind as we engage the gear for change. Say a prayer for us.

Soon, we're also going to need your help and friendship as we start our National Healing and Reconciliation exercise. For our hopes for the future, please read **Obama Visits Queen Latifa**, while for the worst that could happen to Zimbabwe, I refer you to **Farai's Dream.**

The Zimbabwean conflict is a challenge to the human race. It challenges you to explain what you as an individual part of the human race attribute to humanity. What is humanity? What are you? I hope you'll discover that this is much more important than who you are. As Farai reflects in **Farai's Furore**, a lot of us love to identify with certain animals. Zimbabweans, like every other race or nationality, are animals, too. Please, befriend them. Love them.

I'm aware there is a group of people who have given up on Africa, who say the continent's problems cannot be solved. I, along with many more beg to differ. Here's a problem that you and I can resolve, together, forever. Please do what you can to support us.

Zimbabwe is a very rich country, in terms of minerals, agricultural land, wildlife and tourism. We're not beggars. Help us free ourselves from this demonic party and government, and meet and do business with the Best Laughing People on the Planet. You can save this nation from perishing under an unwanted government, as they are doing now, and have been for the last 40 years. For our abilities and potential, I refer you to the subheading **Zimbabweans on the International Stage**, under **Independence.**

It should not come as a surprise that the people who have so much blood on their hands out of the socio-economic mess they create are a tiny fraction of the population, who use another tiny fraction of the military, to play with money and manipulate and control human life, for purposes of enjoying power, standing and prestige, especially on the world stage. But Mnangagwa can't do it, will never achieve a scrap on the world stage. Just look and listen to him

For your entertainment, if you want to know the level of disillusionment with politics across the country, I refer you to **Queen Latifa's Perception of the Zimbabwe Political and Business Environment** and the last few paragraphs of The **Meeting**.

Otherwise the whole book is for you, to find out how dictatorships and military rulers deal with young, modern, intelligent and world-exposed citizens, and how these citizens seek a happy, fulfilling life under such cruel rule.

Kindly wish us luck.
I thank you

MESSAGE TO PEACEBUILDERS, CONFLICT RESOLUTION EXPERTS, ROTARY PEACE FELLOWS AND PEACE ACTIVISTS ACROSS THE WORLD.

When I started writing this book, it was for you. It still is.

I wanted you to read and see how Zimbabweans have and continue to live under extremely harsh conditions, under the veneer of 'independence, with the ultimate intention of appealing for your help in resolving the conflict.

I've had the opportunity to be taught by and interact with some of the best peace builders and conflict resolution experts in the world, especially at the ISS in The Hague, Chulalongkorn University in Bangkok, Thailand, and my local Africa University in Zimbabwe. I resist the urge to name some of them.

I made a lot of changes to the structure and content of the book, among them the appeals to Nelson Chamisa, Zanu PF and the international community.

In addition, as I wrote, a lot of things came to my mind, among them what I would say if you asked what I had in place, for the resolution of the conflict.

That set me thinking of the many courses I went through at Chula and other places, and decided on the action I'm now taking.

Indeed, I'm not a politician and don't ever want to be, or have ever dreamt about being President of my country.

But as you read about the violence and intimidation in **Independence**, **A Fight Over Soccer Game** and **Rethinking Zimbabwean Politics**, the needless deaths in **Little Brendon Falls Sick**, the corruption throughout the book, repression, land seizures in **The Meeting** unstable economy, our bleak future in **Farai's Dream**, our funerals in **Jonah's Funeral** and the impact of all this on family and domestic life in **A Fight with Shupi,** you'll agree with me that there's no point in talking about bad situations without taking action.

All I'm doing is trying to resolve the conflict that has divided my people, degraded them, impoverished them, desert their motherland and fail to plan their lives and future. As a peacebuilder and conflict resolution practitioner, I felt it should be on my shoulders to take centre stage and bring an end to the conflict that has torn my country to rags like this.

On one side are the people of Zimbabwe, and on the other is Zanu PF, the party that brought independence, and we all loved. For the last 35 years, the people have been calling and voting for change, but Zanu PF has denied them.

The events and experiences that the characters in this book go through are my personal experiences, observations and well-known activities in the country, though I gave them a fictional twist.

I ask that you focus on Zimbabwe in the next few days, and ask your support as we go through a new start in Zimbabwe. Your expertise will be needed very soon, when the transformation process begins. It will be an interesting exercise, to which you can contribute your expertise, and draw interesting lessons from.

To my fellow fellows at Chula, Intake 11 of 2011, I say here's an opportunity. I don't want to be remembered as a peacebuilder when I'm dead. Time for peace is now. Let's take it up to prevent unnecessary death and destruction in Zimbabwe.

By the way, part of the proceeds from the sales of this book will go to hosting a meeting for us, in The Hague, the Netherlands. I hope Fay remembers this and keeps it in mind.

THE MINING AND TOURISM SECTORS IN ZIMBABWE

Mining and tourism are by far the largest sectors in Zimbabwe, coupled by rich agricultural land. At some point in the not-too-distant past, the country proudly bore the title 'bread basket of the region'. Mugabe's violent land redistribution policy and activities did not do justice to the vast fertile lands of Zimbabwe, especially in Mashonaland, East, Central, and West, The fertile lands are also abundant in Manicaland for tobacco, tea, and forestry plantations.

But it is in mining that Zimbabwe shines brightest. The country is replete with gold deposits from East to West, North and South, and other points in between. However, it remains largely untapped, due to lack of technology, planning and management. As a result, only politically connected people engage in the sector, with a few selectively chosen foreign governments and companies, especially Chinese and Russians. The bulk of Zimbabweans interested in the mining sector have no tools, and use picks and shovels, and still make a more decent living than teachers and other government workers.

Diamonds were also discovered in Marange District of Manicaland Province. Recent research revealed that Zimbabwe has a third of the world's diamonds under its earth, and of the best quality The diamonds come in all types of quality, and various shapes, colours and sizes. For a bit on our mineral wealth, I refer you to **Queen Latifa's Lonesome Queue**.

The country also has large deposits of platinum, pyrite, tantalite, Rutile, chromite, phyllite, kaolinite, monazite, muscovite and other minerals scattered all over. It is said that overall, Zimbabwe has 80% of the world's best minerals.

Zimbabwe is also known worldwide for its tourism. The excellent climate in parts of the country led to British migrants naming many spots after similar places back home in England.

The Victoria Falls are a world icon, and a one of the Seven Wonders of the World. There are many game parks with live elephants, lion, buffalo, leopard, python and other creatures. Zimbabwean tourist guides are very well-informed communicators, and have no problem with English.

The country boasts of numerous other tourist activities such as mountain climbing, camping, sightseeing, water rafting, fishing and hunting.

Zimbabwean people themselves are a tourist attraction. The people have a strong culture of Ubuntu, and know how to treat visitors with respect, so that they come again. English is widely spoken, even in the remotest villages, by old men and women in their 70s.

Zimbabwean people have a unique laughter, with the women laughing with an exciting, endless ring, and the men moving their arms and legs about, creating a rhythmic, picturesque sound. They also clap their hands or hold their head with both hands. Friendliness is at the core of how indigenous Zimbabweans treat visitors and tourists.

As another tourism boost, we attached a passage titled 'How to Eat Sadza', in this book. Made from maize meal, sadza has been our staple food for centuries, and is still popular with Zimbabweans across the world, especially the men.

FARAI'S EARLY EXPERIENCES IN INDEPENDENT ZIMBABWE

When independence came in 1980, Farai was 20. He'd written his "O" Levels that year, passed, and was on double celebrations.

His father had been killed during the war, by the Rhodesian soldiers in his rural home after mistaking him for a guerrilla as he came from the toilet. Many people said the killing had been deliberate.

Another big problem in his life sprang from the disappearance of his elder brother, Charles. Charles had crossed into Mozambique during the war, but had never returned. When others came back, Farai had visited office after office, in government and private organizations, asking about his brother. Nobody knew him.

He sought out his friends, the ones he'd crossed with, and asked them. All they said was that Charles might have gone to Romania, and that was it.

For years Farai waited expectantly for his brother's home coming, but it never happened, till his memory faded.

Now Farai lived with his mother and younger brother in the Zororo Section of Sakubva.

Fatso's plan had been to proceed to 'A' Level, then university. However, there was no money, and he thought he should accept anything that came his way.

The first offer was temporary teaching, which he did for two years, then plumbing. As someone ever good with his hands, he liked it. He trained for six months and learned the rest on the job.

There was nothing much he could do with the plumbing money those days, so he enjoyed himself with his friends and read.

Politically, his mother worshipped Zanu PF. It was not only for the reason that the family got all their food supplies from the party, but her harrowing experiences during the liberation war were such that she did not want a repeat of that. She was in her early 60s.

"Never in my life, do I want to go through that again," she said emphatically her big 61-year old breasts shaking with every word, and finger pointed at her listeners each time the subject came up. "You people support the MDC because you did not see what I saw. You did not have your whole family wiped out. You experienced nothing. You want war in this country, and I say you can have it when I am gone. Not in my lifetime!"

Nothing happened in her branch or ward without her knowing. They all came to her for advice on political issues, food distribution, party cards, and so forth. As far as she was concerned, every one she knew in her neighbourhood had a Zanu PF party card, and there was no opposition. To her shock and surprise, however, her party lost every election in Mutare and in her constituency.

That vexed and embarrassed her to no end, but she was powerless against it. She however was unwavering in her support, and was the pillar of both the men and women's league in the ward.

Even though most people supported the MDC, they were inconspicuous. They never publicly declared it and you only saw it through the votes, when elections were announced.

At first, like everybody else in the country, Farai had been Zanu PF through and through. Later in life, he got an opportunity to do a plumbing job with a big, foreign –owned private company, One thing led to the next, and he got an opportunity to train as a fitter and Turner, Class 1 That was the time he was really getting hot with Shupi, his girlfriend. During that time, he managed to get a bank loan and built a 6 roomed house in the Chineta Section.

Five years later, he lost his job, and came out with nothing. Even the insurance policies paid nothing, as they crumbled and fell. That was a whole industry, like all others, gone!

He had no option, but to do what best he could with the available resources. He engaged some people he knew in the NGO world, attended workshops and even facilitated some.

After the human rights courses he attended and a further opening of the mind, he could talk excitedly.

, "We can never expect Zanu PF to totally relinquish power to the MDC. That is impossible, judging by how much it has entrenched itself in every facet of our public and private lives. Otherwise we would start from total scratch, like we did in 1980, and that is impossible. It would be retrogression.

"We can also never expect Zanu PF to continue ruling this country alone, without the MDC, because all the people are with the MDC. Besides, the MDC cannot win through elections, violence or the courts. The only solution to our problem is negotiation."

Still, however, things did not get any better for his family. They had their basic needs, thanks to his mother's political connections, but he wanted to stand on his own feet and fend for the family.

He could not live with his wife well enough under the watchful eye of his mother.

When the land redistribution came and Zanu PF was allocating land to those who wanted it, Farai thought he might be lucky. He'd done Agriculture at school, and he was good with his hands. In addition, he could use the large idle labour around the province, as industry closed and people became jobless.

He went to the local Zanu PF provincial office and told them about Charles, and his own interest in owning land. The office was particularly impressed with the part about Charles. Fatso got his land and offer letter.

By then, he was preparing to get married to Shupi, his long-time girlfriend.

Farai's farm was open land. It could be seen that it'd been settled before, but when he took it, Farai was met with tall trees, grass, anthills and stony or rocky parts. Often, he took Shupi or a friend to the farm, making plans on the trip.

Later, he learned that the farm used to belong to a white Boer, who'd fled the war in 1976. Further investigations revealed that the Boer's family had a long history of mining in the country.

That aroused Fatso's interest. A careful analysis of the soil and rocks on the farm showed the possibility of gold on the farm. Fatso kept this to himself.

At that time, there was a lot of private mining activity in the country, especially by government connected people and gwejas. It did not take long before Fatso had an idea about the quality of the gold. What he didn't have was a detector, to help him find out the depth of the gold and its quantity. He would do that in due course.

Then he married Shupi. That meant he had to focus more on his farm than before.

However, just when he became serious about his plans, one day an ISUZU bakkie screeched to a halt near him, on his farm. The driver got out and walked to Fatso.

"Hey, who are you?" asked the man, tall, bulky and oldish.

"My name is Farai. And may I know who you are?"

"I am Colonel Bomber from the ZNA. What are you doing on my farm?"

Your farm? This is my farm. I have an offer letter and everything. I've owned this land for five years."

"No. Things have changed. This is now my land. Here's my offer letter."

Indeed, the offer letter that Farai looked at was written the day before, with the full details of the man who stood before him.

That marked the end of his plans about his land. The man, however, was kind enough to drive Farai to his home in town, but warned him against visiting or interfering with the farm.

THE MEETING

Farai had gone back to the Zanu PF office to launch his complaint about the way he'd lost his farm, and ask for another. They asked his war history, his position, involvement during the war, and stuff that Fatso could not understand. All he did was tell them about his brother, Charles.

"Comrade Bazooka, the man responsible for land redistribution in this province, will be having a meeting with the people in your district two days from today. He's the man to ask about these things. We just follow his instructions and orders. Be there when he comes, without fail."

Farai did not want to go there, or meet Cde Bazooka. However, at least he would have done something about his problem, instead of just sitting at home. So he went. Besides, since losing hs job, hs life had become a mess. He'd taken up a lot of insurance policies when he was working, but by the time he lost his job, there was no money in the country. A lot of insurance companies had closed down, with huge losses, and without paying anything to beneficiaries. There was no social security either, at that time. So farming was his only hope, and Farai went to the meeting with hope and expectation.

At 12 midday sharp Bazooka finally arrived, finding an atmosphere of high expectation in the large rustic crowds commonly defined by filth, dirt and drunkenness. Some carried hoes, ropes, and yokes while others had knobkerries, slings, bows and arrows. One held a dead rabbit in one hand.

After carefully closing the door to his 4x4 Off-road Toyota truck, he strode to the people, a scarf in party colours around his neck and a white cap emblazoned a gun on each side perfectly sitting on his grey head. The war had ended 32 years ago, but they still called him Comrade Bazooka. He was proud of his nom de guerre.

After brief introductions he stood up.

"Comrades", he said in a loud, baritone voice, facing the crowds, "I have come back to you to report on the issues you raised last time. I promised that I would take all issues to do with the Third Chimurenga, which is our land, to the highest offices. I did that, and the following is my report." He cast an eye at his truck.

The people held their breaths expectantly, eyes glued on him.

"The first issue you raised was about the education of our children. We said we needed schools and a clinic. Together with this issue was also raised that of a tuck shop. Comrades, I walked from office to office about this issue until my feet ached. First I went to the War Veterans' office, then to Education, Health, Social Welfare, Defence, and then to the Vice President's Office".

There was wild ululation and whistling at the mention of the Vice president's office.

"However, I could not see the Vice President personally, but after failing several times, I left a request for an urgent meeting with his personal secretary, and I believe this will be soon. All the departments I visited kept saying it was not their responsibility, because there were no populations large enough to warrant the establishment of a school or hospital in the farming areas. As it is now, we await the Vice president's response." Again he cast an eye at his truck.

At these words there was a sudden swing in the crowd's high spirits, and there were hushed murmurs.

"So what should our children do? a man asked aloud.

"Should we just die then, of malaria and other diseases?" another asked.

"No, Comrades," Bazooka said, looking at his truck first and then resting his head on the shoulder as if chastising a child slow to learn, "we should not bring shame to our Government by just sitting back and doing nothing. We need order in this process. Remember, we are in a revolution, and this is the last part. Zimbabwe is ours, but in order to fill our buckets with its milk and honey, we need order."

The people fell quiet.

"The next issue you raised was about inputs, that is seed, fertilizers, and so forth. These will come. The problem however is that the road to this place is so bad," Here he looked at his truck for a full minute, before resuming, "so it would be difficult to bring the inputs this far. This means that we have to travel to the GMB in Rusape. First however, we need to clear the road. Make it passable. As it is now..." he shook his head.

"Second, you all need to be registered. We need all the names of the people here, on the farms in this district."

"But we have all been registered", said a man carrying a pouch across his shoulder. "We registered when we first acquired these farms, and then later for the grain loan scheme, and also towards elections...?"

"Comrade", said Bazooka impatiently, "everything is done for a purpose. You would not be surprised how many people have joined us since we came here in 2001. These are not genuine sons and daughters of the Third Chimurenga, but impostors planted by the enemy. We need to continually check our registers to flush these out."

Again, there was silence.

"Somebody also raised the issue of hunger. Yes, there is a serious drought this year, and our government agrees with us. We need food relief. At present, however, this is difficult, because of the road networks. Not only that, but remember, there is not enough in the government coffers at the moment. The little there is shall be used for campaign purposes in the villages. You all know how the opposition is gaining ground there. We need to counter that with all the means at our disposal. Are we clear?"

But very few people responded.

"Comrades", Bazooka continued, "it was brought to my attention by analysts and researchers that some of you are secretly getting foodstuffs from the same people who sponsor the opposition. Let me state categorically that I will deny you if you are one of these. I warned you not to accept any foodstuffs from Christian Care, WFP, Care, Plan International and such similar organizations. They are our enemies. Do you remember how they opposed the revolution at the start? How they invited CNN and the BBC to come and make false reports about us and our president? Our food and all our needs will be provided by our government. Is that clear? We should never allow hardships to make us sell our sovereignty away."

"Yes!" the crowds echoed in one voice, others nodding and gesticulating with their hands.

"We need our sovereignty!" he barked fiercely.

"Sovereignty!" repeated the people in a loud voice.

"Unity!"

"Unity!" they repeated again.

"So", he said, lowering his voice and wiping his mouth with the back of his hand, "I don't want to deny anybody when the time comes. We must remain united. We need to be resourceful. While we wait for our government to give us drought relief, there are so many activities that we can engage in to get money. For example, we encourage you to form cooperatives and mould bricks on your plots."

"There's no water, Comrade," somebody shouted from the back, and there was deathly silence.

"Water should not be a problem," said Bazooka, walking towards the direction of the voice. "Water is not the only thing that can be used to mould bricks. If you don't want to mould bricks, you can get cash through the sale of firewood. There are serious power cuts in town these days. We told them that they should move out here and be free and independent, but now they are complaining of power cuts."

There was nervous, suppressed laughter at this.

"So, now they are realizing their folly. No power, and they need firewood from us. Form cooperatives and sell it to them!"

At this, a coal black man in a cap with the party's emblem shouted the slogan three times and said, "We could also provide them with meat. There is a lot of game out here, in the mountains and forests..."

"Yes indeed! remarked Bazooka gleefully.

"And honey!" shouted another.

"We could trap birds!" said a female voice.

"And humus," said another.

"We could even sell them our Vhinyu and Zed and Lawidzani here. Town beer is so expensive!"

"You see," said Bazooka, beaming. "You have so much potential in your numbers".

"Yes!

"Right, said Bazooka eyeing his car, "are there anymore issues that I should take back?"

"None" the people said, expressing utter satisfaction and pleasure, and getting ready to leave the meeting.

But just before Bazooka dismissed them, Farai plucked courage, raised his hand and said, "Comrade, I don't know how you can handle my case. I was allocated land five years ago by the provincial office. However, a few days ago someone came to the land and claimed it his own."

Farai was encouraged by the crow, some who said the same thing had happened to them, too. Others claimed that four times they had been allocated a farm, but each time they had been driven off that farm by some chef, either in the political ranks or in the army.

Cde Bazooka appeared to ignore the comments from people and focused on Farai

"Were you given an offer letter?"

"Yes, Comrade".

Two or three people said at the same time: "And the chefs who took the farms from me also produced their own offer letters."

Talking to Farai again, Cde Bazooka continued, "Comrade, listen very carefully, this is a revolution. Expect anything at this moment. Things will stabilize with time. You will get your own... But what is that in your hand? Daily News? Comrade that is not the correct newspaper to read in a sovereign Zimbabwe. Those kind of newspaper spoil you". He seized the paper from Farai and tore it before everyone's eyes. "Perhaps this is why you keep losing your land. Our ancestors don't like this..."

"Sovereignty!" he chanted, fist in the air.

"Sovereignty!" the people said after him.

"Unity!" he chanted again.

"Unity!"

Then he headed for his truck, sat down and chanted again as the car began to pull out, with a trail of young men toy-toying after it, as was the custom.

That was the last Farai saw him, or entertained the thought of owning land again. In fact, many people had told him before that it would not work, and he'd doubted them.

After losing his farm, Fatso was fed up with Zanu PF. He heard many cases of three, four, five people with an offer letter on the same land. First, before losing his farm was the loss of his insurance savings, pension and so forth. He came out of his 17-year job with nothing, except a house he'd built, a wife and baby. Unfortunately, these needed maintenance.

Farai then mobilized with some MDC Harare guys and established several new branches and wards in Mutare and surrounding villages and farms. They were highly successful, and Farai became a well-known key player in MDC politics.

However, he longed to rise higher, and there was much jostling for positions. In one seniors meeting he attended, somebody stood up and said, looking at Farai, @Some people must be vetted before they're accepted in the party. They just come here from Zanu PF after being fired, to spy on us and send information to their masters. I say no to certain people joining the party!".

There was much jubilation at that, and another immediately stood up and said, "It's true. As a hunter in a forest, I run after my hare, and catch it. After cooking and frying it nicely I deposit it into a plate. But Just as I'm about to start eating, somebody appears from the blue and snatches away that plate. Imagine!

"But let me tell you something, this is my rabbit in my plate. I will never let anyone take it away from me. This one is mine!"

At that, the people ululated loudly.

One weekend they travelled to Masvingo, to set up organs there. Dispel rumours and resolve some disputes. As they were about to finish, the room was stormed by Zanu PF men who started beating them up all over the body. There was a terrible fracas as they hit back.

In the end, the fight died down and the police got involved. The entire case had numerous twists and turns. Which culminated in Farai serving three months in jail, for attacking the Zanu PF guys who were 'just passing by.'

When Fatso was in hospital before going to prison, senior MDC officials had visited him and helped Shupi out. They left him word that some compensatory money would be coming his way.

Indeed, the money came, but not to Farai. As soon as it arrived at the provincial office, it stuck on sticky hands from left, right and centre. Some people who were not even involved in the Masvingo fracas took a share of the money. It was suspected that some Zanu guys had also eaten it.

Fatso was powerless against it all. He could not find a difference from Zanu PF. If politicians were of this nature, he was in a wrong camp. From that time onwards, he decided to mind his own personal business only, nobody else's.

GHOST WORKERS

One day in 2007, Farai was with Dube the plumber. Besides his main trade as a plumber, he also ran a stall at the market, where he sold fruits like bananas, tomatoes, oranges and also vegetables. It was not every day that a domestic sewerage or pipe burst and the victim had cash, so he had this stall to augment his income for himself, wife and four children. When the year was good his stall did very well to included pumpkins, melons, nuts and everything else you could think of. He did not grow these, but bought them at the large market in Sakubva for resell. Dube was one of the old guys, and talked fondly of the days he used to manage a plumbing company in town. "We were more than 15 plumbers in that company, and were doing well," he said.

Farai did not have to ask what happened, for he knew. Even though many whites had remained in the country after independence, it was the 'land revolution" that had chased most of them away, plus of course the whites' support for the MDC and Tsvangirai. So feeling threatened, most white companies folded and relocated to the neighbouring countries. Most went to South Africa, while a few went into nearby Mozambique. That left many people without jobs.

Seeing this, and perhaps fearing for mass action, the Government began to talk about indigenization and empowerment. They did not acknowledge any mistakes in the 'land revolution', but proceeded to threaten to take over all white owned companies and factories.

Some brave people with political connections took over some white-owned companies, while those without a clue on what to do or where to start, waited for a sign, which never came. Some of those who took over, and had no strong political connections, had the companies taken over by already rich people, who went about grabbing everything.

Others had not done so well. Their cooperatives had fallen through the ground, for one reason or other. Perhaps the indigenization policy came too abruptly, without the people readied yet. Perhaps the government needed to put certain things in place, first. Perhaps the people did not have any independent work ethic. Perhaps they were poor managers.

Farai did not know. But every time he talked to any indigenous business man, they told him that they were capable of anything. They told him they were skilled enough. "Do you think the white bosses did the donkey work that kept their companies on their feet?" they asked him. "No, it's us, the workers. Go to any farm or company and ask who did the bulk of the work, and you hear that it was us, the blacks. The managed only."

Perhaps that is where we miss it, management skills, Farai thought. He also thought that maybe they did not have any discipline where work was concerned.

To Dube and others, they were simply contend working for the white man. "What we want in life is food on our tables, education for our kids, good health and a generally stable life, and the whites provided that for us".

"But surely that was exploitation," Farai said, "because he took the bulk of the exploits and gave his workers peanuts."

"Not after independence," Dube answered. "After independence things had stabilized. The white man had understood the reality of black majority rule. We could talk. The courts functioned well in delivering justice for the workers. The real problem came with corruption, bad governance and refusal to leave office. Then the MDC came up and the whites saw an alternative, then boom, Zanu exploded."

"Yes. It was all about ingratitude. According to Zanu PF, by supporting the MDC, the whites were ungrateful for the hand of reconciliation at independence, and Mugabe went beserk."

Then Dube began to laugh.

"What?" Fatso asked him.

"It's hard to imagine how our lives have fallen," he said. "Yesterday I was at Sakubva market, ordering vegetables."

"Yes?" Farai encouraged him.

"Where I stood at the huge stalls where the vegetables are displayed, there is a tree, and a blind beggar sat there, singing and asking for alms."

"Yes?"

"I wanted to test him. I had a few old, useless Zimdollars on me, and a fake US dollar that someone had cheated me with. I dropped both notes into the beggar's plate, and he immediately snapped them up.

"He touched the Zimdollar first, felt it, and raised it as if to look at it properly. You know what he did?" Dube asked, fits of laughter filling his lungs. "He tossed it away, shouting, "Iwe, why do you want to test me? Do you think I am a fool? Take your stupid money and get away from here!"

"Then he lifted the fake US dollar, raised it and declared that it was fake, then threw it away as well…" Dube finished.

"You are not serious?" Farai asked, "A blind man detecting a fake note?" he said, laughing also.

True, corruption levels had grown so high in the country that it had encroached children, Farai remembered a popular joke shared on social media, about a photographer who came to a school to take much needed passport-size photos the following morning. He charged $2 per photo. When the headmaster made the announcement to teachers, he said $3 per photo (including an extra Dollar for himself), and when the teacher announced to the class, it was $4. When the child went home he told his mum that $5 was needed, and when mom went to Dad, it was $6. Imagine!

"Hey, Dube, 'Farai said, "who are those two guys?" he asked, pointing at two smartly dressed young men in jackets, obviously second hand from the flea market or bale.

"That one lives in your section of the suburb," Dube said, singling out one, 'and the other one stays across the bridge, to the left side of Phase 2."

"They appear to be loaded with cash. It's been some time since I saw them, drinking lagars and buying stuff in the Spar. In fact, I always see them each time I come around here. Where do they work?"

"Work?" asked Dube incredulously, and looking directly into Farai's eyes, "Work? You talk about work? These bastards don't work anywhere. They are ghost workers!"

Fatso had never seen one before, though he had heard about them especially since the formation of the Inclusive Government.

"So these people actually exist?" he asked Dube, looking more intently at the pair before his eyes, as they danced around each other, beer quarts hanging loosely at the sides, evidently very drunk, or pretending to be.

For it was regarded in high prestige in the locations, being drunk with lagars. It was a sign that one had money to burn, while all around was begging and gnashing of teeth. And there was no money rolling.

"There are so many of them. You know your friend, Sam? The one I sometimes see you with?"

"Of course, I know Sam."

'That one too," said Dube simply.

"Ah, what?" Sure, Farai was shocked.

"And Ray, that violent one who starts fights everywhere?"

"Sure, I know that young man."

"He is another one. They are not even ashamed of it. Most of them are high school dropouts, or have no single pass at Ordinary Level. If you ask them, they tell you they are employed in the Ministry of Youth, and that's it. They simply wait for big event days like Independence, Heroes, elections, and so on. That is only when they do a bit of work. Otherwise they earn a monthly salary for sitting in the sun…"

Farai was filled with rage, but there was nothing he could do. He made a point to ask one of them, Sam especially, and a few days later, he did.

"Sure, Mdhara,' Sam said, rather proudly, Fatso thought. "That's my job, sitting in the sun, but who cares? I don't care for the stupid party or its leadership. I don't even participate in some of the events they pay me for. There are hundreds of us, I could give you names of the local ones only. Most of us are children of war veterans. As you know, a war vet's child is also a war vet. And you know what, I am now due for an increment. If they don't give me, heads are going to roll at the local office, I swear. Do you want a beer?"

In spite of himself, Fatso accepted the beer. He thought it was amazing who people lived with in the country. Soldiers did the same. The police were better, at least they went to work. Farai's biggest question was why that money could not be used for the empowerment and indigenization that they shouted about? Why not channel it to repairing potholed roads, buy medication at clinics and hospitals, books for children, and improve the supply of electricity, and so on? Why not?

The problem with our problem, Farai thought, was that you can't have any enemies. The one you thought was your dependable friend could turn out to be benefitting from Zanu PF, and your enemy could be an active member in the party you loved and supported.

Just look at it; soldiers who blew people away with bullets if they were ordered to, lodged in ordinary people's homes. Same as the policemen who arrested them for demonstrating and striking. The guy who ran the bottle store they drank at supported Zanu PF, and the guy who ran the tuck-shop he bought sugar from was MDC. Something was wrong somewhere, but what to do about it was not clear.

And Strive Masiyiwa, international telecommunications business mogul, who was hero worshipped by millions of Zimbabweans, and at one time rumoured to be presidential candidate, was rumoured to be Zanu PF. He was rumoured to have sponsored the 2008 presidential runoff between Mugabe and the people's favourite, Tsvangirai. Of course, Tsvangirai would not hear the nonsense, and withdrew his candidature, and Mugabe ran alone, on Masiyiwa's millions, and won.

Fatso had many friends among the war veterans, gentlemen whom he drank and shared jokes with anytime any place. And they bought each other beers. When he asked them about ghost workers, or why soldiers should have electricity 24 hours a day while banks and schools didn't, they appeared not to support them, or change the subject.

In the end Farai just thought it was a case of personal survival, aggrandizement and security. This was another case of 'zvangu zvaita', meaning 'so long I benefit'

This is a situation where individuals just looked at their personal needs and affairs, and forgot the next person's. Just mind your own business, they seemed to suggest. But Farai disagreed, the welfare of his country and its people was his business.

INDEPENDENCE

Another Month of April, another independence day looming. But teachers were on strike and children roamed the streets. The TV and radio spewed nothing else besides war and blood. Farai's ears were bombarded with jingles of sovereignty, territorial integrity and the invincibility of people power. "Zimbabwe will never be a colony again! The sweat and blood at Chimoio, massacre at Nyadzonia, and those who lay unburied in the jungles of our land and beyond should not go to waste. That sacrifice, that heroic courage and determination should not be in vain!"

But teachers were on strike. For close to a year now, schools had been closed. Farai wondered if there was any future for teachers, or students in class, across the country. Of course, the government might make them sit exams at the end of the year, and adjust the scale to make them pass, but what was going to happen to those students in terms of their future life? It's survival of the fittest among them. Forever.

Some had already lost interest in school and education, again forever. No wonder why they had so many hwindis and gwejas in town. Sticke thought. And, because they had quick cash (or transport) they got very popular, and kids wanted to be like them. Their role models. Where are we heading? Farai asked himself, shaking his head in despair.

The more compelling question was what was the government doing to integrate these young men and women into the economy, for them to live a normal, healthy life? To Farai, the answer was zero!

In actual fact, the government was at war with them, preventing them from what they termed 'illegal mining, or chikorokoza and forcing them to involve in long, bureaucratic processes of registration, first. The hwindis they chased after, demanding money for protection.

This generation that went for a year or two without education because teachers were on strike, or because of political victimization, Farai called The Lost Generation. He knew that this lost generation had also brought about the Gweja Generation of small scale miners and other so called illegal dealers.

Farai watched on the Tv hordes of guerrilla fighters running all over in the bush, with green tree twigs and leaves on their heads like hats for camouflage. He watched some caught and ripped by the enemy's bullets, then dragged dead to waiting trucks and helicopters. He watched hundreds pulled and shoved and tossed into mass graves, clouds of flies buzzing around them.

He watched but could not hear the speeches of Herbert Chitepo, Josiah Tongogara, Jason Moyo, Robert Mugabe and others. Then some of them spoke, and he heard how the land was the issue, and why it had to be taken back from the whites and given to blacks.

It was war, war, war and bloodshed the whole month. Sellouts be warned, this country was not for sale. It's either you are with us or against us. To the few whites still remaining, please take note, we will forgive, but not forget. We will always remember what you and your forefathers did to us. We died for this country of milk and honey. No one will ever take it away from us. Don't be fooled by Tsvangirai and his handlers. He is nothing but a puppet of the West, and will never rule this country. Never, never, never.

It was all politics, and nothing else. Farai remembered how strong Mugabe was in political games, at the expense of national development. Uppermost in Farai's mind was Mugabe's failure to popularize Ubuntu, the all African philosophy of unity and peaceful co-existence, and it took the release of Nelson Mandela and South Africa's freedom in 1994 for the world to know about it. All Mugabe was interested in was political power, and how to keep it to himself.

Farai was sure that Mugabe's hatred of white people, especially the British and Americans, was rooted in his torture during incarceration. There, people said he was castrated or tortured to a point he could not have children in the normal way. And when his son died while he was in prison, the Rhodesians denied him time to go and bury him. He was his only child with Sally, his Ghanaian first wife.

This time of Independence was the most exciting time for war veterans and soldiers. They bragged about their military might and achievements. They boasted that they had defeated the British, and freed the country for everyone, including the MDC members who were now free to contest elections. This statement made many young men retort,: "Give the country back to the Rhodesians or British colonisers, and see if we cannot free it ourselves!."

This retort caused many quarrels and fights. However, the truth was that the war veterans and soldiers were the new colonizers. There was no freedom, and many people declared publicly that Ian Smith, the Rhodesian Prime Minister, was better than Mugabe.

The truth was that more civilians than armed soldiers died in that war. These civilians cooked for the guerrillas, carried their weapons, or gave them information. The war veterans came to the front with nothing but a gun. He was fed, clothed and cared for by the people in the villages and in town. They ran and sustained the war and, more often than not, were caught in crossfire, or they were hunted down and killed.

The guerrillas themselves killed thousands of their own civilians, especially when one was suspected or accused of giving information to Rhodesians, worked in the Rhodesian army or for a white boss. In the absence of the culprit, parents, relatives or other kin would be killed.

Some of the government ministers and officials did not help the situation at all. For example, one war veteran top government official would declare in interviews on public t television, "We freed you because you are cowards! Where were you when we went to war? You were in school, sitting pretty with the whites, while we were fighting for you! Nobody will ever rule this country, except Zanu PF!."

Mugabe was atypical example of how man loses his chances with God and life. He reversed his countless successes by clinging to power, and what it gave him. He was drunk with power. A typical case of absolute power corrupting absolutely!

Secretly, Farai thought that since his incarceration by the Smith government in the 60s, and the loss of his manhood in that process, the man did not have a penis, or could not sleep with a woman the way normal men did. However, thanks to the miracles of his hardworking friend and personal health consultant, Dr. Timothy Stamps, he managed to father three children with his second wife, Grace.

That he could not father children in the normal way had been established in the 80s, when as per customary tradition, Mugabe's sisters had approached his cousin, Albert, to sleep with Sally and father children for his cousin. Rumour said Sally fell pregnant, but when Mugabe heard it, he went ballistic. The long and short of it was that one morning, Albert's body was found floating in a swimming pool, at his home.

So because he had the energy to father children but could not do it, Mugabe channelled that energy elsewhere and made it productive, for him.

He channelled it towards achieving power and maintaining it. That became his obsession, over time, and he could not listen to different opinions.

Yet he had made countless progress in education, health, and general people comfort in the first 12 years of his career as president. But all that he lost, to power and the luxuries it brought.

Farai asked himself why people didn't love and enjoy the simple life. Of visiting parks and making and meeting new friends, and doing new things? He knew in his mind and heart that Zimbabwe needed an overhaul, as a nation. But where to start, he had no idea. He longed for that degree in Peace and Governance at Africa University.

Farai went outside, tired of the bombardment, because there was no other TV channel and he could not afford DS TV. The atmosphere was tense. He could count two or three people on the streets. He looked this way and that, and got back inside.

There was no food in the house, and he could not stand the look in his mother's eyes. There was no milk. There was no honey. Teachers were on strike. Nothing, no work was going on in the civil service. They just lingered and whispered in the offices. There was no money in the bank. Supermarket shelves were empty.

Farai didn't know when he last had meat or cleaned his teeth. All he did was loiter in the house, outside it, then inside again. He was in prison. The whole country was a prison. Many of his friends he talked to said that they had since forgotten about their parents, now in their old age and couldn't fend for themselves.

He didn't know when he last rode in a car or bus to town or anywhere for that matter. The only news he waited to hear, and he got was about the death of someone he knew.

There was no news, no connection with the outside world. Often, Farai heard that one of his relatives, a classmate, workmate or someone close had passed away and he could not go there. How could he? He stuck to himself and family, just hanging in there.

He sighed, and sat back in the worn out sofa. He wished he could go out into the diaspora like others, but he couldn't. He had no means nor connections. He waited.

He wondered at how few people he knew he met these days. Very few. There were strangers everywhere now, yet they used to know each other all in the neighbourhood, just a few years ago.

And whenever two people met these days, the greeting was the same, "Uchiko?" meaning are you still around/alive? This greeting meant two things, the first was that whoever asked that question had all but forgotten about his peer, and assumed him long dead, along with the others he'd known, or, it meant that the questioner was really glad to meet his peer, missed him and longed to be with him, for some reason or other, most likely, money.

Another popular greeting was, "Murikuzvigona sei" or how are you managing this (hard life?. If somebody greeted you this way, it only meant one thing at the back: begging or asking for a favour.

The greeter would be pretending surprise at seeing how good the other looked, and asking how that person was getting all those goodies. Usually, such a greeting was accompanied by a request for money or other favour.

One funny thing to Farai was that Zimbabweans were not open to discuss their problems. Every one you met, when you asked how they were, the answer was always, "bho", which meant fine, or Im ok. No problem.

Farai realized that culturally, Zimbabweans were trained from a young age not to reveal their troubles and poverty to people they didn't know. That should be a family secret, and we should be proud of who we are. This training begins in childhood, when children are smacked or otherwise punished for eating at a neighbour's, no matter how hungry they were. It was this culture that contributed to the lack of public discussion of social issues, and Zanu PF was taking full advantage of it.

Zimbabweans on the International Stage

Farai had heard of Zimbabweans across the world achieving global feats, such as the Zimbabwean Engineer Irvine Nyamapfene, who had electrified London's entire bus network, as late as June 2019. He knew of many Zimbabwean experts in mining, yet they were working in foreign lands for foreigners, leaving their own mineral rich country untapped, as people went hungry, and those pits becoming burying grounds for gwejas and illegal miners.

Mugabe himself was no pushover. He had seven acquired academic university degrees. When he stood up to speak at international conferences during the early years after independence, he would sway his audience every way he wanted, and they always waited to eat from his hand. Don't forget, at one point, he was friends with the Queen of England. Not now. Not anymore. The world got tired of him years ago, but he could not read the signs. So much for education to the world.

The current Minister of Finance, Mthuli Ncube, was said to have seven other international jobs, including guest lecturer in two international universities. That was something! However, it seemed their books and knowledge could not work in and for Zimbabwe.

But perhaps education was the major problem in Zimbabwe, Farai thought. People did not react to the government ill-treatment because they were too educated to bother with idiots. They would carefully analyse an action or anything before deciding whether to engage or not. It was all about personal benefit, and the need to remain alive.

In other countries, such would not happen. If what was happening in Zimbabwe could happen in South Africa, DRC, Malawi and other countries, chaos would have reigned long ago. No other nationality had the tolerance of Zimbabweans; of normalizing the abnormal. Farai had heard someone suggest that Zimbabweans who lived during Mugabe's era, the GNU. And the Mnangagwa eras deserved some small, international recognition.

Farai and his friends attributed the feats achieved by most of these Zimbabweans to the British culture of hard work and good education being the best source of success and power. Now that culture was gone, and anything else would do.

A good example was the gweja generation, who would do anything, including crime, for a dollar. Only the army was recruiting, and it was hellish competition there. Competition to dominate and reign supreme over public society. What a pity!

Otherwise, the region was also full of Zimbabweans, and their economies run by them. These were mainly the Independence and Born Free generations. At one point, South Africa alone was said to be hosting over 3million Zimbabweans. It was a booming economy then, after Mandela had just freed it and died. White bosses who wanted a good job done at reasonable cost looked for Zimbabweans. They knew their skill, and could communicate very well.

However, because they could not wear the 'foreign' identity and wanted to experience their freedom in a fellow African land, and because South Africans felt 'entitled' to every piece of South Africa, the latter unleashed xenophobic attacks on Zimbabweans, between 2008 and 2019, killing them with machetes in broad day light. They wrapped tyres around their necks and burned them, watching their flesh drop with the fire and tyre.

Stories were numerous of South African goat herders who went into Johannesburg in numbers, visited surgeries and other critical services departments, pulled out screaming surgeons and other specialists, and accused them of taking their jobs. Imagine that!.

And they would kill those specialists in broad daylight, while the police and other spectators watched. Farai thought for people who brought Ubuntu to the world, South Africans needed to do a lot to appease the human spirit. He thought a good Zimbabwean ambassador would one day open that door, for open discussion, but ultimately for compensation.

Farai giggled to himself when he thought of the embarrassing experience involving Mnangagwa. While Rwanda, DRC and Malawi pulled out of the World Economic Forum to be held in South Africa starting September 2019, in protest against Xenophobic attacks on Zimbabweans in the country, and Zambia called a soccer friendly against Bafana, President Mnangagwa was already in South Africa, waiting for the Forum to start.

Nothing could show more clearly that this leader did not care about his people. There was the evidence.

Meanwhile, South Africans were sending messages, warning every foreigner to have left the country by the 10th September, 2019, if they still wanted their lives.

As a matter of fact, the human race should not continue to watch what is happening in South Africa, without taking any action. A strong international peace force should enter that country and instill order and stop the killing. The international community must teach South Africa a lesson.

If what is happening to black foreigners in South Africa is bad, then it could happen to you, because you are also part of the human race. It sure will, if you cannot stop this stupid madness in South Africa.

In spite of their abilities, intelligence and victimhood in the terrible xenophobia attacks, Farai was also aware that Zimbabweans could take full advantage of their plight, wherever they went. They would keep on receiving, to no end as long as the goodies kept coming, and as long as they had the intelligence, skill and ability. In their endless receiving they know, but ignore or forget, that their country is rich, and they can afford to buy those things with their own money and live the life they want. Yet they do nothing about it but crack jokes about their plight. He had heard stories of Zimbabweans and other blacks in Harare and Johannesburg living in huge debt but staying in mansions and driving huge automobiles bought on credit, while real billionaires like Ted Turner drove around in 3 series BMW. There was a huge lack of Ubuntu in that, and needed to change.

A FIGHT OVER SOCCER GAME

With nothing to do at home one Sunday afternoon, Farai went to watch a soccer match between the national soccer team (the Warriors), who lost again, to Mozambique, of all teams. There was a time Zimbabwe would thrash Mozambique 5-0, at home or away. Now this!

Throughout the entire match there were Ahs and Eighs from fans, both in the stadium and those watching the game on TV at home or in bars and restaurants across the country.

This was becoming the trend with the national team. Last month they had lost to Angola, 1-0, at home. That was the return match. In the previous one in Luanda they had lost 3-0. Before that they had also lost to Malawi. It appeared as the economy got worse, so did the national team. Yet it was everyone's pride and joy. It was the only hope for heroes, and the children saw in it their hopes and dreams, and nowhere else. Everywhere else was below mediocrity.

Anyway, this story you're reading happened before now, when Zimbabwe is placed in the same AFCON group with Somalia-and losing a match to them. Honestly, Somalia! With its warlords and mafia type of government and general way of life? It's not surprising how we got this low. It happened right before our eyes, and it is happening now, on a daily basis.

Anyway, to continue my story:

Apparently, after winning their first game against Mozambique at home, the President had nearly declared himself patron. He had invited the entire squad to State House, fed them and told jokes, in the hope that they would win.

Farai thought this was the tragedy with the country's politics and general way of life. In the midst of the doom and gloom across the country, when Zimbabwe's politicians saw a glimmer of success in any field, they were quick to grab it and claim responsibility for that and subsequent other successes.

That was how Gideon Gono was created. He seemed to have been doing well at his CBZ, Bank, until the politicians snatched him up and put him at the helm of the Central Bank as Governor.

And he presided over the worst Reserve Bank in the history of any nation, including America during the depression and Germany after the war, or even Zambia during Kaunda's reign. And to prove it, it was during Gono's tenure as Governor that the nation lost its very own currency, which was their flagship and identity. And the politicians ululated and showered praises all the while. Talk of serving one's people, thought Farai.

So, Farai was in Chikanga Bar, watching, along with scores of other patrons as the national team lost at home to Mozambique. It was Ahs and Ugghs throughout the game, because of lost chances and near misses. Finally, the whistle to end the game blew, and people trickled out. Farai was so angry, so furious. Deep down inside, however, he was not surprised at the loss, because everything else in the country was rotting away.

As he stepped outside the bar, he put his frustration into words, "How can we expect them to perform?" he asked no one in particular, "when the entire country is underperforming? We cannot expect miracles from these idiots when there is rottenness everywhere. Until we change this below mediocre government of looters and killers, we shall continue to be the whipping boys of the region…"

Then he felt a hand upon his shoulder.

"What did you say?" asked a tall, light-skinned guy, dipping his fingers into Farai's shoulder bone

Fear took the place of anger, but only for a moment. He knew he had expressed the sentiments of many people in that bar that day, or the nation at large.

"How can you expect them to win," he said, "when the country is losing everything it ever had, including teachers, workers and goods?"

Farai's confidence threw the inquirer off balance a little, but like him, he too quickly gained his composure.

"Who told you that?" he asked, in an unmistakable Ndebele tone.

"I know it. I see it every day. Teachers striking, some leaving for the diaspora, people leaving every day. Factories closing, shelves empty in supermarkets. Where do you think the players can get the food to build stamina?"

"Where do you stay? Where is your home?"

"Here in Chikanga," Farai replied.

By then some of the people getting out of the bar had formed a circle around the two. This was bad, the circle. It was as if these people were expecting a fight, and encouraging it by forming the circle.

"What did he say?" asked another guy, a soldier whom Farai always saw in the bar, but knew little about.

"He is mocking the country, blaming the political leadership for the national team's failure to qualify…"

"Does that have anything to do with politics?" said the soldier, looking directly at Farai.

"Everything has to do with our politics, at least in this country. What aspect of our lives is not controlled by politics? Education, health, transport, you name it. And that includes sport."

"Politicians do not train any sportspeople, but civilians do. Where do you live?"

"Here in Chikanga…"

"Nobody lives in this bar. Where is your home? What job do you do?"

Before Farai answered, someone in the crowd shouted. "That one is just a teacher".

"Just a teacher, heh? He extended his hand to Farai's collar.

You are the people who teach our children politics at a young age. Come here…" The soldier pulled Farai to himself by the hand, half dragging him behind the bar. The onlookers followed, silently, from a distance.

He pulled Farai against a civilian blue truck, slapped him hard on the left cheek, then the right, and slumped to the ground, his spectacles fallen, too.

"Next time you say something stupid… I'll kill you!" he said.

He turned around the car, opened the door, shut himself in and drove fiercely out, the crowd creating space for him.

And after that, everybody started to talk.

"We should have done something, guys" some said.

"He was only one! Alone, and all we did was watch!"

"Next time he does this again, we will butcher him."

"But you told them the truth, Fatso. That was really brave. They don't want to hear the truth", said a teacher friend.

While some gave Farai a wide berth, one or two helped him to his feet and left him on the road home.

After this incident and many others involving the army, Farai had time to reflect on the changes that had come with independence, and its impact on people's lives. He found that society had changed, even its hierarchy and order had changed. At the top of the social ladder in most communities were the war veterans, followed by soldiers. Soldiers especially ruled the roost, especially if they were also war veterans. They would rule the entire shopping centre. They could urinate everywhere when drunk, say anything to anybody, and demand to buy anybody anything.

A private soldier, even without a single "O" Level pass, earned a salary that was higher than a teacher's, no matter the service or age differences. This gave soldiers immense power. The government also gave them powers, especially at provincial level.

At one point, they had the responsibility to distribute land and mining claims to people. Such processes were fraught with confusion and chaos. Soldiers also could do the work of the police, oftentimes beating up and harassing civilian suspects to no end. They walked around in numbers, drawing fear out of people.

The soldier bosses or 'chefs', as they were called, would send a driver 30km to drive their wives 2km to collect a school child or see a friend, and return to the barracks. Such was the luxury of being in power.

As a young boy growing up, Farai had been made to believe that schools were the source of human resources to fill up gaps left by those who died or retired, now it was muscle, and not education.

Farai also marvelled at the tides of time: Only a few years ago when he was growing up, people did not just mix with everybody. Soldiers especially were at the bottom of the social ladder. It was not socially proper for a Christian young man, who was a part of the Youth Fellowship, to be seen in the public company of a soldier or uniformed police man.

These two groups were associated with crime and violence, and so nobody liked to be associated with them. But now things had changed. To Farai, it was plain to see that blood and violence now ran the show in the country. He wondered where the country was headed.

Mugabe himself never benefitted from his huge investments in education. He ranted against university students and graduates who criticized him, from as early as the 1980s and failed to pay them, and when they found they were in demand outside of the borders, they fled. And Mugabe continued to insult them, to the point of hunting them down, denying them citizenship, barring and torturing them.

What a loss, what a theft, what a waste! Mugabe stole the lives of his fellow citizen, and crashed them on the wall. He killed a lot of dreams, wasted a lot of lives, and did a lot other things.

He remembered reading Ian Smith's book, 'The Great Betrayal', in which he compared Zanu PF with a Mafia Gang. He said there was no difference between them. To Farai, it was plain to see.

Farai, along with the majority of Zimbabweans in the country, believed that soldiers had no place in a poor, developing country like Zimbabwe. They had no respect for human rights. Video clips had circulated through social media of uniformed soldiers beating up women in public places. That was horrific, and of course, the army had said it would investigate. No news came after that. The point was, that was how they ruled, by fist, Mugabe style.

The most common news and complaint from his teacher friends was that classrooms and schools were filled with soldiers' children. Whilst they were the naughtiest and caused the biggest problems of drug-related incidents, the bulk of them just vanished into thin air after school, never to be heard of again. The explanation for that was because they went into the military or so called security sector. Very few of them ever went to university, as compared to children of civilians. So, the country was slowly but surely turning into physical militarization, in all spheres and ethos of life.

RETHINKING ZIMBABWEAN POLITICS-16 JANUARY

Dear Farai

I acknowledge receipt of your letter dated 04 January. As it happens, I shall be visiting Mutare on 16 January for the official opening of the American Corner at the Turner Memorial Library. Is it possible for you to come there so we can meet and discuss your plans and proposal further?

Regards
D. B. Wharton

Farai received this email from the new American ambassador, a day before the date, and was very excited about the coming meeting. That night, he slept very little, turning ideas in his head and thinking of the best ways of presenting those ideas. He saw the meeting as an opportunity that did not come every day, and so was determined to make the most out of it. Attached to the email was a programme of events. Besides opening the American Corner, there was also a speech to be delivered by the ambassador followed by a question and answer session. It looked like it would be a beautiful day, Farai thought.

As he crossed the small footbridge that linked the library to a supermarket, Farai saw hordes of placard- carrying men and women ahead. They turned and walked down the stairs to the library basement, where the talk was going to be held. By the time he got down those stairs and entered the basement, there was pandemonium already, with the placard wielding people on their feet, singing and shouting Zanu slogans. They were about a hundred, mostly young men and women. There were also a number of elderly men, with national or party symbols, pins and badges on the lapels of their jackets. They were unmistakably the country's war veterans.

There were about 10 whites, mostly women, including evicted mayor, Brian James and his wife. The singing and hand clapping grew louder by the minute, with the mob slowly moving deeper in the American Corner section, a beautiful place of quiet reading and internet access. They moved further in beyond that, chanting and waving placards. Some began to strike at tables with wooden sticks and iron rods as they sang and danced. One woman stripped off her dress and bra, leaving just her pant, and shouted insults about the whites and opposition supporters. They did not touch or pull down the books from shelves.

After a while they turned back into the hall and faced the fear-filled whites.

"Go back to Britain," they shouted.

"Remove the sanctions," some said

"Wharton, go back to America. We don't need you here."

"Give us jobs. We need jobs."

"We want our land."

"Zimbabwe will never be a colony again"

Meanwhile, Farai stood against the wall, along with a few friends. They visibly shook their heads in disgust. "Is this the dialogue that we were invited to partake in?" Farai asked aloud.

He knew quite a number of the youth, very nice and cheerful on the streets and in the neighbourhood. While their body language showed disdain at what was happening, later he saw them join in the singing and sloganeering.

One of them slapped Obama's hard paper statue in the face three or four times, then tore off the head before pushing the rest of the body to the floor. Others struck at cameras on the table. Meanwhile, four of the elderly men sat at the front table where the dignitaries would sit, then lulled and toyed with gadgets smiling at the audience still brave enough to remain in the room.

A striking thing about these young men and women was their dressing and general demeanour. Some of them were ill-clad. Shoes and shirts had depleted soles and gaping holes. Some were evidently ill or in dire need of nutrition. Others were drunk, and openly drank the illicit Zed spirits from bottles and cans.

Farai asked one of them what the issue was about, and his answer was "Our diamonds. They are stealing our diamonds."

He also asked another why Zanu PF always lost elections in Manicaland, if it had this much support. He did not know.

As the mob moved towards them threateningly, the whites left the building, a group following them. In the foyer stood Brian James and his wife. One war veteran Farai knew very well approached the ex-mayor and said," Brian James, you are no longer mayor, get out!"

But James refused to budge. Two or three others joined the war vet and tried to pull him by the hand. The man stood his ground, hanging onto a high wooden desk. He said he would not go out. His wife stood a distance and produced a camera and began to take shots of what was happening.

Eventually they left him and joined the large group that had gathered outside of the library. The big war veteran spotted Farai, then with his face cast aside, said, "Certain people are worse than dogs. No matter how many degrees they get, dogs still think better than them. What does a white man give you? A dog knows the source of its problems, but certain people don't!

Farai grinned to himself, shaking his head in puzzlement. Meanwhile, the mob had surrounded the ambassador's 4x4, where he was closed in with his staff and family, may be. They continued to sing and chant and dance around that vehicle.

As all this was happening, the well-known state media journalists were having a field day. They mingled with the dancing crowds, pens, pads and cameras openly displayed. They demanded a room inside the building, where they would take photos and recordings. The people loved that, and sang and danced the more.

Farai said to the ZTV news crew (whom he knew) that he wanted to be interviewed and give an opinion, but he stared at him, then walked away.

As all this was happening, there was no sign of the police. Farai however spotted two policemen that he knew well. They were in civilian clothing, busy taking notes and photos.

One young man remarked that most of the demonstrators had been offered free beer to do what they were doing. They went for him.

He fled, past a large building nearby (Courthauld Theatre) and out across the bridge. But like hounds that had tested blood they chased after him. They brought him, dragging him by the collar of his shirt as he quaked with fear. They sat him down under the Municipality building across the road. The crowd on the other side could not tell what was transpiring, but shouted that they should not beat him up. The situation relaxed after a while of interrogations.

The ambassador's vehicle slowly began to move out, the mob in front and behind it. A white banner inscripted something about sovereignty and sanctions was held by two men on either side of the vehicle. One man behind the vehicle sang and kicked the car as he ran by its side, until it got onto the main road.

More talk continued, mostly in hushed voices, about the implications of all that for elections that year. Most wondered whether this was the right platform for a demonstration. If President Mugabe would be glad to have a chat with the ambassador, or with the US President, why cant others? Why cant people boycott such events, instead of disrupting them? It is allowed to stick placards on the walls, then sit down and listen, or walk out, isn't it?

This was a futile attempt, because people had satellite dishes in their homes and watched and listened; they could still know what was happening in the world, whether the US ambassador addressed them or not. They had social media, the internet, sms etc. Farai thought that Zimbabweans politicians needed to think better, if they wanted to win the coming elections. Disrupting public meetings was a sign of weakness, a failure to think and a clear sign that there would be violence in the coming elections.

One by one the mob dispersed, until there was no one by 4.30

Farai had a number of questions for the ambassador, but the biggest was how as Manicaland people they could be helped to organize against the exploitation of their resources and people. The government never explained how the Mutare people failed to get even a single investment from the diamonds that were theirs. They could not explain why people from Manicaland had to travel to Harare to apply for a job at Chiadzwa. He wanted to ask him if Mutareans could get assistance to avoid the murders, rapes, arsons, beatings and other human rights violations that always happened at election time, especially as elections were drawing close.

If that was selling away, Farai didn't know what was not. So many other people had questions. Others wanted help to form business partnerships, or access scholarships, and so on. Though that chance was lost, Farai still believed there was room for tolerance in the nation's politics. There was need to inculcate a culture of tolerance, of respecting individual differences and perceptions.

The world was becoming smaller and smaller, and Farai did not know for how much longer his country should remain in isolation. While China had opened up to the west, Zimbabweans were fooled into thinking that they were self-reliant and self-sustaining. Honestly, how could they do that while at the same time calling for investments? Worse still, the nation was using their currency! Farai felt that the need for organizing and civic education was more vital then, than ever before.

Two Kinds of Politics

To Farai Zimbabwe had two kinds of politics: the politics of thought and that of spontaneous, unthinking habits. The politics of thought did not support a political party, but the policies of that party or what that party stood for. A person of thought asked a political party to explain its position on key issues, and interrogated whether those issues served his interests. Only on that basis did he vote that party. A person of spontaneous and unthinking habits did not interrogate. He had no reason for supporting a party except that his father or uncle supported it. To him, politicians were demi-gods, (according to hierarchical positions) with everything to give away to the have-nots, so the competition was on pleasing them and making them happy.

HE HIGHS AND LOWS
OF GHETTO LIFE

This Christmas 2014 Diasporas are very few. Over the years, by Christmas time the town would be teeming with them. Wherever you went in town or in the locations, you would bump into a long lost familiar somebody, who'd been to the UK, Ireland, South Africa, America, Botswana and elsewhere in the world. Christmas was the time they all flocked homeward to see their old folks and show off their latest cars, flash a bit of cash and fashion, and generally touch base with all and sundry. It was like rural Christmas in the sixties and seventies again, when some guys who were lucky to get gardening or messenger jobs from white people in Harare would come home loaded with bread, margarine, jam and sweets, and we would not sleep that first night, dancing to gramophone music till we dropped dead with fatigue. That was also when a goat, cow and chickens would be slaughtered for meals.

On the day itself Farai and his friends would gather at the shopping centres, looking immaculate in their best, watching Harareans rule the roost.

Yes, so those times were very similar to those just past, the 2007, 2008 and 2009, when we locals lived at the mercies of Diasporas. For why not? A South African Rand fetched hundreds of Zimdollars, while a US Dollar or pound could literally wipe out a whole market stall. So these Diasporas rolled in the money, and we locals followed them like bees after nectar.

But that was then. This is now. After the Unity Government in 2009, things improved greatly, especially with the multi-currency system. The US

Dollar was the most widely used, and the guys from South Africa found it difficult to compete. Even those living and working in the UK found it futile to send money as they used to: "What the heck?" said Tsano Mbuu, who used to wipe out all the stocks in the local bottle store each time he was around. "You guys are made of sterner stuff, and I raise my arms to you. How do you manage, especially with the unemployment and how difficult the US Dollar is hard to come by?"

And the guys would stand proudly erect, a broad smile across the face, to show they were made of real sterner stuff. Tsano Mbuu loved them for that, and would buy them anything they wanted, and often had to borrow money from them, to make his start back in London. Such was their bond.

So, the majority of Diasporas did not come home at all, because they knew they would not compete with locals, or would be broke in just two weekends. Only the serious ones, those who were not the show- off kind, came and hid in their homes and families. Most of these declared that they no longer drank beer. But Farai and his crew knew better. In Europe, for example, a can of Heineken cost 50c, but in Zim it went for two US dollars or more. At one point pints and quarts were sold in billions of Zim dollars. Check…The same goes for many other goods now available in our shops. They sell at double or treble the price in Europe, and still business flourishes. At such a question those around smiled confidently and proudly, to show that indeed, they had tough mettle.

Fatso remembered clearly that a few years back, the jokes were about Zimbabweans in the diaspora, and how they took up nursing jobs in the UK and other countries, just for survival. Those jokes tell you or anybody how proud indigenous Zimbabweans were of their heritage. Now, the jokes were about their politicians and the run down economy and social life.

Farai always thought that the problem with Zimbabweans was their own fault, and always cursed them for it. When a strike or mass action to boycott expensive bread, or transport costs was called, not everybody joined in. Even when a person had money for a day's loaf, or transport money for one day, he considered himself covered for the day, and so did not worry about tomorrow. He viewed the problem as belonging to people who did not have the money that day, and not his. Because he had the money that day, he did not join the mass action, and considered it as for the poor. Another culture, this one called 'bling' emerged.

There was no unity, like in South Africa, where everybody would come together for a common cause. There was no unity among them, and that was why their peaceful mass action failed to bring required results, every time. Such protests almost always ended in violence, and that benefitted the government, which had stronger muscles.

Thus those who took part in any industrial action were eventually rounded up and thrown into prison, and lawyers got fame and publicity-but all for nothing. It was the same cycle every time. To no end, until they gave up demonstrations altogether, for a long time. Still they suffered in silence. These days they were saying strikes, marches and demonstrations cost them money. They would go to work on the day, only to find that their customers don't come, because of the stay away. What rubbish, they say.

Nobody saw any reason at all in leaving their source of income to engage in demonstrations, from which they saw no immediate benefits.

The other reason some of these Diasporas said they did not want to come was 'political'. They accused the locals of having voted wrongly in the 2013 election, and so they had to face the consequences alone.

They said they had supported Zimbabweans at home strongly over the years, with money, accommodation, air tickets and stuff, hoping that they would change the government, but had not. Instead they lied that they hated zanu PF, and voted for it behind their backs.

Of course, the locals knew better, and they too knew better. It was just an excuse.

For years, elections had been an issue in the country, as far as Fatso's fading memory could recall. There had never been an uncontested election, except the one that brought independence. That one had no dispute. But all others after that one were disputed. This went as far back as 1995, if Fatso remembered correctly. And it was not a safe or pleasant subject to discuss or think about.

So this year's Christmas was a much localized affair. Of course the locals looked for the Diasporas, for free beer, etc, but very few came. Farai's sister, two brothers, an uncle and aunt did not, and so did Shellaz brother. Tendai had a niece, but she too did not come. They still saw cars with foreign registration around, but very few parked at the bottle store.

The funny thing, according to Fatso and those around him, was that those who purported to be going to work did nothing at their jobbing places, except loiter, gossip and go home. Everyone tried to put as little effort in their work as possible, and save the energy for something else, more profitable, hopefully.

The only thing people concentrated on, especially now that there were cell phone, was gossip and sharing group messages on WhatsApp. As things appeared to Farai and other people in the city, those who spent their time at work for a salary appeared worse off than those who had no jobs at all.

The latter had all the time to look for means of getting money, while the former spent it at work, where they got hardly enough to sustain themselves for the coming month. Because of this, a lot more people resigned from their jobs and spent time on the streets, looking for money.

Farai wondered which the informal and formal sectors of the economy were. To him, the government was evidently informal. This was further aggravated by the fact that nearly everything was obtained on the so called informal market, from health needs, education (private schools sprouted up and were better run than government and council schools), food, clothes and anything else that a person wanted. Clearly, the government had no control over the national economy.

Everywhere across the country, people looked for money to feed themselves and nothing more. It was like a war zone, with people all over, evidently hungry or starving, but looking for money, just for the day. Most of the money circulated on the streets, not banks or legal businesses, because most business happened there, for example, dealing in donated second hand clothing, dealing in forex, and selling anything that could raise money, and offering services.

Very few people invested their money or bought things of value. The money just wasn't there, or it lost its value any time. Very often, prices of goods on supermarket shelves changed prices four or five times while a customer was in a queue to the pay machine.

And outside, on the streets or homes, people always shouted at each other about money. The biggest arguments were on the fact that the money was lent or borrowed when the US$ was at a certain rate, and now if that money was returned at that old rate, the lender had lost. These adjustments happened every day, sometime twice per day, and caused countless quarrels, fights and court cases.

It was not profitable therefore to lend people money, or borrow, without carefully calculating the trend of the rate, or the anticipation of a reasonably big figure of money.

Farai thought that Zimbabwean politicians employed large teams of people to monitor and delete the bad messages that were spread about them on WhatsApp. If they knew what people said about them, Farai thought they would immediately, voluntarily resign, or run amok shooting everybody in sight.

Zimbabweans were not kind in their criticism of their government. Their vent for stress and tension was in their jokes. They said anything that came to mind, regardless of who the target was. Whenever three or more people met and stood or sat together, Farai had no doubt that the subject they discussed was their political situation. They joked about the politicians' clothes, their scarfs, dances, their speeches and anything else that came to mind.

Others went around declaring that the country, or lucrative parts of it like the Victoria Falls and the mineral rich Great Dyke, had long since been sold to various others, including Chinese and Russians, who were mining gold.

Nasty jokes were also spread about the top brass in the political leadership. Some people got caught and were arrested, but the lawyers always tried to do a good job.

The other embarrassing thing was that alphabetically, Zimbabwe was the last country in the world. This was embarrassing, because many Zimbabweans also saw it as the last, economically and socially. At one point Zimbabweans were said to be the least happy people on the planet, and that did not help. Ever creative, Zimbabweans accuse Mugabe and team of naming a country after ruins, of all things! How could they?

And others say our currency became useless the time we started printing bearer cheques and bond notes without an inscription of a human head. A human head is a symbol of life, and any money without that is valueless, useless and can be tossed away without any thought. Such was the Zimbabwean currency.

One Saturday around this time, Farai struggled out of bed, pulled his trousers and shirt from the chair by the bed and staggered towards the door. Outside, he stood by the windowsill, facing the rising sun. Jesus, he needed a cigarette, but the shops were quite some distance away and he could not just vanish without telling the wife. He looked around, but failing to locate her anywhere, he ambled out the gate and headed for the shops. Not that he had any money on him, but there would be many people at the shops, and he would get a cigarette from any one of them, or someone would 'cut' him one.

It was difficult to understand, he thought to himself, how when he had no cent on him, he rarely found a friend, or anyone to offer him a sip. But when he had just enough for a pint, offers were extended left, right and centre, and he would be spoiled for choice.

As he walked, a thought occurred to him that he should pass by Tendai's house, just to check on him and see if they would go up together. They had drunk together the previous night, and he could not remember where or how they had separated. He would be a suitable companion, just for being on the same par and catching up.

Sure enough, after knocking the lock of the gate on the iron pillar that supported it and two loud shouts, Tendai announced that he was coming out. In no time he was, and together they walked.

But after only two steps, Farai spotted a pair of jeans trousers tossed carelessly under the hedge, and a pair of black spotted underwear beside them. The two stopped dead in their tracks.

"What could have happened?" Tendai asked.

"Robbery", Farai replied briefly, moving closer to the hedge.

"Or sex," said Tendai. "The guy might have failed to pay for services rendered…"

"Then what? You think the prostitute striped him and dumped the clothes here?"

"You're right. No sense in that…But I bet there is money in there", said Tendai, joining Farai close to the hedge

"Forget it," said Farai. "Whoever mugged this guy did it for the money, and so would not leave any…"

"I still think there could be money in there. However, I do not want to touch the trousers…"

"Why? Then how are you going to find out?"

"I won't touch the trousers. The victim will certainly go to a sangoma or Nikuv to fix whoever mugged him… and I don't want to be involved."

The mention of Nikuv sent shivers down everyone's spine. To some people, she was a saviour, and a blessing, while to others she was the devil himself. She was believed to possess magical powers that could turn you into whatever her whims fancied, a snake, a bird, jackal or smoke. She herself was believed to be all those things, and so was of no fixed abode. Everyone agreed that she did exist, though.

Then suddenly, Farai had an idea. "Let's get to the shops and see Mosey," he said.

"Or Bruno", added Tendai, brightening up.

"Yes. Or Professor.

"Or Bhonono."

"But should we leave things as they are? What if some courageous someone, or even Bhonono himself comes along and searches them?"

That was a problem, and for a moment or two, the two pondered what to do. Tendai suggested he should get back into the house, take a bed sheet and cover the lot, but decided against it after fearing for the sheets. Farai suggested they cover the jeans with leaves from the hedge, but Tendai thought it was not safe. Finally, after looking around, they picked up a stick and shoved the clothes deeper into the hedge, then walked hurriedly to the shops.

Sure enough, the place was already teeming with people, and Pedzi's disco was already booming. Farai and Tendai headed for the Breeze, next to a tree where all the guys started the day with all kinds of toxic drinks from vhinyu to opaque beer to ganja and everything else. Professor was there, and so were Bruno and Mosey.

Tendai immediately took charge. "Guys", he said to all and sundry, "we are in. *Tapinda*, boys."

"What do you mean?' Mosey asked, eyes like two red moons.

"We are in for Christmas. It's going to be ours this year, after all."

"How?" Bruno asked, eyes also bulging out.

Then Tendai proceeded to tell them what he and Farai had seen. But he added, "From one of the back pockets of the jeans we saw a corner of a twenty US Dollar note, protruding…. Only we were afraid to take the money."

"Twenty dollars?" Mosey, Professor and Brian said at once.

"Yeah, twenty," Farai said, looking bored.

For a moment, everybody fell silent, talking only with their eyes.

Brunno was the first to recover. "Lets go," he said, rising from the rock on which he sat.

"Me too. I want to join you," announced Professor.

"Okay," said Tendai. I will go with you two".

So they left. Of course the others were part of the deal, and would benefit too, otherwise they might blow the whistle if things got sour.

When Tendai left with Bruno and Professor, Farai remained behind. There wasn't any drinking taking place, and all those around him wore long, forlorn faces. "Guys", Farai said, "you see what elections have brought us? Nothing! Let me tell you something, this year the politicians were shouting the slogan: Bhora Mugedhi. I tell you, next year it has to be Dhora Mubhegi. It should all be about money, and not politics".

"The only way our situation can improve is when our President marries Graca Machel," said Mosey, tobacco smoke spilling out of his mouth and nose.

"How is that?" asked Simba.

"Well, she married Samora, and he died. Then she married Mandela, and he also died. I am sure if she marries our President…"

"Hey," said Simba again, "do you know that some South Africans are complaining about how long it is taking before Mandela is buried?

"Ten days? Of course that is very long, but well worth it. You cannot bury such a great man the day after his death, like we do most people."

"According to some people, there is too much of Mandela in South Africa as it is. There is Mandela Day, Mandela Park, Mandela Stadium, Mandela Hospital, Mandela Street, and so on. They are afraid that the days of the week shall be named after Mandela. Thus they will have Mondela, Tuesdella, Wednesdiba, Thurstata, Fritata, Saturdella, Sundiba."

"And that is how dictatorships begin," said Farai, "only that Mandela himself never showed any signs of it during his brief time in office. But all that must be coming from his cronies…the dictator type…"

"Yeah, the bootlicking dogs…"

"Sadistic dunderheads who celebrate at the pain and suffering of fellow beings…"

Just then, the three who had gone to search the jeans came back. "Tough, guys", said Tendai extending his hand to Mosey's cigarette.

"Nothing? asked Farai. 'I knew it. Whoever stripped the guy of his clothes did it for the money. There was no way they would leave it in the trousers."

So with their hopes dashed, the guys settled for hot illicit stuff that they diluted with water, and thus began another long day of tales and dramas.

A week later the trousers and underwear had an owner-a young man who worked in a shop in town. He said he'd been robbed. Meanwhile, the trousers and underwear had long gone.

Another three weeks later, the story had another turn. Brunno proudly professed that he had actually seen the trousers before Tendai and Farai, and had pulled out $20 US Dollars out of them.

Many other twists were added to it, but no one cared about it anymore.

A WAY OF LIFE

With a few exceptions, November Saturday mornings were usually bright and shiny. For Farai, however, the difference was the same. He had a splitting headache from last night's heavy drinking and, besides, there was little or nothing to feed the family on. Hanging around at home and watching the long faces of his wife and two kids filled him with guilt. Not that the fault was his: his company had closed two years ago and in spite of his high education and qualifications as a fitter and turner and before that as a plumber, finding another job had been a real mountain to climb. But this morning seemed different.

For the last two days the upper lid of his right eye had been twitching continuously. Whenever this happened, he knew luck was on its way. For as long as he could remember, it was always like that, and he had grown never to doubt it. It was only a question of time. He wondered why it was always like that to him, being ruled by signs and signals.

The events leading to the termination of his employment stood uppermost on his mind. For two weeks the lower lip of his left eye twitched incessantly, and then bam, the sudden announcement of the closure of the biggest paper making company in the country. Yet he had been doing quite well. He even remembered as a lad growing up in the locations; each time his lower left eyelid twitched, he would cry. Much as he tried to avoid it, tears would roll down his cheeks by the end of the day. Some boy would hit him, or either of his parents would. There was never a miss.

And then he remembered his marriage to Shupi, the apple of his eye. Even before that, the very first day they met and fell in love. Two doves had flown past his home as he left for town, and then silently, he had said, "Two for Love!" They had always said that, as children growing in the streets. During those early days, however, they would shout it, even competing and coming to near fistfights as each child claimed the two flying doves to themselves. And then of course, on that day he had met Mandy in town, fallen in love, and with time, proposed and, nine months later, they were married.

And then later, he discovered that numbers also played a part in determining the course of his days. Each time a series of the same number appeared, say on a calendar, he would make a wish, and that wish always came true. It was always something immediate and pertinent in his life.

For example, once the time was 8 minutes past 8 o'clock in the morning on August the 8th year 2008. That meant five sets of eights, and he made a wish to be promoted at his job. That very week, he received a letter to that effect. Oh his life was ruled by signs and numbers, of that he had no doubt. Unfortunately, the frequency with which the positives happened were fewer than the negatives, especially as he grew older, and he had no explanation for that. This led to a decrease in faith, but more often than not, the negatives were almost always forewarned.

Coming out of the house this bright Saturday morning of November 2015, he stood by the kitchen window, hands buried into the front pockets of his faded jeans. He looked at the rising sun but, blinded by its sharp rays, lowered his eyes and slowly walked towards the gate, hands still deep in his pockets. He did not see Mandy anywhere and, guessing that she had gone to some neighbour or other opened the gate.

He walked up the road, looked left and right then took the left turn, towards the main road. He was always careful which way he took to Spar because it was determined by which way he had creditors, especially at the tuck-shops. He didn't want to be asked for money for cigarettes he'd borrowed, especially on a day like today, when he'd no cent in his pockets.

He did not mean to go anywhere, but as he turned a corner onto the main road he saw chickens in a coop placed on the ground. A young woman he vaguely recognised stood by the coop. He greeted her, and asked how much the chickens were selling at. "Seven dollars, cash, or eight dollars credit," she had said.

"Can I have one on credit?" Farai asked hopefully.

"Of course, Mr. Fatso. You still live there?" pointing at his lodgings.

"Of course. Where else? You know me?"

"Ah, yes. You work at the Board and Paper Mill?"

He hesitated a moment, then, "Yha, that is where I work." Then bending down to pick up one of the chickens, "You will come and collect your money on the 30th. Or my wife will bring it to your house. Thanks!"

So, instead of proceeding to nowhere, Farai returned home, chicken under right arm, which he deposited onto the kitchen floor. He shouted to his sons to tell their mother to fry the chicken for breakfast, and went out again. Now he had reason to go to the bottle store! With the wife busy on the fire, and the family with the prospect of a nice breakfast, why should he hang around? He kicked away the flip-flops under his feet and slipped into sandals he saw by the fireplace, then he was out of the house. He had no cent in his pockets, but what the hack, everyone went to the bottle store on a morning like this! It was promising to be a beautiful day, after all.

And sure enough, as soon as he turned that corner again, where the chickens were, two doves swooped past him at high speed right before his eyes, like two jets in synchronized flight, turning this way together, then that way, until they vanished into the thin blue air.' Two for joy!' he said silently as he watched them turn into dots in the distant horizon. Farai's spirits rose and he quickened his pace.

Not that there was much drinking at the bottle store these days. Times were hard, and very few people could afford a beer, let alone two meals in a day. Oh but the boys loved to get high; "just a slight wave", they said, but they always ended up rolling in their urine and vomit. Some hardly ate, but quaffed all day long. Many had died this way, but who cared? Who lived forever, anyway?

And so in their desperation, they got high on anything. As a result, many illicit liquors were sold at the vegetable market stalls near the bottle store, and the market itself was always full of drinkers. The police raided the area from time to time, but that was only after Pedzi, the guy who ran the bottle store, paid them to do it. If his bribe was too small, and the shebeen queens in the market paid more than he did, then the police did nothing, and complained about manpower shortage. And often the drinkers would pay too, or offer the policemen free liquor. So literally, the market stalls were a 'liberated zone' for drinking, and even had benches and big rocks and piles of bricks, on which revellers sat.

It was to the market stalls that Farai headed. He scanned the place from a distance, as he approached it. It was full, but there was nothing unusual, just the usual riff raffs, quaffing and laughing away. Then he saw Tindo, the ex-teacher he used to drink with. But he was a stingy, selfish bastard who took much more than he gave away.

Besides, today he appeared down and out and, hands clasped in front of him, was dozing off the brick he sat on. Then Brunno, the market's permanent fixture. Oh he was shirtless and staggering drunk already, lashing out his shirt and incoherent words at the queens, who went about their business as if he did not exist. Other people sat in threes and fours, sharing concoctions which they poured from a one-litre plastic Chibuku bottle into a small plastic cup cut out of the base of a small whisky container. Cars zoomed past, raising dust which settled on the mangoes and tomatoes and cabbages, into eyes and hair and everywhere, such that the whole place was white dust.

Farai left the market and walked up towards The Breeze Corner'. This was a favourite drinking place for those who did not want to drink in the market stalls. It was actually nothing more than a part of the wall that surrounded the huge Chikanga Bar. Closer to the bottle store, it commanded a good view of the entire area. That meant any potential raids could be spotted from afar. Monday the teacher was there, and so was Bomber the war veteran gambler. Peter the pickpocket stood against the wall, and Benji the Rasta sat on an axe he had been chopping wood with, but there was no liquor. Farai sat down among them.

A car parked under the tree right next to them, and a man came out and dashed into the butchery, leaving a woman and baby inside. Then, "Hey, Fatso!

Farai turned and looked at the car. The woman inside beckoned to him. In threes strides, he was beside the car, and lo, Elizabeth!

She was huger now, but he could not miss that gap in her teeth. She had been his boss's secretary at the Mill, then left unceremoniously before the company went bust. He remembered reading something about her marrying the head of a rival indigenous company.

"So, what's up?" asked Farai.

"Ah, I'm not crying, my brother. God has been good to me. My husband and I are doing well…. What about yourself?

"Jobless. I have been jobless for two years, and things cannot be worse than that. And the wife, as you remember is useless…"

"Oh don't say that. Which church do you go to?"

"Right now, I have no church. I feel that going to church is a luxury I cannot afford. I need to feed the family, send the kids to school, you know, to be practical…For me. Living in this country is similar to eating sadza with sugar cane as relish. On one hand you need to swallow the sadza and fill up the belly, but on the other, you need to spit out the sugar cane roughage."

"But how can you do anything without God? Impossible!" Elizabeth said, laughing at Tindo's joke. "What about your wife?"

"I don't even know…Look, my guys and I are really dry at the moment. Can't you do for us just a little thing…?"

"Ah, Fatso. You never change!" And with that she flashed out her purse and pulled out a bill. Without even looking at it, Farai said "Thanks", and shoved it deep into his jeans. Just then, the husband came out of the butchery.

"'BaTino," said Elizabeth, "this is Fatso, one of the best technicians at Mutare Board and Paper Mill. I told you about him, remember? Years back, when we needed an additional fitter?"

"Ah yes. Hello Farai. Where are you working now?"

"Ah, he is actually looking for a job. He is unemployed."

"In that case, here is my card. There's my phone number there. Give me a call Monday morning, and we'll see what we can arrange…"

Farai was thrilled. As soon as the car moved out of the bay, all the guys were upon him. The exchange of money between him and Elizabeth had not escaped their sharp eyes. They all wanted to know how much he had been given. Fatso flushed out his pocket, and was as shocked as his peers to see the US fifty dollar note between his fingers.

"Plus a job…" he said, smiling like he did not remember when he had before.

"What a joy!!" he exclaimed.

And then he remembered those two doves he'd seen and wished for joy.…

So he went to the bottle store counter, asked the day's rate, and bought a quart, just to have his money changed. He bought two small whiskies for his buddies, which they mixed with water and began to drink. And so the day began. But to Farai's shock and surprise, the lower lip of his left eye began to twitch. Oh no! What could possibly happen? He had plenty of money, there was chicken at home (which he wasn't going to pay for with this money. Not yet), and he was in sound health. What could possibly happen?

Wait a minute: there could be a fight, yes that was possible. Or he would lose his money. Yes, that was it. It had to do with the money. After drinking up the quart, he decided to go home. At least stash the money away in one of his jackets, then return with five dollars or six. That way, he would make sure nothing would happen to his money. But then, why not drink at home? Buy whatever beers he needed for the day and drink them at home, watching the madam play with the pots and pans and the children hollering and playing about? It was a good day. But nay, Mandy would start talking about her hair needing a retouch, or some few dollars she owed a neighbor. That wouldn't do, because he needed the money for the children's fees, and a few more beers with the guys…

Eventually, he reached a compromise. He bought one more quart and headed for home. His friends derided him for being stingy with free money, but he told them he would be back, soon. But they would not have any of that, so they pestered him until he parted with enough for two more whiskies, then left.

NEW FARMER COMES TO THE BREEZE

There was an internet Café at the Chikangaz Shopping Centre. This shopping centre, just a year or so ago, used to be very thriving and popular. One of the big businessmen there had won a franchise with the Spar brand of supermarkets, and the whole place became known as Spar. Even today, in 2013, long after the franchise has gone and the businessman has since gone broke and died from it, the place is still called Spar, not Chikanga Shopping Centre. So, if you are new to the area, or are on a kombi and you want to get off there, just tell the driver or hwindi to drop you off at Spar. Three other businessmen have tried their luck with the large supermarket, I mean, renting it, but have all gone bust. Now there is a seventh or eighth, and this one seems to have some measure of tenacity, for he has been there a year now. I guess it's because he hires cheap labour, most of them who act as security, for they are scattered all over the shop. There is a butchery section, a section for drinks, and the general groceries.

Besides this big store there were several others. In the same line with it was the popular Douggies Bar, a two storey building. There was also a takeaway outlet downstairs. The owner also abandoned it and went into the diaspora. Several people have tried running it, and failed, but there was a new one now. Next to Douggies was a butchery, owned by one of Fatso's friends. He too went bust, and someone else is renting it. Farai wondered how these genuine businessmen could be successful when there were rows and chains of tuckshops littered around the centre, all of them competing for the same customers. And now the old street wooden shops were returning again, those ones destroyed by the Government some five or six years ago in Operation Murabatsvina. They are sprouting again right before everyone's eyes.

In front of the shops was the market, The Open Market, where a lot of quaffing and ganja smoking went on.

Behind this line of front buildings was another chain of small shops. Some sold sadza, ice cream, motor vehicle spare parts, a hair salon, a hardware, groceries, you name it. Four or five of these were into groceries, and three or four in the hair business. Farai could not understand why these small shops were authorized at all. They gave the whole place a poor shape, and showed lack of proper planning. No doubt, money changed hands. Some people, however, believe that the shops were necessary, to prevent monopoly by the big ones, and created competition. This, they say, gave the customer wider choice.

So, above one of these grocery shops was an internet café, which Farai visited from time to time. He'd managed to convince Shupi that things had been very difficult, and it was safer to wait for the right time.

Like every business centre, the local Spar Shopping Centre had its regular patrons. Some people called them 'fixtures' of the place, but they liked to be called 'owners' of the place. These were the local roughnecks, the guys who woke up just to come to Spar every single day, come rain, cold or sunshine. They were the first to get there, and the last to leave, whatever the time. There were eight or nine regulars there, but the numbers invariably changed. They hung around in a corner, which they called BREEZE. The guys called this place the Breeze because right above where they sat, on the high durawall for the Chikanga Bar, there was a bold advert of a brand of cigarettes called Breeze, complete with a green packet and green lettering. There, under this advert they sat on empty tins, metal pieces of car parts, half bricks, rocks, stones, chair shells, logs, benches and anything else that their bottoms could rest on.

Like the people who drank in the open market, the guys at the Breeze did not buy their beer at the Douggies, the main Chikanga Bar or the Beer Engine. They bought all their alcohol in the market, and took it out to their corner. That meant they drank the same illicit stuff, mainly Zed, Vhinyu, and such other, though they never drank together, or mix. So the difference between these two groups of people was in place of drinking only, otherwise they drank the same liquors, from the same source, hence they suffered from similar diseases and died of the same. The slight difference was that those who drank at the Breeze were long time loafers, who had lost all hope of being employed again. The market drinkers were regular job owners who could afford credit at the market stalls.

After visiting the café, Farai joined the guys at the Breeze. There were four of them, including the guy who sold firewood and airtime credit. There was no beer, and Bruno asked Farai for five rand, or 50c. It was a wonderful morning, promising to be sunny and bright, in spite of the dark clouds and wind rising from the east. Farai replied to Bruno he had none, even though he did have a two dollar note, curtesy of one mourner. But then he realized it was a Monday, and he needed just one beer, especially after the funeral rigors and horrors. If he didn't give them, he might find it uncomfortable and rather embarrassing to drink while they watched. So he handed over a dollar. "Bring back my change!" he yelled at him.

"Thanks Mungezi[1]," and he darted straight into the market and brought back whisky (It was the highly intoxicating Zed, actually, disguised as whisky on the label).

"Unza ndishepe," said Mozey, eyes bloodshot and tongue hanging out. They mixed it with water, which was called 'shaping' in their lingo. They poured it into a plastic bottle, and settled down to drink. Tendai bought himself a Pilsner beer and sat with them.

Just then three others popped up, they must have been hiding behind John's butchery, waiting for some liquor to materialize.

"We won't drink with you!" declared Bruno. "Yesterday you had a mungezi who bought you, and you drank alone!"

But the others protested, "No we did not. It was just half a mug of masese, and a small quarter of whisky."

"Liar. I saw you. You got into the bar, came out with a mug, got into the market and bought two or three whiskeys. I saw everything! Am I lying, Mosey?"

"No, you are not lying. I saw them too. They drank a lot. None of them is going to touch our beer."

They haggled on a while, until the three gave up and sat down with others. For their patience and quiet they finally got a sip each, from the bottom of the plastic container. "For our luck," Brunno said, and the others laughed.

Then Peter, the war vet and new farmer came up, dark as ten midsummer nights.

"Hey, vafana[2]," he said in his authoritative voice. "How is it?"

"Bho," they all said.

"So what's the latest news in town? I'm just coming from the farm, you know. Been away for a whole month and a half."

"What did you bring us?" Farai asked.

---

[1]   Bring so that I shape it

[2]   Young men

"Everything that you want. This year I planted everything from maize, beans, tomatoes, bananas, okra, you name it. I even have a section of potatoes. Hey, our government loves us, guys. Can I have a cigarette?"

The guys all looked at each other, some suppressing smiles and outburst of laughter.

"So you didn't grow tobacco? I hear it's the in-thing these days. Lots of money there", someone said.

"That's for others. I want to feed the nation, first, then make money later."

"Oh, that's great. Very patriotic. Where is this farm of yours?" Farai asked again

"Correction-don't say 'farm of yours'. Say where is your farm?"

"Sorry"

"That is the problem with you urban loafers. You are cynical about everything. You somehow dream that one day you shall have your own land from somewhere, and everything we have achieved so far will be reversed. Well, dream on! Tsvangirai will never give you anything, because he will never rule this country. If you had vision, and were really Zimbabwean, you would grab this chance and get your own piece of land. I tell you, one day your children and children's children will spit on your grave. They will curse you in your death for not utilizing this opportunity and get them land, which they shall inherit and leave to their own children. You are so shallow and stupid!"

"But what's wrong, blaz? Why get all worked up?"

"Worked up? *I* get worked up? Listen, I don't get worked up over you people! My energy is spent on my land, not on sell-outs!" and he walked away, proud and dignified, but evidently worked up.

"What's wrong with him? Why is he so short tempered?" Farai asked no one in particular.

"There is nothing on that farm," Mozey volunteered smoothly, lighting a cigarette.

"It's a harvest of thorns," Brunno added. "I saw him yesterday as he got off the kombi. He had a basket in one hand, and inside were a few bananas, nuts and nyimo. Nothing more. These guys are starving, I tell you. Most of their farms are deep inside forest, where there are no roads but forests all around. The nearest clinic is 30 kilometres away, same as nearest school. The next neighbour is ten kilometers away. They live on wild fruits, hunt wild animals, and drink from rivers."

"Hey," someone said, "it's like the Bushmen days are back. I hear they live on selling firewood?"

"Yes. Firewood, grass thatch and honey. If you want any game meat or loads of firewood, just get connected with these guys."

"And vineyard[3]…" Bruno added.

"Yah. They brew a lot of illicit liquor, especially on these farms close to town. Oh, those guys drink from one morning to the next. Did you notice his darkened complexion? In the drinking arena, they are definitely kings!"

"But this guy has a house here in town, doesn't he?"

"Oh yes, he does. But town life got too tough for them. They saw their bosses' flourishing farms on TV and thought they could do as well. Forgot that those bosses took prime land, in good and excellent rain areas and with dams and stuff, well equipped with tractors, machinery and even stock…."

"They are coming back, I tell you!" said Mozey. "All those new farmers are coming back! Where do they get the manpower, inputs like seed, fertilizers and stuff? Last time around they got these as start up from the government, but they sold away those inputs for a song. Now they are chopping down trees and chasing after animals, until everything gets finished. Talk of Command Agriculture! They love to command everything, but can't command the economy.

When they finish with the wild rabbits and fruits, they will come back. This one, this guy who's just been here, I don't think he's ever going back to his bush farm. I swear, he will not…"

That could be possible, because as they years went by, the war veterans seemed to have run out of their power and allure. Most of them were perpetual beggars. The majority wore pitiable looks on their faces, and complained over and over again that they had 'died for nothing'.

The guys changed the subject, for they saw he was coming towards them as he opened a pack of cigarettes

"Ask him when he last smoked that brand…Madison, Kingsgate or Everest…." Bruno chuckled in a whisper. But the others did not want a fight with him.

But later Farai heard from another war vet that this guy, Pets, was an impostor. He was not a genuine war vet, but had only joined them at cease fire in 1979, without firing a single bullet. That didn't make much difference to Farai, because instead of declining with time, the number of war veterans was actually increasing.

Pet's story, however reminded Farai of his uncle, another war veteran.

His uncle was all elegance when still at the post office counter. He was smart, elegant, handsome, clean shaven and all: well-built even. Tender, soft well washed skin, black suit on white shirt. White clean teeth. But what did he see the day he met him? A complete opposite image of what he used to be. Dark skin with blacker spots all over. Unkempt hair, woollen jersey in that sweltering heat. Long, dirty finger nails as he extended a hand. Shifty eyes,

---

[3]   Rough and coarse, unrefined wine from grapes, also called vhinyu.

husky voice. Weight had been lost, now a bony frame. Tattered collar, loose trousers, cheap Chinese shoes that were worn out, no socks.

Still he smiled confidently at Farai, though his teeth betrayed him. Yellowish brown. But he proudly promised a bumper harvest. He planted everything this year: tobacco, maize, nuts, beans, etc. "Come and get!" he said proudly, an arm in surrender gesture. "You get to your fill!".

JONAH'S FUNERAL

arai doubted that there were any genuine tears at his Uncle Jonah's funeral as he and his crew buried him at the new Yeovil Cemetery the following afternoon, after meeting Elizabeth at Spar. At 57 and single, Uncle Jonah seemed to have completely abandoned all hopes of making it good in life. He drank every type of concoction that they brewed or brought to the shebeens at the community market stalls, and there were many kinds: vhinyu, Zed, Lawidzani, Skippers, you name it. These were outside of the regular lagers, scuds and other legal strong stuff.

There was another latest drug called Bronco, which was sending the youth wild with bliss. It was aalso called N'Ghoma, and came from South Africa. The guys spent lots of their hard earned money on that drug. Fortunately, it was not sold at the market stalls.

For the good part of his adult life Uncle Jonah was at that market every hour of the day. He had never been employed, as far as Fatso knew, and would arrive there as early as 7 AM, with absolutely no food in his tummy or cent in his pocket. He would curl his legs on top of one of the stalls, his face very close to the bottles containing the concoctions, breathing in the smells and watching the shebeen queens pour out the stuff to clients who had the money. His eyes bloodshot and thirsty, Uncle Jonah would lick his dry lips in futile anticipation. Oftentimes, however, he would get a sip from an excited customer or the shebeen queens. This way he would get high, little by little.

When it so happened that hunger was getting the better of him and there were no prospects of an early sip, he would stagger home under the blinding sun, or tightly wrapped in pieces of cloth that made up for a jacket. And the way he walked alone was some sight. When it was hot, he walked with arms wide and outstretched, a little to the sides. This was to aid the locomotion of his legs and body; lifting, thrusting and landing the feet. Each stride was a result of some negotiation, and took some time. As a result it took him about 20 minutes to cover the 100 or so metres between his home and the market.

This kind of walking Uncle Jonah himself called 'swimming'. As his close friends testified at the funeral, their Jonah took pleasure in equating himself to the biblical Jonah, who was swallowed by a fish. To him, he never understood what swallowed which, that is, whether the fish swallowed Jonah or Jonah swallowed the fish. This confusion usually came whenever he was really drunk. In such a case, the alcohol he had taken became the fish, while he remained himself, Jonah. So, the analogy assumed a different dimension in that he did not know whether it was him who had drunk the alcohol or because of his unfeeling, drunken stupor, he had been consumed by it. In that case, he (Jonah) had been consumed by the fish. So, the real Jonah was determined by how much he had drunk that day.

Either way, however, he would be 'swimming' rather than walking home.

Soon he would turn and swim back, depending on what he had found to eat at home. Sometimes there was some remnants from breakfast, but usually because of the large numbers of people in his household, some hungry kid would have snapped it up already. He would raise hell, calling people names and demanding they leave his brother's home and seek their own accommodation. They said he often chased them out at night too.

So, with nothing to do at home, he would swim back to the market, loose shoes often coming off and collecting soil as he swam, till he arrived and took his position and waited for luck to strike. Often it struck very late in the afternoon, at sunset, when crowds swelled-some who came to buy stuff for supper and others arriving for a drink or two after work.

Anyway, Fatso heard that his uncle, Jonah had died. He was his uncle on the mother's side, and Fatso liked him somewhat. He often shared a mug with him, ignoring his long whiskers that sprang from all over his face, especially when they dipped in the beer mug. They said he had died around 1.30 AM, after a day of excruciating stomach problems and passing water and blood. They took the body to the hospital but in no time it was back, in a coffin.

Farai could not believe the crowds that came to mourn and bury his uncle, Jonah. The evening of the day of his death, three pastors were at the ready to give sermons. Three. Yet Jonah never set foot in a church all his life, and he abhorred the double standards and hypocrisy of Zimbabwean church goers and their priests. His mother, 94 years old, went to the United Methodist Church, and so it was only fair that a pastor from that church presided. Farai and his team were outside and it was dark and there was no electricity again that night. So the priest plucked out a verse from his head, about Methuselah and his life of 969 years, and bearing children.

Farai remarked to somebody standing next to him that he had heard this same priest quote and preach on that verse before. Surprisingly, he too had heard him preach on the same verse, at a different funeral in another suburb. Sure enough, his sermon was the same, verbatim, A to Z, word for word. His message, as before, was that Methuselah was known only for having children, something even a lunatic could do. So what are you (listeners) known for in your lives? He went on to talk about some people being known for chasing women, gossip, drinking, desire for power, stealing at funerals, etc.

The sermon was good, but only to those hearing it the first time. When the priest was done and time was open for testimonies, songs and anything else, a young man (Farai recognized him as Uncle Jonah's mate, and often drank with him) rose, staggered to his feet and stooped before the crowd.

"I have a serious problem, men and women, especially those from the church, which I hope you can help me solve. Yesterday I saw Jonah going to the market, and he asked me for a cigarette. I looked into his face, and decided that he was too sick to smoke, so i said, "No, Jonah, I cannot offer you a cigarette," and proceeded past him.

"I was shocked this morning to learn that Jonah, the man I had refused a cigarette yesterday, was no more. Now, please, my conscience is bothering me. Can somebody from the church please tell me if I did right or wrong by refusing Jonah a cigarette/"

He sat down, waiting for an answer to his question. None came. Instead people laughed and some began to leave. Most, however, stayed.

The following morning there was an even bigger crowd at the funeral. Strangely, they dressed Jonah in a suit and tie, and Farai chuckled at that. They shaved off his long, white whiskers, leaving his dead skin shiny and pimple- free. The coffin too was decent-a smooth, wooden affair complete with silver handles.

Fatso had never seen Uncle Jonah in a car before, but there were seven or eight cars there, including a Navara and an E-class Mercedes Benz. People hung from the tails of full-loaded trucks as the hearse moved out to the cemetery. There was even the comfort-cum-menace of a ZANU PF 4x4 truck, which stuck with mourners throughout the funeral. Yet Jonah was far from political, and did not even bother to vote in any election, let alone talk about it. Farai did not think he even knew who was running the country at the time, or who his local MP, Senator or councillor was.

For some reason, the priest who had preached the previous night refused to come. They said he literally refused. None of the other two from the previous evening was there as well. A different one, from ZAOGA, ably took over, and Farai could see two more who had not been there the previous night.

There was cooperation at filling up the grave, with a mix of Christian and social songs, drums and percussions. It was really a jocund affair, with lots of skirt sways and body gyrations. All the shebeen queens closed down business for the burial, and came in their numbers. They sang plaintively, spicing each song with jocular statements and lyrics. There was laughter and merrymaking, all round.

"Jonah is only half dead", said one, "He is in one of his drunken stupors and will wake up soon, when hung over, or when the earth on his grave becomes too cold or too heavy for him".

"Jonah was bloody lazy and never bought his own beer, he was a tick (gupa), drinking other people's sweat" others said.

"How could he claim to be a builder, without a shovel or trowel?" others asked

"Ah yangu yaenda kani Mhai hwe! (My penis is gone!)" moaned one of the queens.

As they filled up the grave, the men would drop a cigarette here and there in the rising mound, pour some bit of alcoholic concoctions, for Jonah to smoke and drink if he felt the need. Some said it was so that they would not be haunted by his demands for these, since they often denied his requests.

As it happened, the grave filled up when people still wanted to sing and hang around some more, but eventually they had to leave and go home. Farai joined the family back at their home, for a bit of filming.

Everybody wanted to be captured on video, saying praises and eulogising Jonah. Farai interviewed so many relatives, till his battery got flat. The most common statements were:

"Jonah was a great man. People ignored his wise counsel because they thought he was drunk, but the counsel was insightful and very beneficial."

"We will never get another person like Uncle Jonah. He was always giving sound advice. He preached peace in the family, and was very patient and understanding

"Everyone thought he was a drunkard and ignored him, but he did not give up."

The closest to the truth came from his daughter, in her late twenties: "It was difficult to live so close to someone who was always drunk, but in spite of everything his love never failed. He was always there to give advice and help to those who would listen".

"Jonah had many talents. He was a bricklayer and ex-teacher. None in our family was like him".

"As a young man Jonah was a member of the United Methodist Youth Assembly, and showed a lot of promise. It's unfortunate that he failed to quit drinking once he started, and this is what has become of him..."

Because his battery had run out Farai had to go, leaving people scrambling with more eulogies. This as they drank Coca Cola, Fanta, Sprite and ate biscuits, seated comfortably in sofas and sharing a laugh from time to time. Meanwhile, delicious dishes of beef and chicken stew were simmering in large drum-like pots on the open furnace. At the end of it all, Farai did not know what to make of Jonah's funeral. One thing he was sure of was that it breathed something into his life that day. Was it sunshine in his heart? A gentle breeze? May be, because he did not really feel sad for his loss continually, but often caught himself thinking of very different happy things, and he felt a certain light heartedness inside.

THE NOVEMBER 2017 COUP, AND A HARVEST OF THORNS

Towards the 2018 elections, there was a lot of political activity in the country, mostly in the ruling Zanu PF party. There were clear divisions in the party, each wanting to contest the presidential post, the G-40 faction, headed by Mugabe's wife, Grace, with a team of Mugabe die hard supporters, and the Lacoste faction, headed by Mugabe's long term ally and colleague, Emmerson Mnangagwa, and his mostly private supporters.

Mugabe was 93, old and frail, but he wanted to stand in the elections as a presidential candidate at 94, despite. Grace, organized rallies and told the people, "You will still vote for him even when he has to travel in a wheelbarrow. Even if he dies, you will vote for him!"

She publicly named names of deviant politicians, especially those in the Lacoste faction, and dressed them down in public. Unbeknown to her, however, Mnangagwa had a secret deal with the military generals. He remained quiet over her rantings, until Mugabe declared that he could fire him for his underhand dealings and plans to topple him. That was when he fled, first to Mozambique by night, then to South Africa, A lot of stories were told about his escape, but the long and short of it was that he successfully escaped. After that escape, things began to move fast.

Apparently he had left a letter expressing his love for his country and the party. Mugabe was placed under house arrest by the military, and General Sibusiso Moyo, now Minister of Foreign Affairs, announced on television that the coup was merely to restore the legacy of the war of liberation. He said that a lot of people who had not taken part in the struggle for independence, had occupied influential positions in the parry and leading the party astray. For some breathtaking days there was expectation in the country as Mugabe refused to hand over power. Parliament was also making moves to impeach him, Announcements had been made by war veterans and the military that people should come and march to State House, and force Mugabe out. They did. Hand in hand they marched up and down the streets of Harare. Seeing no way out, Mugabe resigned on 14 November, 2017.

The use of civilians by the military to remove Mugabe received a lot of negative comments afterwards. The truth was that if you talked to them after Mugabe was gone and Mnangagwa came in, they said that they were used. They were paraded and marched across the city, under the protection of soldiers. Unbeknown to the people, this was a ploy by the military to show the world that this was a popular protest, and the people were tired of Mugabe. So, feeling protected, the people marched side by side with the military, feeling as compatriots bothered by the same man.

If the military had removed Mugabe 'alone, without the people, SADC and other countries will have intervened and stopped them. As it was, the people felt used again, for nothing, as they had been used during the liberation struggle, from which they benefitted nothing but poverty, general lack and a shorter lifespan.

To say there was jubilation is an understatement. People poured out of their homes, offices and workplaces to celebrate. The army knew that the majority of the marchers were MDC supporters, who came from far and wide, and they silently supported and protected them. Video clips of Zimbabweans celebrating the end of Mugabe's rule circulated the world, and at one point, Zimbabweans were described as the happiest people in the world.

I remember, even I, writing for Peace Direct at the time giving my story the title 'Zimbabwe's Beautiful Coup'. However, thanks to Ruairi Nolan at Peace Direct at the time, for being cautious enough to change the title to **Zimbabwe in Limbo: What's happening on the Ground?**

True, the coup had nothing Thai about it, except parading civilians.

Some observers especially in the legal fraternity issued a statement castigating the coup as setting a bad precedence, but nobody listened to them. Mugabe had thought he would rule forever, but now he was gone, and the nation would breathe.

Because of the huge MDC supporters countrywide, everybody though there would be another Unity Government between the MDC and Zanu PF. Rumours of this spread across the country, and were beefed by other rumours of previous secret meetings between Chamisa of the MDC and Mnangagwa.

However, when Mnangagwa announced his government, it was full of Zanu PF ministers and officials only, with no single MDC. People were astounded, but wait, elections would come in a year.

In his cabinet, Mnangagwa picked many soldiers from the military. This was clearly a military government being formed.

This was blatant cheating, stealing, of power from the masses by the Zimbabwe National Army (ZNA). However, like we always say these days, the chickens are coming home to roost. The army itself is divided, and the younger soldiers are complaining bitterly about their 'chefs', for 'eating alone' while they starve. Besides, evidence across the country is clear that they've failed.

During that time and after, people in Zimbabwe and across the world thought the new start for Zimbabwe had now come. All Mnangagwa had to do was hand over power to Chamisa, who had won the previous election, form a unity government or announce elections, and he would be a hero. He would have been a bigger hero than Mandela if he had immediately formed a unity government with Chamisa, run the course together, and then hold elections. But he went alone, as Zanu PF, to the disappointment of many Zimbabweans, who felt used.

At first, Mnangagwa was relatively popular with his 'New Dispensation' and 'open for business' mantra, in which he announced to the nation and world that the country would no longer continue in its pariah status, as was the case under Mugabe, but would engage the rest of the world. He bemoaned the backwardness against the mineral wealth in the country, which he said would be used for development. He also tried hard, travelling across the world for economic investment meetings with world leaders. After a few fits and starts, a few businesses were formed, but mostly from China, Russia and a few other countries. The major ones. Like America and Britain, adopted a wait and see attitude.

As an afterthought now, I think Mnangagwa, being very African and from very rural Chivi, staged a series of shows celebrating his coup, with his stupidly funny dance, in which he was communicating something to his rivals, and seemed to be concentrating more on perfecting that dance than the economy or Zimbabweans, for that matter.

That was why he hired Mthuli Ncube as Minister of Finance, and poor Mthuli had no idea how deep the difference between his employer (zanu PF) and the people was. The chasm has grown since 1995, and the people hate everything Zanu PF, money, law, people, roads, hospitals and all. They are sick and tired, but being Zimbabwean, they trudge on. But while Mthuli and Mnangagwa say one thing, the people, all of them in unison, do a different thing. Each time, however, they win and the government backs down. What they refuse to back down from is political power when the people say so at elections and other times.

Military rule and power spread across the country, with soldiers dominating social, economic and political discussions.

The 2018 harmonised elections were hotly contested. This time around, there was not much public harassment of civilians. The voting was peaceful, to a large extent, and the first unofficial announcement of results showed that the MDC had won. However, this was overturned as more results came in. In the end, Mnangagwa was declared winner.

The MDC launched a high court appeal against the results, but in drama filled sessions, Justice Luke Malaba declared Mnangagwa winner, as everybody knew he would, even before the court began. He charged that the MDC did not have evidence that it had won. There were many irregularities in the election, featuring some of the high placed officials in the Zimbabwe Electoral Commission (ZEC), including the Chairperson Justice Priscilla Chigumba. in the presence of Chamisa himself, and failed. What had changed, to make him trust it now?

It was funny to notice that like Mugabe, Chamisa was going legalistic. How could he go to a Zanu PF court of Zanu PF judges using Zanu PF laws and expect to win?

Surely, he had to use other creative methods. Tsvangirai had tried the courts before,

And after being sworn in Mnangagwa publicly pronounced a new dispensation, a second republic, and pledged to deal with all forms of corruption, even at senior level. He hunted down his enemies in the G-40 faction of the party, and arrested them. Some fled abroad. He also hunted down money launderers and other illegal dealers, but did nothing after catching them. People wondered what happened, after such declarations and the culprit being caught. All cases of corruption, it seemed, were swept under the carpet. Perhaps money changed hands?

Mnangagwa also declared that the country was 'open for business', and travelled around the world meeting with governments and world business leaders, inviting them to invest in Zimbabwe.

As it appeared, this did not bear much fruit. This could be as a result of the militarized state and its concomitant instability.

The next elections will be held in 2023 and, for most Zimbabweans that is a long way off. Things have to change. The only party that can get the nation out of its quagmire is the MDC. It has the people's support, and not Zanu PF. In any case, a lot of people will be dead by 2023, and Zanu PF always puts that to advantage, especially at election time.

A FIGHT WITH SHUPI

"So, how did you spend your day today?" Farai's wife asked her husband as she dropped rather heavily into the single sofa in their lounge.

"Oh, I wanted to water the vegetables, but the water ran out, so I ended up playing with the children, then went up to the shops", answered Farai, trying hard to appear sober.

"Playing? Did you say playing? Some people surely have the whole world under their feet," she said sarcastically.

For a while, Farai kept quiet. He was slowly getting used to Shupi's sudden mood swings and outbursts. Last week, for example, she had suddenly accused him of 'throwing away the children's food to a dog'. All he had done was throw crumbs of last night's remains at his mother's dog, which had followed him to his home. And then there had been other small, seemingly harmless comments like "Don't put too much sugar in your tea," or at night when he was watching TV "I don't know where I will get money for the ZESA bill this month."

It was two months after his return from England, and it seemed like there'd not been any break in the Zim life cycle. It was the same, a matter of being asleep or awake. And when awake, nothing much would go except breathing and watching the sky.

This made Farai wonder what all the beef about removing Mugabe was about. Bread cost 80c during Mugabe's time, now it cost $8. A lot of families, including his own were going without bread. Eggs cost $1 for for 8 during

Mugabe's time, now they cost $1 each; a quart of beer cost $2, 50, and now it cost $10. Many other things had quadrupled in prices.

The funny thing to Fatso was that people were beginning to say Mugabe was better ("Mugabe anga arinani") was now a common statement. Fatso remembered during Mugabe's terrible reign, the same people used to say, "Smith was better" Smith anga arinani)

Some even proceeded to wish that he stood for election, so that they would vote for him, rather than Mnangagwa. Yet the country was full of fresh, active minds that could catapult the nation out of its quagmire. Unfortunately, Mugabe himself had died only a few days before.

Perhaps they had nothing else to compare with, but people should not always look in the past, but future. Books used to open one's mind when he was growing up, but this time, Mnangagwa was killing that.

Funny, in an attempt at diplomacy and to hoodwink the world into thinking that he was multiracial and liked females and whites, Mnangagwa had included a white lady, Tracy Coventry into his cabinet. Farai knew, however, that she was a carrot being dangled. She would be heartily welcome into government at first, then later used to raise money from her international connections, which they would loot and abuse, then dump her. Fatso knew the Zanu trend well enough to suspect that, unless she could read it in time.

It appeared Shupi didn't notice how Zim life was negatively affecting him, killing him slowly. For example, she didn't notice how thin he was becoming, or how many times he'd pricked holes through his belts, adjusting the waist of his trousers.

"What do you mean 'the whole world?" Farai replied. "The whole morning I was here, waiting for water, and then the maid went to town and left me with the children. I only left when she came back".

"Is that all? And what does that bring us here? Other men are busy fending for their children while you play and get drunk every day. Tomorrow I am going back to my parents'. I will leave you with your children," she said, standing up and going into the kitchen.

Farai had heard that line before. Several times Shupi had threatened to leave him, but he knew that she would not go anywhere. He had reminded her that her parents, like many other people, were struggling to get two meals a day. But she had retorted, "I would rather spend the little that I earn with them than on you!"

That had hit a soft spot, and he had burst out, "OK, you go. Go right now and see whether you will find us starving to death here. Do you think you sustain my life? You are so quick to forget!"

"Forget what?" she shouted from the kitchen. "Do you think we feed on the past? I did not come here to look after you, but for you to look after me. Am I the man in this house?"

He did not respond, but busied himself with arranging sticks in a matchbox. She came back, plate of cold sadza in one hand, and sat down to eat.

"I see now that is why you left your job. Just to sit and expect me to feed you and give you money for beer. I shall never do that again. From now onwards, you will not get a dollar from me!"

"Since when have you bought me beer?"

"Sadza. I am talking about sadza. And all the food you gobble in this home. It is not my responsibility to feed you."

"Then whose is it?" he asked provocatively, sending her even wilder.

"Shameless!" she spat out. "You are so pathetically shameless. A strong young man like you spending his youth in beerhalls like an old man!"

"If only you knew how sweet beer is, you would not work yourself up like that!" Farai said.

"From tomorrow onwards I am not going to work anymore. I quit. I want to see what you will eat!" she shouted.

"Just do it. Don't go, and see if we will starve. You know that I do provide when I get the money. Look everywhere, things are tough. Tell me one teacher who is managing. I am much better off doing piece jobs.

Indeed, many times in the past Farai had got some piece jobs in town; a workshop to facilitate, and so forth, and he brought the money home to Shupi, even before he did anything else. It was she who would give him a little for a quart or two from that money. But that was in the past, and it had been a long time now since that had happened as piece jobs were hard to come by.

But tonight it seemed Shupi was serious. "Whatever you say, I am going," she said between chewing cold sadza and dry vegetables, which infuriated her further. "I work my life away every day, only to come home and eat this rubbish! This time I am definitely going. Watch me!" she said.

But as she ate, little Brendon started to cry. They both ignored him. Farai rose from his seat and went out. However, when Shupi finished her meal, she rose from where she sat, and took the baby in her arms and began to feed him.

By the time Farai came back, more drunk than before, she and the children were asleep.

This was typical of a time he felt so low and hopeless about losing his job. He got almost suicidal at such times. One thing he hated was disappointing his wife. Oh how he loved her, but only his way. According to him, he would do anything for her. Several times when they had no firewood for meals, he had wished he could give her the file full of his academic and professional certificates to make fire with. They were useless to him now. Indeed a file full of college notes had burned on the fire, cooking sadza.

But she was putting him under immense pressure now. They were a small family, and he thought that they were managing. At the bottle store and in town he heard many tales of families going for days without food. Some had sadza without relish. Cooking oil was a real luxury when it was found, but Shupi always got it. The same went for margarine.

The time Farai lost his job and farm was also about the same time the MDC was spreading its wings and becoming very popular. Farai immediately joined the party, becoming very central in the provincial management of political affairs and organizing its expansion.

Just a few years after losing his job, when Farai looked at how miserable teachers and other government workers looked and listened to how they complained about everything, he surely felt that he would rather be patient and wait for something else. He also felt that being unemployed was far much better. These days you hardly saw a teacher at the shops or the bottle store. Of course, he knew that he was wasting away his life, but better this way, in a happy than sad and miserable atmosphere. Life was hard all round, but since he knew his town well, quite often he had a 'deal' from which he got a little money to cover a few things. Only that Shupi did not see it, he thought to himself.

He was surprised at how women changed. In particular, he found a strange similarity between women and Zanu PF politicians. They thought they knew what they wanted, but when they got it, they cried the same, wanting more and more, while delivering nothing. How they changed like chameleons!. He yearned to have a chat with representatives of women and domestic violence organizations, and ask them if they had researched and analysed the thought and feeling among some men that women were largely responsible for the larger percentage of the domestic violence and related divorces and separations that were rocking the country.

Farai could never forget how Shupi treated her one day, when they had gone to bury her cousin in her village. Because he had lost his job and was no longer working, he'd no money, even for transport or a beer. Because he was the eldest son in law in Shupi's homestead, he had to perform a few rituals, which needed money. He knew Shupi had the money, because she'd told him. However, when they got to the village and the elders approached him for traditional beer for the grave diggers, as per custom, he approached Shupi, and she flatly refused to give him any. She didn't say she didn't have, but simply ignored him. Farai tried and tried, even in front of people, but she refused. In the end, he withdrew from the funeral activities, opting instead to spend his time at the nearby shops. He felt very humiliated, throughout the funeral, and borrowed transport money for home before it was over. According to traditional custom, he'd violated custom, for which he had to pay his in laws.

Later, when the issue was discussed further, people said that Shupi was under stress that was why she could not give him money. Farai smiled at the explanation. From that experience and other similar ones, Farai learnt that in African tradition, it was not proper for a man to depend on a woman. If a woman or wife was employed and had money, that house was destined for problems. Women took long to make decisions, and at times they used their hearts instead of minds. They had their own interests, which were not always necessarily of the family or occasion at hand, but personal. It was their money, and they used it as they saw fit, while the man, who was referred to as head of the family, had nothing. Such was life in Zim.

He also remembered the last time Shupi had told him he would never get a Dollar from her for his beer.

What had happened was that he had run out of clean underwear, T-shirts and jeans to wear. When he mentioned this to Shupi during super, she answered that she was overwhelmed, and couldn't he help out?

Farai readily agreed, and the following morning when Shupi had left for her job, he collected his underwear and socks, and put them into a pale, got a bar of soap, sat on a chair and began to wash.

Guess what? As he went through his washing, he met a strange underwear. It was brownish, blue and yellow. This was not his style. Fatso's colours were black, blue, red and grey, mostly.

Later that evening, he asked Shupi about it.

She (sleepily) said, "May be it belongs to the boys."

Fatso was sure it didn't belong to either of his sons. To avoid a quarrel and put an end to the issue, he dashed into the bathroom and brought it to her.

She immediately woke up.

"What? It's your underwear. I've washed it before."

"No, it isn't. And it's not the boys', either. May be you can tell me more?"

"Me? Why me? I don't wear that stuff!"

"This underwear belongs to somebody who does not reside here. And it's a man."

"Am I a man? Did I bring a man here?" Then the reality of his suspicion hit her, and she sat up.

"Fatso, are you accusing me of something?"

"Im just talking about this underwear…"

"After all that I do for you in this house, this is how you pay me?"

"I'm not talking about anything. It's just…….."

"That's it. I now see you more clearly, now. I now know you. Listen, from today onwards, if you see these hands of fine giving you money, ask me."

"Even for a beer?" he asked to lighten things up a bit.

"Worse for that!" she retorted, angrier than before.

Farai just kept quiet, wishing the moment would pass. What could he do? She was her whole world now, her life, and he could not afford to offend her, even one tiny bit. Otherwise, he would die slowly, but surely.

He knew that if he'd been employed, their conversation would have gone differently, and she would've been the sweet Shupi of old.

Now he could not even exert his rights as a man, husband and father. As things stood, she had all the powers. According to the recent Bill passed by the Mnangagwa government, a married woman could have boyfriends, enjoy and go out with them anytime, whilst still married. In such hard and difficult times for most men, it was like Mnangagwa was castrating them, and taking their wives. Only that the women were too skinny and hungry, too.

The other thing was that she blocked him from borrowing from her friends and people she knew. She said it was embarrassing, but she did not give him money, even a dollar when he needed it.

He had noticed long ago that she had lost respect for him. This she demonstrated by giving his favourite part of chicken meat to visitors, or even their son, Brendon. That part was a husband's part, in every home anyone went in Zimbabwe, and may be even Africa. The gizzard was a husband's piece, but Shupi didn't care anymore.

The reality was that like most Zim men, Fatso could not help but feel that their life and its privacy was laid open before everyone's eyes. They owned nothing. That was further aggravated by the recent Bill under discussion in government, which was about giving women the freedom and right to have a boyfriend, even though she was married. To Farai, life in Zimbabwe was like stripping unemployed men like him of everything, a house and family then rape his wife. Indeed, he felt deeply abused.

Whatever job he did at home or anywhere was of no value to her, as long as it didn't bring money. He could dig in the garden, fix a door, a hose pipe or anything, but got no respect or 'thank you'. Because she was bringing the money, she remained boss, and distributed it herself, according to her needs and wants, first. Fatso's ideas, opinions and views were secondary. This added to further turmoil when monthly bills went unpaid, much to his suffering and regret.

Hard times like these took their toll on men. What was worse was that most working women did not know how to articulate their new bread winner position with men. Men also remained rigid, unfamiliar with their secondary role. In the end there was endless friction.

Farai also remembered one day that he sent Shupi to a tuckshop as she went to town. "If I come back, it will be a success, but if I don't….I might as well go straight to the combi rank. It will be a failure."

"But I want you back". Farai protested. "You come back and tell me if you fail to get what I want, then I make another plan."

"No!" Why waste time coming back? If I don't come, you know there was no success."

Farai just eyed her and let her go.

He remained at home, waiting and waiting for her to return, but she did not.

In the end, Farai thought that she'd failed to get what he wanted, and so had gone to town.

He went out himself.

After two hours of absence, he came back home, only to hear from neighbours that Shupi had been looking for him, but had gone to town.

Farai was somewhat relieved, but wondered why she had not telephoned him or sent a message?

Except for that problem in the village, and the underwear, Shupi, belonged to the less difficult group of women because she understood, otherwise she would have stopped providing food long ago, or spend time on her phone, always.

Fatso knew how painful it was for her to part with money easily. He remembered that a few times, he'd borrowed money for her transport from her.

The situation was that because combis were becoming too expensive to ride, Shupi would often walk to her shop. Fatso didn't want her to walk, and he'd no money to give her. He knew, however, that she had some US Dollars stuck away somewhere. So he would plead with her to change just a little, for her transport, and he'd pay her back when he got his own money.

Most times she would comply, but you could never tell with her.

However, he knew that if she decided to leave him, there was nothing he could do about it, especially with the overwhelming support she would get from the same women's organisations and ministry. He would wait for time.

The whole town was full of split families. Many parents had left their children for the diaspora, for money. With the money, they lodged their school-going children into expensive lodgings in leafy suburbs and sent them to expensive schools.

Much of that did not help, because the children would drop out of school for one reason or the other, sacrificing their education and future... HIV/Aids wreaked havoc, along with drug abuse, sex and other forms of mischief. In the end, it was death, and Fatso had attended many funerals of dead children with their parents, and it was a sorrowful sight.

The funny thing was that in the midst of such poverty and lack, Mugabe and his ministers insisted that Zimbabwe was far better than most African countries. To Fatso and his gang, that statement was meaningless, because Zimbabwe was never a banana republic like these countries she was compared to. The fact was that Zimbabwe was different, and it had been ruined.

One day the City Council men were outside again, to demand payment for water and rates. They visited every house with outstanding bills.

"So what do we do now?" That was their hymn question. They always asked that one, no matter who they were. Whether from electricity (ZESA), government or parastatal, that one was the key question, "What do we do now?"

"I don't know," Farai said, thinking fast and buying time. He had absolutely no dollar, neither did his wife, and so there was nothing at the moment to give them, or anything in the day or the next. No hope. "But you know what, as I said, I am just getting into town. If my money is there, I promise to pay about $350 or $400, then finish off the rest later in the month. But if there is no money in town, I promise you guys something, you know, for my appreciation (for not disconnecting me), say $20 or so".

Yes, that did it. They looked at the ground, then one of them extended his hand to Farai for the bill, which he gladly handed over.

"What time shall that be?" Toothy asked.

"Around five. I think I will be back by then." Yes, he had to push the time as far away as possible, so that they might fail to pitch up the same day.

"Can we have you cell number?" He gave them, and they wrote it on the flipside of the bill. Immediately, they led the way out of the yard.

"OK guys. See you later. Let me see what I can get in town", he said as he left them headed for the next house.

This was how almost everyone in the neighbourhood was living those days. Bills, bills, bills, especially from the City Council and ZESA. Mutare water was said to be in abundance, from the perennial Pungwe River, and people didn't understand how it could be that expensive. Granted, there was added the supplementary charges as well, but refuse was hardly ever collected in time, as there were dumps all over the locations.

Farai knew that as soon as he was done with the Council, ZESA would be at the door. He owed them around $150. This at a time he was struggling to put food on the table, and was sleepless over where he was going to get $1 000 for the kids' school fees at crèche and primary school later in the same month.

All that was beside the point, however, which was corruption. That was how everybody lived. And this extra money that they paid these boys, the one outside the bill, which Farai liked to call "Delaying Tact', went straight into their pocket and not towards his account. Of course, they honoured their promise and did not come again for a month, but the fear was that someone else from the same office might come and demand payment.

This usually happened with the police. You grease one policeman's hand, and a docket is withdrawn. Papers do not get to the courts. You should never rest and think that it is over. Two, three months down the line, another constable will come to serve you again. You grease his hand again, but then another will come, and so on. This was how they survived, Farai knew. Better deal with the magistrates and prosecutors, in the end, but who knows...?

The same thing had recurred to Farai. In the end you think there is a racket: Policemen watching every case to its conclusion in the courts, and court officials instigation policemen to raise again issues that they had corruptly benefitted from, so that they were always in 'business' together.

At around half past four the same day, Farai received a call from the young men from the City Council again.

"How far?' one of then asked.

"Who is this?" Farai asked, perplexed.

"Vakomana we Vat. Tambouya nenyaya yemvura makuseni"[4]

"Oh. Ok. But I said around 5PM, didn't I?"

"Oh, alright, mdhara."

He stayed out a bit late, but when he arrived home at 6 sharp he heard they had been. Shit.

He slipped them out of his mind, but no sooner had dawn broken the following morning than he was called to the gate by the maid. Sure enough, one of them, slim, light and tall and with a big adam's apple that gave him the look of a bird, was there, huge, shining spanner in hand.

"So what's up, Mdhara?", he asked, adam's apple bobbing up and down.

"Oh tight, munin'ina. I failed to get anything yesterday. But you know what, my wife is in the census deal, and they are likely to get something today or tomorrow."

"So shall we say, ah... in the afternoon, then, around two o'clock?"

"No. They finish around 6, and she arrives here around 7. Why don't you try tomorrow morning? Yes, I think that would be fair."

Eyes shifting, he finally said, "OK, tomorrow morning then. See you." And he was gone. Farai couldn't go back to sleep after that, but got out.

---

[4]   The water boys. We came earlier in the morning for the water issue

As he walked about, he didn't know what he would tell him if and when he came back. But this was a matter of life or death. He would never allow them to disconnect his water, come hell or high water. He would always think of something to tell them. Something juicy, for he had not the money at the moment, nor were there signs of him getting it anytime soon.

FARAI NARROWLY BUT BRIEFLY ESCAPES THE ZIM ROT

Life now had become unbearable to Farai. Since the coup, soldiers took over society and communities. They did whatever they wanted to do, whenever. He discovered that the process had started at independence, and maintained throughout. Funny, the beautiful teacher or nurse so and so, was married to a soldier, or war vet.

Except it was not the case in other spheres. Most of soldiers' children did not do well in school, neither did they go to university. They almost ended in high school, from which they went to military training, like their fathers. And the cycle would be repeated with the next generation. A generation of soldiers, Fatso thought, where there was no war. All this to protect an individual's grip on power!

It was mostly soldiers who had cars, a house, and money to splash at the shopping centres. Children wanted to be soldiers when they grew up, because it didn't need a lot of hard work, except to bury dead heroes and a few other trades, but which no one saw or knew about.

It was clear to everyone that soldiers worked for only three or four days throughout the year, on Independence Day, Heroes' Day, and their own Defence Forces Day. They took three or four days to prepare for these days, and paraded military gear in stadiums and grounds across the country, on these days. Of course, they buried heroes and did other jobs according to their skills and trades, but no one knew about such, and so did not benefit from it.

Farai remembered reading somewhere how the Zimbabwe National Army came to be what it was. It was plain to see that the army was full of old men and women, especially at the higher ranks. This was because in 1988 Zanu PF declared that soldiers would retire after 20 years of service, or 25 for pension. This Act was targeted at soldiers who had served in the Rhodesian army, so that they would retire early.

So when these retired, Zanu PF filled the gaps with their own men, and changed the Act, to extend their years, even ensure they don't leave the army, with benefits.

So at the present time when a senior soldier wanted to retire he was told, "Where do you want to go? Can't you see the MDC is threatening us? Do you want to leave the country to puppets and their handlers?" And the soldier would stay put, old as he was. At least he had farms, his children got free education, he had an endless choice of official and unofficial cars, was assured of a good monthly salary, and plenty other things.

To Fatso and his crew, there was no doubt that soldiers' lifestyles promoted laziness and brainless things all around, which were the daily affairs of Zimbabweans. They just enjoyed money without working.

Fatso observed how education had been rendered useless in life, right before his eyes. Mugabe spent billions of borrowed money on education, and just as it was beginning to pay dividends on its own, Mnangagwa comes and destroys it. Now soldiers ruled the roost in Zimbabwe, not education. By God, Fatso thought, it looked like they were at war! Indeed, the entire city and country looked like they were at war; people running around, looking for the day's meal.

On the other hand, Farai's life had taken a deep end. Besides the lack of activity at home or in life, he felt guilty about being taken care of by Shupi, his wife. Though she bought most of the stuff in the home, he chipped in whenever he got some money. His biggest worry were the prices. Since Mugabe had been deposed, prices had shot up. The worse still, money was harder to come by.

The other thing was that Farai no longer took care of himself the same way he used to. For example, since water and electricity were now rare commodities, he could go for days without a bath. A shower was out of the question. Though he had installed a shower with beautiful curtains and marble bath tub in his bathroom, these were rarely used. There was too little water for that.

He took his bath with two tins of water in front of him, one cold the other hot, sometimes standing in the tub. He used a stone, these days, and would scrub and scrub his skin until it became sore. This he did to avoid another bath soon. After the scrubbing, he felt fresh.

"I bathed yesterday." Became his favourite statement to Shupi, and an interesting thought to him.

He bathed standing up, as they used to do as young boys in the river, in the rural areas.

The tub was now used for laundry.

If that was not going backwards in time, Farai thought, he didn't know what was. Evidently, the people of Zimbabwe were going backwards, and not stationary, as some people suggested, while the rest of the world was going forwards.

He also needed to be careful with the soap, because the same was used for plates and the dishes, and Shupi did not want her soap in the kitchen with hairs.

She also was stingy with her dishtowels, but gave them freely to visitors.

With the critical shortage of power, water, food and other goods, Zimbabweans were clearly going back to the primitive mode of living. If anyone doubted that man was created from soil, here was the proof.

Under Zanu PF., Zimbabweans were slowly returning where they had come from. Some people said they were taking them back to the forest, where they'd liberated the country from, but it was clear, it was back to the soil.

Usually, Farai wore long T-shirts. This was to allow him to wipe his face when he needed to, or wipe off sweat or tears that came out from the smoky fires and dust all around. People didn't notice it, so that was his personal little secret. He would walk about like that, pretending to be in his own world.

Besides, he was ruggedly handsome, above average height, and ladies found him interesting.

One day around Christmas 2017, as he wandered across town, Farai wondered at the coincidence that whenever there was lack, such as of money or food, the streets were filled with ugly women. Wherever he went, he was met with the same types of women, short or plumb, pitch black and fat. The hair skyrocketed in all directions, unkempt. He did not like these, for he preferred them slim, full-breasted and smooth-skinned.

Even outside of town, the further out he went, the uglier the women. They were written 'poverty' and 'classless' all over their faces, and had absolutely no style. Such were typical African women, according to Farai, and he wondered if any social development was taking place. That was another clear sign that they were going backwards.

He also discovered that he'd lost sexual appetite, or interest. A lot of it was gone, and he had to struggle to satisfy his wife. Even when a woman looked beautiful, he had no interest any more, unlike before.

All around Mutare and Zimbabwe, the common response you got from a greeting was "zvakadhakwa", literally meaning life is 'drunk'. This means it is meaningless, senseless, and insensitive, like a drunken man.

To Farai's surprise, even priests, pastors, ladies, schoolchildren and everyone else was freely using that expression to describe Zim life.

That meant these people knew what they were talking about. They knew how it felt to be drunk. In other words, they too were drunks. That was the way Zimbabwe was degenerating into. Everybody, everything, was drunk.

And he reflected briefly about how easy and cheap life in Zimbabwe was. He knew how sacrosanct life was, and how awful and scary a crime like murder was. To most Zimbabweans, murder was scary because of the avenging spirit of the victim, who would not leave his murderer in peace until fully avenged. Today, however, it was widely rumoured that if you commit murder, the victim won't avenge, but bless you with money, wealth and property as a 'thank you' gift for freeing them from Zimbabwe's hard and tortuous life.

He slowly ambled along the pavements, trying hard to ignore the ugly, grating sounds of power generators all over town. The atmosphere was worsened by smoke, dust and fuel spews as old trucks and cars sped past.

These days, nearly every shop was filled with Chinese solar power gadgets, from self-charging bulbs to panels and generators. Business was booming for them in the tears, misery and starvation all around.

As he approached the city centre, he heard, "Farai!" He turned, and there stood the caller.

Farai could not remember her, so he moved closer.

"Don't say you've forgotten me…? She said coyly as she smiled.

Farai extended a hand, which she took and looked directly into his eyes.

"Maiwe, Sis Cherry!" he exclaimed.

Charity was older than him by a year or two, but had grown up in the same neighbourhood. Farai thought she'd always given him a teasing eye. After greetings, he invited her to a restaurant with seats outside, and they sat. She bought drinks for both of them, and Farai relaxed. He learnt that she was divorced from her Zimbabwean husband in London, and had come for the holidays.

The rest was easy. Apparently it was clear that each wanted the other. So that day Farai went to Charity's house in Hospital Hill and spent the rest of the day, and night. He knew how to pacify Shupi. There were a lot of funerals those days and people slept out a lot. Besides, there was no power to charge his cell phone.

Meanwhile, his time with Charity was made in heaven. Farai felt it closely that this would be a life-changing opportunity and relationship. He did his best to please her, until one day she said, "You know, Fatso, my time here is almost up. I will be going back in two weeks."

Farai waited. Just before he said "I'm going to miss you." she uttered those words, with a kiss on his lips. "But," she continued, "I have an offer for you."

"Let's hear it. I have an offer for you, too"

They played about the offers, she demanding that he give his, first, until she said, "My offer is that we fly and live together in London. Just the two of us."

Farai could not believe his ears. London!! It had been his dream for a long time. In fact, many Zimbabweans were flocking to the UK, and were scattered all over the island. Now it was his turn to leave all the rubbish around himself that was Zimbabwe.

He quickly accepted Charity's offer. When pressed to declare his offer, he said he wanted to marry her. They discussed the pros and cons, and decided that it was better they lived together, first, before they discussed marriage, which could be very difficult and complicated, because they came from the same neighbourhood.

Thereafter, they went over details and conditions of their living together. The first was that Farai only dated her, and no one else, while in London. The second was that he would not leave the house they stayed without her knowledge.

This was an opportunity he was not going to miss.

How am I going to get money?" Farai asked.

"Don't worry. I will take good care of you. Jobs are there. I will look for a nice, well- paying tie- job for you. Even a plumbing or fitting in one of the counties."

To say Farai was super excited was an understatement. Here, at last was his dream coming alive. He always felt too superior to be still living in such a backward, underdeveloped country like Zimbabwe, which was going backwards, to the Stone Age century, while the rest of the world was going forward. He thought that the root cause of the country's problems lay with its name. How could Mugabe and his gang name a country after ruins? Why name the country after Zimbabwe Ruins?

At home he told Shupi that he had met a friend who had offered him a ticket and accommodation in London. Shupi too was excited. She imagined herself visiting her husband in London, and him coming home for the holidays. Every family these days had someone in the UK, and they seemed the only ones left out. She discussed with him the potential dangers those days, such as human trafficking, but Farai laid her fears to rest.

Indeed, human trafficking had also come to Zimbabwe. Stories were told of innocent girls who were lured to countries in the Middle East, where they had got domestic jobs, but faced a lot of abuse, such as work without pay, sexual and other forms of harassment. The same happened to some local girls too, here in Zimbabwe.

On the day of travel, Shupi accompanied Farai only as far as the bus terminus in town. It was because she had to save the little money she had for the children's upkeep. Farai made vehement promises that he would secure a job as soon as possible, start work, and send money and goodies home. He travelled alone to Harare, where he joined Charity at a local hotel. Their Air Zim flight took off at 10 pm.

The first thing Farai discovered in London was that Charity stayed in a flat. There were many other Zimbabweans on their block of flats, and they came to welcome them. Farai was at his best behavior, focusing only on Charity. When she went to work the next night, she locked him inside the flat. In fact this became the trend. Whenever she went out alone, Charity locked the flat, with Farai inside watching movies or reading. He also cooked for Charity and himself. He never went outside, except on a few occasions with Charity.

Yet he was curious to explore and discover London. He had heard of a lot of guys from his location who now lived in London. For example, he desperately wanted to meet Gidza, from his neighbourhood, and Chikwenaz. He wanted to meet them. However he had to be careful.

When he brought up the subject of a job one day, Charity repeated her statement that she would look for a job for him.

One day he asked to call Shupi's boss, who had a cell phone, and ask him to bring Shupi to the phone. When she talked to him, Shupi cried and cried about the hard life in Zim, the critical shortages of food, and other needs. She pleaded with him to send money quick.

It struck him that he had not even found a job yet. He could not ask Charity for money to send to Shupi, so he decided to act for himself.

One Friday night, when Charity had gone to work, he broke out. He used a block of iron to unlock the door, and was out. He didn't go far, but to a flat to his right. He knew from peeping through the window several times, that the door opened around 11pm every night, and a Zimbabwean woman lived there.

The woman recognized Farai as soon as she opened the door. She opened the door wider so he stepped in. When they sat down, Farai talked about a teaching job, to which Jane responded that it was difficult but could be arranged, with the right connections. He spent that night in Jane's room, and creeped back to Charity's around 4 o'clock in the morning, two hours before Charity knocked off.

It became a pattern with him. Each time Charity went to work, he would get out to Jane's. He had discovered that he could make the lock appear normal most times, but could disengage it whenever he wanted.

He learned from Jane all the Zimbabweans who lived on the block of flats, and the next. Sometimes, Jane would invite a friend or two, and they would enjoy time. This expanded Farai's circle of places to visit. In the end, he had been to all the single ladies' flats, and slept with them. He was on demand. However, still he stayed with Charity,

It did not take long before Charity discovered Farai's games. She received an anonymous call that informed her of Farai's movements and doings. That evening she came home and told him that because he did not have the right papers to stay in the UK and had come as a visitor, she no longer wanted him. So he had to go back to Zim. He could use his return ticket. She hired a taxi for him to the airport and bade him farewell. When he mentioned bus fare from the airport, she threw a 10 Pound note on his lap and withdrew into her flat.

LITTLE BRENDON FALLS SICK

One mid-morning, about four weeks after his return from London, Farai was sitting in his worn sofa reading a newspaper, when he raised his eyes to his son and saw something amiss with him. His eyes were blurred and sleepy, and the breathing was uneven and low. Farai dropped the newspaper and looked closely at his son, turning the head. Brendon immediately slumped into his hands. Farai scooped him up and went outside. There, he laid him on the veranda and waited. There was no movement from him, however, and Farai panicked. He quickly made long strides towards the gate, to try and see if he could find a car to the hospital.

Yesterday evening there had been a rumour of critical fuel shortages. But he was hopeful. He saw two cars at the shops as he got near them. He went to the first one. "I'm afraid I have no fuel, my brother," said the driver. Farai went to the next, and was told the same thing. He tried one or two others that came in, with the same result. The problem, Farai thought, was that he had no money. If he had money, he could offer any large amount. There were countless dealers in fuel across the location.

He went back home, and saw two elderly women by his son's side. "It's the fontanelle", said the older of the two. Fatso had heard about this common affliction that affected children. Without another thought, he scooped his son into his arms, threw him on the back and began the long walk to the clinic. All the way he prayed ceaselessly for his son to survive.

He saw large crowds as he entered the hospital gates, milling or just walking about. One woman stepped up to him and said, ": They're on strike. We've heard that all nurses countrywide are on strike. What's wrong with him?"

Farai told her and she responded by telling him that such a disease was not for hospitals, but traditional medicine. She further said that she knew of a woman who was an expert at such matters, and proceeded to give directions. Farai did not wait. He knew the area described by the woman, and proceeded there.

After going round the place and getting lost, he found the woman in her yard. She took a quick look at Farai's son and declared, "You're too late. You want to put my life at risk. This fontanelle has been delayed for long, and it is dangerous to treat. Your son might die, and I don't want to be held responsible."

Farai pleaded with her, but the woman was adamant. She advised him to go and see a doctor, another traditional medicine woman she suggested. But Farai knew only one doctor in the area, who made his charges in US Dollars. Fatso had none. He walked on, hopeless. He met the other traditional medicine woman at her house, but one look at Brendon gave her fright. She again said that Fatso was late to bring his son, and there was nothing she would do.

Fatso had nowhere else to go but home. There, he found his wife. He explained the matter to her, amid fighting tears welling in his eyes. Shupi too began to cry. This raised Farai's emotions, and he picked up his son again and walked out, Shupi right behind her. Now it was mid-afternoon. Several times Shupi told him to try for passing cars, but he did not seem to hear. He kept walking, head bent down, and crying.

When they arrived at the Mutare General Hospital, they found the yard deserted. They proceeded to the Outpatients section, where they saw hordes of people sitting or sleeping on benches. Farai went up to the desk, but there was no one. He hung around there for a while, then went to sit at the tail end of the queue, followed by Shupi. They sat there, in a stationary queue. Next to them was a man or woman covered with a white hospital sheet.

Then a man came in. He stood by the door and announced that doctors and all hospital staff were on strike that day, and probably the next, and so there was no treatment. Farai raised his hand to ask if there was any emergency service. The man walked up to where Farai and wife sat, and said no, there was no emergency service. He took Brendon in his arms, looked at Farai and Shupi, and said, "This child is lifeless…"

Those words triggered horrific feelings in Farai and Shupi, who both wanted to reach for their baby at the same time. They cried and cried, round the waiting room, sometimes sitting in the corner, on a bench, outside, and everywhere else, but there was nothing they could do. Brendon was wrapped in a hospital sheet and deposited on a separate bench. That was when Farai and Shupi realized that they'd been sitting next to a dead body. In fact, there were several such white sheets covering human bodies in the waiting room.

Days after Brendon's funeral, Farai wondered how it was possible that people would die in a hospital queue. This was not the first time. Several people had told him that the General Hospital was now one big mortuary. People did not go to hospital to get treated, but to die. Such was life in Zimbabwe. He heard from nurses and people who visited the hospital that outside every department of the hospital was a queue of dead bodies. The mortuary was full, and people were dying in large numbers, so the hospital could not cope. The biggest drawback was medications and well-trained experts in certain key areas.

At the hospitals themselves nationwide, staff and workers became the main source of medicines, outside the hospital. They sold tablets, injections, bandages and anything you wanted on the black market. That was how they lived. Teachers and other workers elsewhere did not have this source of extra money, and so they suffered, along with every Tom, Dick or Harry.

The other thing was that nurses, doctors and other hospital staff were almost always on strike. The causes of the strikes were varied, and ranged from low salaries to corruption and transfers, and so on. Some people (especially in the military) compared these strikes and demonstrations to treason, and the government agreed. They tossed and harassed such people, until they ran away to other countries, never to come back.

And there was also a sudden outbreak of cholera, of all diseases, in this age! Harare, Chitungwiza, Bulawayo and other cities and towns were engulfed in cholera. Fortunately, this happened at a time when there was no strike or any kind of industrial action, and resources were mobilized locally and internationally to fight the disease. In the end, hundreds were announced dead in Harare alone, with other cities providing their own figures. Still the government maintained its grip on power, saying cholera was God's disease, and there was nothing any human being could do to avoid or prevent it.

One puzzling thing to Farai was the government's economic mismanagement, and how it affected people's finances. While at independence, the local Zimdollar was at par with the British Pound sterling, now it was millions of miles off. After the knock the economy got from the war veterans' payment of $50 000 each in the late nineties, the government started printing bond paper and newsprint. then mixed it with grass and sand and called it money. They played around with this money, sometimes slashing zeros to reduce inflation, but costing people their investments and savings. A trillion Dollar note, for example, could not buy a loaf of bread. When people discovered that it was useless and could not buy them anything, especially outside the borders of Zim, they cried to their relatives in the diaspora for help. When the money came, they discovered that it could buy a hundred or two hundred times more than the so called Bearer cheques, which the government made out of paper. Everybody wanted to go to the diaspora, or to have a relative there, so that they could have the money.

In town, including across the country, the Bond Versus US$ rate continued to fluctuate. For example, he saw a packet of potatoes downtown selling at $5 cash, or $6 Eco cash. He liked the potatoes, but had no Eco cash yet, and would buy on his return trip. When he got his Eco cash, he saw the same type and quantity of potatoes selling at $8 a packet. However, if he wanted two for ecocash, he had to pay a total of $19. The woman explained rates per $10 Bond that Farai could not follow.

That was the Zim way of life, most times. Everyone wanted to maximize their profit.

The other troubling thing to Farai was the government's inconsistencies. What was said in the newspapers and radio was totally different from what was said and seen. The Herald, the government's main newspaper, had headlines of good living, and mega deals being signed with Chinese or European governments or large conglomerates, only to see nothing on the ground for years, until everybody forgot the mega deal. This was always the case, and people wondered where the deal had gone to. Mega deals were pronounced on radio, in the newspapers and tv, but nothing happened on the ground. Life actually became harder.

He wished people would join Pastor Evan Mawarire, the lone individual who was fighting the government and getting arrested every time. Politicians had cost them many lives, and had brought forth nothing, except empty promises. He hated the tendency among Zimbabweans to use jokes as a release for their painful and harrowing experiences at the hands of this government. If people did not joke as they did, perhaps their anger would rise and spill, leading them into action. This was the case and advice Zimbabweans got from people in South Africa and the DRC. The statement, "Zimbabweans normalize nonsense" was commonly expressed in combis and bars across the country. How could the people tolerate such nonsensical behaviour by their government? they asked. And yet nobody took any action. It was a case of one man for himself.

The popular expression these days was 'So long life'/As long as you're breating, or 'Chikuru kufema' in the vernacular Shona. This in short meant as long as you're breathing, why worry about anything, including pains, problems, troubles and suffering? Indeed, chikuru kufema, but what about the means that enable that breathing?

The economy stabilized somewhat, especially when the government adopted the multicurrency system.

But then the same government felt threatened, or weakened, so they banned the US Dollar and multicurrency system again. People were wild with disbelief. "What kind of government was this, which banned an international currency in preference for bond paper and tree leaves that they call RTGS or Ecocash?" they asked. Ecocash was electronic money, which one could deposit on one's phone and make payments from there.

In the latest development, the central bank and the government introduced another currency from paper and tree leaves and called it Bond notes. They lied to citizens that bond notes and coins were only for facilitating change and support exporters. The governor had assured the nation in 2015 that he would tender his resignation the following year if his plan did not work. His plan failed dismally, but he was reappointed to his post every year, up to 2019. At one point the Bond note was pegged at 1 to 1 with the US Dollar. What cheek!

To Fatso and his peers in the ghetto, all the government was trying to do was steal people's hard currency, the US Dollar, while they gave them the bond paper. In this way, the government was committing daylight bank robbery against its own people. Everybody knew the government was broke, industry was dead and there were no exports. In the previous crisis in 2007, the government had raided Foreign Savings Accounts of private companies and individuals, taking their foreign currency without asking or telling them. Fatso thought the same tactic was back. The local Zim currency was useless without industrial backing. Analysts and other level headed economists said that many times over, but nobody listened.

To Fatso and his friends, Gono reigned high as the worst reserve bank governor in the world during his reign from 2003 to 2013 It was during his governorship that Zimbabwe lost its currency, and plummeted into the fiasco it is today. And Gono would put on a cap and jeans and distribute his printed trillion dollar notes to his and Mugabe's gangs of crooks scattered across key towns and borders, even in streets, to buy ordinary people's US Dollars in exchange for the bearer cheques, which again were made out of newsprint and grass thatch. And people suffered, because the bearer cheques were worthless outside the country's borders.

It took the inclusion of the MDC in the inclusive government in 2009 to apply the multicurrency system, which sustained the country until the MDC was unceremoniously booted out and Zanu PF remained alone, to do its monkey business again and here the country was' back to 2008, the worst year in the living memory of many Zimbabweans

Farai wondered how the situation would end, and when. A lot of people Farai talked to, said that this time around, the government would find it difficult to steal from a wizened citizenry, who were determined not to part with their hard currency. They still used it among themselves, avoiding banks and certain bureau de charges.

But they seemed not to know Zanu PF, which prided itself in doing the undoable, such as fighting a war with the British army, and defeating it! Time would tell.

This time around, there was a new Reserve Bank Governor. There were money merchants in every town and city, with millions of the Zim currency, which they gave out to people in exchange for the banned US $. People said that a lot of whites were involved, as well as Mnangagwa's cabinet ministers and associates. They offered irresistible, lucrative rates, and had offices all over. Queues of people could be seen everywhere.

And Farai thought how difficult it was for someone to receive money from abroad. Usually, there was no electricity, which meant phones could not reflect the money. And when there was, there was no cash at the banks, including the sent money. It was scarce, and went to government priority areas By the time one got one's foreign currency, one's door would be full of people lining up to beg. One wondered how the news spread, or how people had seen one.

The foreign currency was also changed in the streets, on the black market. It was the politicians who ran the black market foreign currency cartels. Trying to buy all of it from people. It was understood that the country's political elites supplied the local currency to buy off the foreign currency. One wondered how they could term the currency market, when they actually fuelled it. And when one managed to receive the money from abroad, the next problem was changing it to local currency. That depended on the rate, which was not static but fluctuated several times, even in a day. Local currency was scarce, too, and banks were giving it out in coins, mostly.

A person who changed US$50 would for example get $500 in 50c coins, and had much trouble packaging it and getting home safely with it. Always one had to decide how much of the local currency one needed as cash, or Eco cash, or to remain in hard currency (the US Dollar). Sometimes, depending on need, the money was also changed into the South African Rand, Botswana Pula, and so on, depending on need. There was no single currency in the country, both officially and unofficially.

Most people Farai knew lived on buying and selling goods. They would find much needed goods in a shop, buy them in bulk, then resell on the streets. Often, they would buy from a big supermarket like TM or OK, then step outside and spread them on the veranda of that shop, for resale to incoming customers and passers-by.

ON THE ROAD AGAIN

Sometime in 2017, Farai found himself on the road again, to Chimoio in Mozambique, about,90 kilometres away to look for a job. It was funny, he thought, how Zimbos were relying on the poorest country on the continent, if not the planet, for survival. It was not so long ago that they were the beacon and shining example in the entire region. Mozambique, Malawi, Zambia, Botswana and even South Africa-they outshone them all in life style-as determined by their economy, education, agriculture, infrastructure and everything else.

But now the tide was turned, thanks to independence, and they were at the bottom of the barrel, the dregs at the base. So there he was, at 56, with a diploma in Fitting and Turning, Class 1 qualification, going to Moscan to look for a job. Funny, he thought, they could not even afford to pay him. But as things stood in his household, anything could do. He could take anything also in the form of payment currency, meticais, dollars, shillings, Kwachas, you name it. Because Zimbabwe didn't have any standard, single national currency. And he could change any of these currencies anywhere on the black market.

For a long time, he waited at the combi station, waiting for his ride. These days things were difficult. There were not that many combis on the road anymore because they were in the fuel queues, waiting their turn to fill up, then get on the road.

Rumours spreading on WhatsApp said that the fuel shortage was worsened, or even caused by bosses in the fuel industry, who diverted national supplies to the black market. What could they do, in the midst of corruption everywhere? They had to eat from where they were.

Then suddenly, Farai saw the combis speeding fast towards him, each trying to be the one to pick him up. It was fierce competition for passengers among the drivers, and this caused accidents. There were even no police to enforce road rules as they tried to overtake each other, or the soldiers, who said they were running the country, now.

Farai remembered a few years back, when the police would detect a drunken driver from the way he drove straight, on his side instead of swerving left and right, negotiating the potholes. Anyone who drove this way was the sober one, not the one who drove straight.

As they were bumped more on the road Farai couldn't help but think that only at independence, these township roads, like all other main roads across the country were tarred. As they deteriorated, more money was poured into tarring them, but a shoddy job was done, and the money eaten by some big sharks in the city council, party and or government.

Now there was nothing but dust, dust, dust and dongas. The roads also had signs and public phones, but these were struck down and the material used to make water containers and coffins, by private metal workers.

A surprising thing he noticed about people in general, and Zimbabweans in particular, was a tendency to like to drive the latest model cars on such roads. One wondered whether it was the car that was more important, than driving it, and doing so comfortably.

He also couldn't help thinking that the problem on Zimbabwe's roads was that the real honest, humble and respectful citizens were not the majority of drivers. Because they didn't have the money to buy cars, roads were taken up by those who could afford cars. And these were the gwejas, hwindis, whiztechs and some crooks and dealers.

Besides lacking the experience and education, these people just drove the same way they lived their lives; rough and tough, with the devil may care attitude. Many tales were told of road experiences and the carnage.

They picked up more passengers along World Bank Road, even entering people's gates. Sometimes these hwindis were so desperate for money that they would wait for a prospective passenger who was still in the bathroom, to finish off his bath and toiletry before boarding the combi.

Passengers would complain, and often, it depended on the character of the hwindi. Often they would wait for such passengers when the hwindis said, "That is my money I'm waiting for. I'm at work. It's not my fault that you woke up late, but yours. Let me do my job".

That would seal it, and passengers would keep quiet or drop off for another combi. That however, depended on the number of passengers, or the distance covered by the first combi, in which case the passenger had to pay. It also depended on whether there was a soldier among the passengers.

To make matters worse, some of the combis had outlived their legal life span. Farai remembered one combi which he boarded. A woman sitting in the window seat just behind the driver fell through the floor, right to the tarmac. There was a hole under the floor.

Fortunately for the woman, people screamed so loudly that the driver immediately stepped on the brakes. The woman sustained head, facial injuries and a broken leg.

After a few more passengers, the road got back onto Bonda Road By then the combi was full.

Whereas the standard number for passengers is 4 per seat, this time they were six. Farai couldn't help noticing that in South Africa, it was three passengers per seat.

This combi however continued to take in more. Some stood by the door, and others hung their heads loose for easier breathing, as long as their feet found space stand. That kind of overloading was dangerous, Fatso thought, and there was no police in sight. Soldiers had taken over, and they were not in sight either.

Soon as they were back on the tarred Bonda Road to town, they relaxed somewhat, at least those who could.

"Do you know where I'm going?" asked a man behind Farai.

"I don't. Where are you going, Sekuru? responded a woman right next to him.

"To Zimunya. Do you remember that friend of mine I told you about, the one I told you I work with?"

"Yes, I remember him. From Zimunya?"

"Exactly. He attempted suicide yesterday."

"Suicide? Is he mad?"

"No. He's not mad. And he was very sober."

"Then why? Why would he want to kill himself?"

"I had chatted with him at work earlier in the day. He had asked me if Rogo could really kill, and I'd told him yes. I had no idea he intended to kill himself."

"But why?" persisted the woman.

"I don't know. You know what saved him? When he arrived at home, with his rogo in pocket, he went behind the house and drank it up. After that he called his wife who had visited her parents in sakubva, and told her that he'd just drank poison. The wife phoned the man's brother, who apparently lived with them, to check on him. He did, and found him holding his belly behind the house. This guy knew something about traditional cures. He ran into a bush nearby, plucked up a green damba fruit from the forest and fed him. That's how he was saved".

"Really?" said the woman. "Does an unripe damba treat poisoning?"

"It sure does. Alternatively, you can use cow dung. Feed the person raw cow dung, and he vomits out everything."

"I know someone who committed suicide by taking rogo last year," said a young man in his twenties.

"Me too. I know two people who took poison last year alone," said a big-breasted woman in a window seat in front of Farai

'Ah, two only," said the driver. "I know about five in Sakubva alone. Some of these cases go unreported. You never hear of them.

Then the conductor shouted, "One more, one more who hasn't paid?" He looked into the eyes of his passengers as he said this, standing on the inside of the door.

There was no response from the passengers.

"One passenger who hasn't paid me, yet?" he shouted again.

Again there was silence.

Later, a woman in the second seat from the back asked, "Do you accept Eco cash?"

"No, we don't," replied the conductor.

"I was waiting for money in my wallet…but now the power is finished," continued the woman.

"But I asked who hadn't paid and you kept quiet. Now, we'll have to return to Chikanga with you, and you pay double," insisted the conductor.

Fatso wondered why people were not helpful to each other anymore. Long ago, that woman would have been helped by a fellow passenger with cash. Not these days. Each person looked at his own interests.

Farai was more concerned with the conversation about rogo, poison and people committing suicide. His own cousin had taken poison in 2005 or 6, and died. But throughout the discussion on the combi, he'd kept quiet and decided to suffer in silence.

However, as soon as they got into town he wished he had made a contribution to that discussion. And he wished he knew about green damba or raw cow dung. Of course it mattered.

His first mistake on the trip was failure to change his US Dollars on the Zimbabwe side. The quality of money he got from the Mozambican side was not good. He knew that if he pleaded and asked for something better looking, the answer was always the same, "look, brother, I don't make this money, and neither does the government. We don't have a printer or bank here that renews this money. Do you want it or not?"

And you take it, because it is legal tender still. Farai looked at the 8 two US Dollar notes in his hand wondered where he could shove it. Certainly not in his pockets! He turned and walked away towards the immigration building, with the notes in one hand-all eight of them. But soon enough, he had to pull out his passport from his jacket and as he did that he dropped the dirty dollars in there.

The formalities at Immigration were easier now, except that the official did not return his greeting. But, surprise surprise, the guy at the exit did-even to the extent of asking how the wife and kids were. Amazing.

And soon as he was out of the gate and Zim area, trouble began. Young Mozambican men surrounded him with wads of meticais, their currency.

Farai's journey took only $6, to and fro, but he had to consider lunch and a fw other things. Eventually, he changed $30. And of course, he got cheated. This happened every time, and he didn't know why he never bothered to calculate the amount he should get, even with a calculator on his phone, right inside his pocket. This time the young man who served him used a different trick, he said, "Mdhara, the rate is US$1 to 32 Meticais. How much do you want to change?"

"$20", Farai said, "but I have $50, so you give me $30 change, and the rest you give me in Meticais."

"No problem," he said, and even before Farai handed him the $50, he gave him the $30 change.

He counted the meticais, and said, "Here is 650 Meticais. You owe me 10 Meticais…"

"But I don't have any Meticais on me…" Fatso said.

"In that case, do you have $2? Then we are done"

Farai immediately thought of the rotten dollars that were probably causing his jacket to smell.

"Sure. I have $2," he said, and proceeded to dive into his jacket pocket and fished out the money and hand it over to him.

He took it, gave his thanks, and turned. Farai proceeded on his way, but at the back of his mind he felt, that he had been cheated. This was not the first time. Each time though, he had recovered his money on the return journey, just like he did with this young man, as you probably have noticed that the he should have given Farai 704 Meticais, and not 650.

So he went, crossed the Rio Munene, and was at the Moscan side. They were much slower there, naturally, and when he was done, went out the gate to the waiting kombis. One was already filling up and he got a middle seat.

It was the usual, typically unmistakable breed of border jumpers they had on this one. Short, plump or obese, big breasted and fat cheeked women of between 30 and 40. There were a few men too and, in that early month of June, all were tightly clad in cheap jackets and overcoats and woolen hats and high boots. They talked at the top of their voices as they argued and haggled with vendors of all types and wares.

"But this seat....your seat, was already booked," said a woman at the window, next to Farai.

"Oh", he said, "but they will fit in. It sits four, doesn't it…?"

"Yes. You may sit, I think. We will see when he comes."

And this woman had piles of bags and paper bags and more stuff wrapped in newspapers. She shoved some of the stuff under the seat, then held a few items in her lap. Farai squeezed in, and sat.

Then a man came in and they were three. Another came in, but the third did not shift towards Farai, preferring the window, forcing this guy to squeeze in between him and Farai. He was not very big, but oh what muscles he had over his arms and shoulders. Farai felt the air squeezed out of his lungs. Shit. He shifted and moved, but he was solid as a rock, and did not move an inch to Farai's shifting. He gave up, having at least attained some comfort.

The seat ahead filled up fast, and the kombi was full. But there were more passengers. Space was created just behind the driver, so that 4 more passengers sat or stood facing the rest of the passengers, with their backs to the driver. Farai counted 22 passengers (2 more in the driver's cabin) and 2 staff, making a total of 24.

The driver started the combi, and the buying started.

"Hey," one woman said, head out of the window, "give me one drink and a packet of biscuits! Hurry up!"

"Iwe," says another, "do you have Buddie airtime?"

"Mcel", shouts another, "Give me Mcel airtime. Chop-chop!"

"Drink! Drink! Give me a coke!"

"Hey, change these 5 dollars for me. I need just a few Meticais!"

"My stuff! Hey Compradore, are you sure all my stuff is safe up there?"

"Have you seen my small bag anywhere around here? I had it between my thighs... just now now."

All this somehow reminded Farai of a story a diaspora friend had told him. He said he knew that the people he had met during his flight out of Zim, or into Zim were Zimbabwean, because from the time they entered the plane, and right throughout the flight, they spoke in English

And he was also reminded of an observation made by someone decades ago, that if you offer someone (African) a ride at the back of your bakkie or lorry, he felt very lonely, but the moment they became two or three they would start singing, no matter where they were going or the distance or occasion. Some would start insulting those on terra firma, saying silly jokes and being smart alecs. Farai thought this notion still prevailed. Especially among the younger generation.

He also had a friend or two who had the ugliest of voices, and hardly knew one musical note from another. But the moment they got into the bathroom they suddenly became Pavarottis and undiscovered talents, or so they thought. It all ended, of course, soon after they stepped out of the bathroom.

Finally, the combi pulled out onto the tar mac, and they were on their journey. And the talks got excited again, this time on mobile phones.

"I am gone! I am already in Mozambique. Yes, Chimoio. No I'll be back today. I am just leaving now…But you know what? Yesterday you bored me…."

"Mai Ngoni? Ko where are the evening prayers tonight? Hoo? Ah today am out shamwari. In Mozambique. Yes. Yes. Thank you. Bye."

"Hallo? Hallo? Can you hear me? Tell Mai Tsitsi to give you the money for our weekly rounds. Yes, it's my turn to get it this week. Tell her to give you, and you take $20 from there and give it to Tete Shami… Then keep the rest till I come, wanzwa?"

"Hi, Mike? Is that Mike? We are off now. Yes. I know. Don't worry. Iribho. Sharp. Ka hwani."

And it was like that, phone chats up to Manica, after which the Zim transmission was lost, and Mozambique took over. And after Manica, one by one they fell asleep, right until Chimoio. The windows were tightly closed, and no one attempted to open any one of them, in spite of the intense heat. At one of the road blocks Farai asked one to be opened, and three opened at the same time, only to be closed soon as the kombi picked up speed again. He gave up, and joined his fellow travellers in the alternate game of dozing and waking up. That way, they arrived quite early, actually this time they beat the last record by taking only I hour 40 minutes.

FARAI'S FURORE

There was no electricity again that evening, the third in a row. Farai and crew had been told by ZESA that the prepaid system would ensure constant supply, but alas. This was two weeks after his return from Mozambique, where he'd stayed only four days, because he'd found no job, or anyone to stay with as he searched.

By 5pm every day, in 2017, the entire neighbourhood was enveloped in thick, grey smoke from the cooking fires, and dust from cars passing by. The smodust filtered into the houses, settling on window sills and furniture, making Farai and his family cough and sneeze. Smoke also came from burning rubbish on almost every street. Refuse trucks were no longer coming to collect, and so rubbish dumps were all over. People would sometimes burn these dumps, without prior warning. There was always a pungent smell in the neighbourhood as a result.

In the mornings, women and girls would sweep the dirt around their yards and roads with thatch brooms. This also raised and spread dust. The entire location was a greyish smoke or dust.

All cooking was done on the open fire, these days, because of critical power shortages. The government said water in the great Zambezi River had fallen to levels that could no longer power hydroelectricity, and the Kariba coal power station had numerous faults that needed urgent repair.

However, people wondered how Zambia, which shared a border with Zimbabwe and drew electricity from the same Zambezi, was getting power.

The stories were many and diverse. Some people talked of unpaid bills that ran into millions, but how that debt was accrued was not explained. Others even said Strive Masiyiwa, the communications mogul, had offered the government the US$80million that ZESA owed, but also buy the ZESA parastatal and it becomes his personal company. People chided the government for refusing that offer, because it rescued the people. A lot of industries would reopen. But others said nay, the government, for once, was right. They knew Strive Masiyiwa from past dealings, and were not prepared to sell him the parastatal.

Yet others talked about Mnangagwa's address to the nation, when we had no power. But then the news filtered through, that in the address, he'd assured the nation that power would be restored to a certain level soon.

Anyway, back to my story, about the grey city. Now the whole location was covered in smoke from cooking firewood. But there was a threat to even that, too. The government was banning the use of firewood due to deforestation and other environmental hazards. The question most people asked was, the government knew very well that electricity was scarce, and firewood was the only source of energy for the people (gas was very expensive and could only be accessed by a few), what did it want the people to use as energy?

An alternative would be cow dung, or such other fossils. Who would like to keep that in their house?

The grey colour of smoke everywhere made Farai think of Zimbabwean award winning journalist Hopewell Chin'ono's popular Facebook Page, in which he remarked, "All this is happening in a country where politicians are driving Lamborghinis and Rolls Royces."

To Fatso, the guys in Zanu PF danced to Chopper Chimbetu's song, 'Pane Asipo', with automaton feet and a deaf ear. They thought the missing person was always the one dead and buried somewhere without a grave, during the war. Yet the missing people were there, going hungry in front of their eyes. Yet they loved the song and danced to it over and over, as their tradition.

The country had sunlight throughout the year, including June and July, the coldest months, but the government had done nothing to harvest that sunshine, let alone encourage the people to use it. What a pity!

The firewood itself was not easy to get, and at the worst period, cost more than electricity in a month. Besides firewood, you also needed matches and paper to light the fire. Matches especially was not easy to come by. Sometimes one had to walk hundreds of metres going round, looking for a stick of matches. And Farai had many experiences of having a single matchstick in his pocket, and failing to get supper because the stick could not light.

Farai always tried to forget his notes and certificates that he used to light fire outside. Whole files had gone into cooking sadza. Shupi had often derided her for keeping files of education certificates, while the family was starving. However, he later learned not to panic when times like these happened.

Farai discovered the many stupid things that fire made him do. For example, he'd recently lost a whole crate of empty scud containers, plus their plastic container, in a fire.

He also remembered his cousin, Haru, who had thrown a whole packet of double chicken n fresh chips into the fire, while hungry faces with parched lips stared. She'd been miffed by some political Zanu PF comment. Now, however, that tiff had gone and the Zanu PF people were back again, begging as before.

He wondered why these people never learned. They could see, read, feel and talk about things, but never learned anything to improve their lives.

It was important to flow with the tide. Go out, observe, and watch. That way, you're kept in the flow.

If a person who died in 1980 would resurrect today, he would watch the same Mvengemvenge on ZTv, listen to the same songs like 'Bhutsu Mutandarika, 'Madhebhura,' and travel the same.

It was a wonder that there were still any people supporting such a party. To Fatso, Zimbabwe and its people died in 1980. There was need for resurrection.

Farai remembered some of his friends of yester year, who could even set the trend for the entire community when things were that tough. They set the pace, and dictated it. Such guys had large followings. In the ghetto, they were called 'Masters'.

Some of them who came later, tended to be violent, against the culture of being 'master'. Thankfully, that ended when soldiers took over, and the ghetto was no longer what it used to be.

In addition, the coal from cooking fires was also used for ironing clothes and other laundry, not electricity as before. Hot charcoal was put into an iron cast iron, for pressing.

Meanwhile, Mnangagwa and the military continued to rule. While Mugabe had destroyed people's hopes, dreams and lives through his legalistic dictatorship, Mnangagwa held a hammer in one hand, and a gun in the other. He made sure nobody made a noise as he bludgeoned them into submission.

There was virtually no progress or development in any sphere now that Zanu could claim. They'd destroyed all the gains that their two governments would ever claim to have made.

At one time, a journalist asked him live about the skyrocketing prices, and he answered, "Its up to you to do what you can. I'm not there to deal with bead prices. Affected people should deal with it themselves. My bread is cheap. Deal with yours."

Many comments were made by listeners, to that. Generally they felt he was insensitive to their plight and needs.

Farai remembered some of their desperate efforts to get electricity. The funniest and most successful was when he and his friends in Sakubva ganged up and wrote a letter to Mugabe. In it, they expressed deep respect for him. However, that unanimous respect was being threatened by employees at ZESA, who were adamant MDC supporters for change. They said they'd been assured by someone that the MDC was determined to oust Mugabe, by introducing severe power cuts nationwide, and people would abandon him for that.

For a whole week, they had basked in the glory of electricity. The power cuts were reintroduced after somebody had written a letter to the Sunday Mail newspaper, in exactly the same words as Farai and his crew had used, and the lie about MDC was discovered. No one was arrested, however.

But the days of darkness were back again, and new methods of coping had to be found. Farai was thinking of introducing what he called 'cave games' to his family. Since they often had no candle or matches, they stayed in total darkness, whether by day or night, especially night.

Farai thought that since the house resembled a cave at night, what could be wrong in entertaining each other before super, and after super, before they went to sleep. It would be a long night and, as he joked, some of them might never wake up at all. So the cave games would keep them entertained. They were easy, safe games, such as guessing someone's voice in the dark, or finding something hidden nearby or in the next room. Of course, when they wanted to talk about the cave games in public, they would refer to them as CGs, so that people would not know.

Lack of spending money, coupled with absence of electricity, cuts you off from the world. That way, you are in a real cave. And yet you had scores of people in the international circle that you want to engage with.

As things stood, there was news across the country that patients were dying on the operating table in theatre, because there was no power. Sometimes, there was also no phone network and money could not be moved to the specialists who needed it to do their job. There were also widespread reports of certain doctors refusing to treat patience before they were paid, in full. In more cases than otherwise, the patients died after the operation, when the doctor is gone, with the money.

So, because of power and network connectivity, a lot of patients were dying in hospital queues.

Meanwhile, soldiers ruled.

Sure, Fatso thought with a giggle, they were going backwards. If there was anyone who doubted that human life started in Africa, Zimbabwe was the perfect proof. Man was going backwards, into the soil, where he started off, and it was in Zimbabwe that it was starting.

Interestingly, Fatso had heard a tale about the black man being like soil. "Wherever you go", the speaker had said, "if you look closely at fertile, productive soil, it looks like black skin."

Fatso could see sense in that.

Zanu PF was taking them back where they'd all started, where God had made them from into the soil.

Recently, ZESA had just increased power charges,-even when the power itself was not there. This was 'booking money in advance' for themselves.

They were also threatening to charge those who used solar panels, yet ZESA did not feature anywhere on the solar energy deal.

If they could do that, what could stop them from entering people's homes and blowing out candles, as they had threatened for Stage 5 of their power cuts?

Sure, Farai thought, Zimbabweans were above normal people. They tolerated the intolerable, and normalized the abnormal. Where else in Africa, or anywhere in the world, could this be tolerated?

He'd heard of people who claimed to love animals. Such people identified very closely with elephants, cats, dogs, zebra, pythons and other wild creatures, yet they left their closest animal, the Zimbabwean, out in the cold. Farai secretly and silently cried and prayed for such people to turn on Zimbabweans and help them out, despite their wrongs, mistakes and omissions

Much as he knew the family needed his company in dark moments like tonight, Farai banished them to their cooking and headed for the shops, for the temporary comfort of generator- powered electricity in the bars and bottle stores. At least there, they could commiserate their plight of living in Zimbabwe in numbers, ignoring the finger-numbing cold from the inclement weather and the beer bottles fresh from the fridge. Not that clear beer was still affordable, but some guys had guts. The good thing, Fatso observed, was that unlike in 2008, this time around, goods are available in shops.

In 2008, everyone had piles and piles of bearer cheques and agribonds, but could not find what to buy with it. This time it was the opposite. Shelves everywhere were full of goods and foods, but people did not have money in their pockets. Completely dry.

What we learn from this is that the government did not learn anything from the 2008 experience. They just fumbled in the dark, to extremes.

A group of guys sat in a circle at the Breeze, a billow of smoke curling and churning up the wall to the sky. I could tell soon as I approached the bottle store that Farai was in a foul mood. He had got over the sudden loss of his new job at Pritchard's Diesels. Elizabeth and husband's company had shut down a few weeks after Fatso had joined it, due to failure to access foreign currency to buy spares and goods abroad. And now he was jobless again.

Four scuds between his legs, cap drawn to cover his red eyes, and an ever twitching moustache were enough evidence. No one touched Farai when he was this angry and, I repeat, no one. Even the police avoided him, and that meant ordinary folks like myself could drink freely; no police raids for public drinking. But that also meant keeping Farai's *bhavha* in constant supply with the scud stuff. And that was some big problem.

First, though, I wanted to know why my old guy was in such a bad mood. Tendai (or Tindo) was not there, and Sizzler could not be seen at the braai stand. So I had to ask him directly, but first I had to grab a bottle of water for myself, for some sort of confidence boosting, you know. I sat down next to him, on the bottle store stairs, facing the milling crowds at the market stalls.

"Hey, Fatso," I said, without looking directly at him, "*Ndeipi?* What's up this time?"

He took a longish gulp from his mug, wiped some drags off the corners of his mouth, coughed, belched loudly, then looked at me. "Have you ever been to Chiadzwa?" he asked, taking me by complete surprise.

"No. Why?"

Silence.

"What happened at Chiadzwa? Any news?" I prodded.

He took the mug and covered the mouth of his scud with it, upside down, before saying," Can you believe how they employ people at Chiadzwa? I heard there were jobs there, so I woke up at 5 this morning to see if I just might get something.

When I got there around 8 I saw hundreds of people already there. And you know what the authorities said? They said we have to go and apply to their offices in Harare. Harare! Can you believe that? Harare! I was born in Chiadzwa, went to Chiadzwa Primary, then Chiadzwa Secondary. When I was sick I got treated at Chiadzwa Clinic. I dipped our cattle in Chiadzwa Dip Tank, I married in Chiadzwa. I have Chiadzwa blood in my veins. I am Chiadzwa, and those fields are in my territory! Those diamonds…." He poured more scud to cover up for the tears welling up in his eyes. Farai crying? My, my. This earth my brother!

To be honest, I wanted to laugh. I also wanted to say, "And when you die, you will resurrect in Chiadzwa". But how could I? The guy would make mincemeat out of me. So I said, "Harare? How can that be? You mean for anybody to be employed at Chiadzwa they have to go to Harare, first?"

Fatso ignored me. Silly me. But I wanted more, so I said, "Why did you not find some connection first, somebody who works there and could pull a few strings?"

"Only this one guy I know, Widzo, and he said they were recruiting. But they're not, at least from here, they're not. This is not independence. What kind of independence is that, when you lose everything that you ever had, to the people who liberated you? I think we have to start another war of independence. This is not freedom!"

'May be it has to do with skills, you know. Employers want certain skills, and you locals may not have them."

"Skills my ass," barked Fatso. "What skills? Do you need skill to shovel earth? I am a skilled plumber and Fitter n' Turner, all rolled into one. What more do I need?"

There was relief when Tindo arrived, but he was in someone else's company, a guy who looked vaguely familiar. Farai had to tell his story all over again.

"Ah," said Tendai's friend, whom everybody understood was called Uncle Pets, "your problem is an easy one". With that, he grabbed Farai's scud and cup, and poured himself a fill. He drank long and hard, his adam's apple bobbing up and down in an automated fashion. "The thing is,.." he continued amid hiccups, "you need to get into the structures. Get into structures, *mudhara,* and the whole of Chiadzwa will be yours."

'What structures?" Farai asked.

But before he answered, Uncle Pets reached for Fatso's scud again, at which point Farai shifted his big foot and prevented the scud from escaping between his legs.

"What structures? Fatso asked again, his temper slowly rising.

"Political structures, of course. Who knows you? Whom do you know? You cannot do anything from outside. *Chara chimwe hachitswanyi inda, madhara angu.*[5]"

"And which party is this, if I may know?" Sizzler asked, quite amused.

"It's obvious, isn't it?" he tried to reach for the scud again, but Farai was still firm.

"No, it is not obvious, you tell us," Farai insisted on my behalf.

"Actually, I do not belong to any political party, but am an analyst.

"What analyst?" Sizzler asked, now baffled.

"Madhara, we are all over, these days as we move closer to elections, we analysts. You hear us on TV, radio, newspapers. You guys look educated to me. Don't tell me you have never heard of us. Analysts. See?"

"Tell us what you analyse, maybe we can understand better."

---

[5]   No man is an island, my elders

"We are on television, newspapers, and radios. Haven't you ever heard of analysts? We analyse news, politics, employment, elections, everything in the country, including sanctions."

At this, Tendai began to roll with laughter. Bald, shiny head in the fading sun, he bared all his teeth and held his face in both hands, saliva drooling from an open mouth, laughing loud and clear.

"Guys," said Tindo amidst laughter, "did you know that Air Zimbabwe has one airplane, 28 directors, 49 pilots, 800 employees? Somebody asked Zanu PF what they should do to make the airline profitable. Y'know what the answer was? They said, "Add a chairman to the Board…""

"You talk of that?" said professor laughing away. "At a recent investment drive that the president attended this week, a Zimbabwean journalist asked one international investor why he invested in Nigeria, rather than Zimbabwe which was peaceful. The businessman replied, "The world knows that there is Boko Haram in Nigeria, and we all see the efforts the government is making in fighting them. However, the case is different in Zimbabwe, where the government is Boko Haram.""

The laughter that ensued encouraged Farai.

"Scram, "he said in a gruff voice.

"What?" Uncle Pets asked.

"I said get lost. Get away from here, right now!'

Sheepishly, the guy stood up and ambled towards the bottle store.

Fortunately, there was no sign of soldiers around, and there was no scene.

"Analyst my foot," said Tindo. "The guy tells me lots of different stories each time. Most times, he has some cash though. I wonder where he gets it from."

"Must be a ghost worker," Fatso chipped in.

"Very likely," I said, and left to join Sizzler who was now at the braai stand.

We continued like that for a while, with Sizzla doing his tricks at the braai stand. Again, there wasn't much braaing going, but Sizzla being Sizzla, he never left the braai stand. Now he was braaing some birds from Wengezi junction, which no one, except some street kids, was interested in.

Then suddenly the generator went silent. This was because ZESA power had come. But, however, the ZESA power had come only for seconds, then switched off again. So there was darkness all around. To make things worse, there was no moonlight.

Apparently, the guys had been told that the President would be addressing the nation that night. Now there was no power, and they wondered how many people he would address.

They were however assured of power the next day, the Defence Forces Day. There was no way the president would let down soldiers by failing to broadcast live their displays across the country.

"I'm going home," I told Fatso and crew as I stood up.

"me too. Let's walk together," said Fatso as he fumbled his hand for his scuds. But there was no scud. There should be two left.

Fatso went silent for a while, even his shadowy features portraying shock and anger.

"Who took my beer?" he asked in a strong, baritone voice, his body ready to pounce on anyone.

Nobody answered, and nobody had any scud with or near them.

Fatso looked at the faces that stared at him. "Let's go," he said to me.

But a few steps from the stairs where he'd been sitting, we bumped into that Analyst, drinking a scud, with another one in his left hand.

Fatso went for him. "You!", he said, "that is my beer. Give me back my beer."

The Analyst was dumbfounded. He stood there, puzzled.

"This is not your beer, but mine. I bought it in…"

Before he finished, Fatso was upon the scuds. He seized both of them and marched homeward, me following behind.

FARAI ATTENDS A CHURCH SERVICE OCTOBER 2018

"Heee, varume[6]
Musaputse sungano[7]
Sungano yacho ndeyaMwari"[8]

And on and on the chorus went, repeatedly. The organ accompanied the song, almost drowning the voices of the people. Everyone clapped loudly, and others danced round and round. From 3km away the song could be heard.

He had tried everything in his power to sustain life and improve his family's welfare, but had failed. Church seemed the safest hiding place. Like many other people he talked to, Zanu PF would rule forever, with or without opposition. They would continue in their position until they got tired, or someone in the party saw reason, and decided to serve the people, in whatever form or quantity.

For example, cabinet ministers and their deputies alone, who numbered up to 40, could donate a million dollars each to the nation. They could afford it, especially with the millions they were always accused of stealing.

A recent case was that of Minister Prisca Mupfumira, accused of fraudulently acquiring $95 million. The case was publicized in newspapers

---

[6]   He-e men
[7]   Don't break your vow
[8]   The vow is before God

under pressure, but Zimbabweans had no doubt that that was its end. She would not be prosecuted. If she was, she would not be found guilty and sentenced, but would go scot free.

This was the case with many other corrupt government officials, many of them who were enjoying high class life in the world's best tourist attractions. Ignatius Chombo was an example. He had destroyed cities and towns across the country as long-serving Minister for Local Government and Development, under the Mugabe rule, was tried under Mnangagwa and found guilty, but was nowhere to be seen or heard about. Instead a picture of him in Dubai, shirtless, circulated on social media.

Or, Farai thought, the cabinet ministers would donate a month's salary. Surely, that would not be asking too much by an impoverished, unemployed population? Top government officials and cabinet ministers were getting their salaries every month, while some people had spent four or more years without a salary. If they really cared about the people they served, surely there would be nothing wrong in donating just a month's salary?

That, to Fatso, was the middle case scenario for Zimbabwe, if things remained as they were. Rescue and respite would only come from a thinking Zanu PF official, because they would rule forever.

If nobody saw reason, then Fatso was prepared to face his destiny. He had no power over that. Parties and people had tried to dislodge the party, without success. So be it!

By now Farai was tired of the singing in church and, shoulder leaning against the window, he clapped lightly. His concentration began to wander. There was that young woman singing her mouth off, and that young man clapping and dancing like possessed.

It was a couple of days after his return from Chimoio in Mozambique, where he'd stayed just for four days. The trip had brought forth nothing and, having no relative, money, friend or anyone he knew to stay with, he had returned home.

In the church, Farai felt very at ease, and was glad he had finally agreed to join his wife and sons, and come. What he saw in particular encouraged him. The church was almost full of people he knew. It appeared he was the only one who did not go to church. Nobody was new. There was Mai Tambu, only last week accused of keeping snakes in her house, singing her lungs out. Up in front, he craned his neck to catch Ntombi's eye.

They had met in a bar in town deep in the night, and she was so scantily dressed you could see the edges of her panties. Right now, however, she was completely transformed, and looked so genteel and ladylike in a coffee brown suit. She too was singing at the top of her voice, head almost touching her left shoulder.

And there was Sticke's young brother, a renowned pick pocket, on the bench right behind the church elders. He looked so serious and far from picking anyone's pocket.

Behind him was Agatha and her fourth or fifth husband, arms in the air and praising God for something he could not hear. And finally, there, in the right corner was Gina and his small-house, resplendent in green and blue.

Sure, Farai felt encouraged, and wondered what he had been afraid of all along. He felt at home. He could not understand why he'd refused Shupi's advice. She had spoken to him passionately about giving their problems to Jesus.

Last week, a visiting pastor had spoken strongly about Zimbabwe's problems being on Jesus' shoulders. He'd said that only those who brought their problems to him would be rescued and relieved.

Shupi had brought the message to Farai and, hard though it was to take, he had taken it. And here he was now. In fact, the whole town was full of churches. Some broke away from main ones, but others were brand new, with everything new. It was fashionable to belong to a church these days, never mind your way of life or means to it.

However, Farai had a slight worry of late. He had a strong suspicion that Shupi was having an affair with the shop owner she worked for. The hours she kept at work were too long, plus the boss often invited her to work from his house. This was on weekends, of all days, when she was supposed to be with her family!

But Farai didn't mind the affair too much. A quick recall of Brendon and Melissa's facial appearances convinced him that they were his children, though one was now dead. He would wait for Shupi's next delivery, which was four months away.

By now Mugabe had been removed from power, and people saw hope in the air.

Finally, with a wide beaming smile the pastor stood up and in three strides was behind the pulpit. When he turned to face the congregation, Farai's heart missed a beat. He had seen that face before.

Amazing how everyone was a pastor these days. This guy, for sure, was Takesure. The last time Farai had heard of him, he had been sentenced 7 years for rape. He'd raped his wife's sister under his keep. At that time he was an elder in the ZAOGA Church in Harare, and worked for a bank. Farai did not know whether the 7 years had all been served or Takesure had been released on some account.

And now he looked so well fed: round, fat cheeks, nice glasses and protruding buttocks. Not bad. He also looked smart in a yellow jacket over a blue shirt, and a bright red tie. Fancy and overly done, but ok by these standards

Pastor Takesure, opened his bible and the singing stopped, only the organ continued a little longer.

"Haleluia!" he shouted when the organ had stopped.

"Haleluia!" the congregation responded, hands raised and waving.

"Haleluia!" the pastor shouted louder.

"Haleluia!" the people responded, even louder.

"God is good!"

This went on for another minute or two, until the pastor said, "Yes! That is what we do in the house of the Lord. There should be joy in the House of the Lord. There is happiness in the House of the Lord. Tell me, where else can you find such joy, such happiness, hope and life? Nowhere...!"

And he started the chorus again. This time the people shrieked and pranced and skipped, everything with their most energy and voices.

Farai clapped.

Then there were announcements; about last week's attendance, the Bishop's imminent visit, the need to build a church (instead of using this classroom), the pastor's parsonage, last Sunday's collection, the pastor's visitation rounds, the next big prayer meeting and so on.

"Now," said the pastor, "if there are any new people who have come to join us, or have just come to visit, please stand up so that we greet you."

There was a good number, about 6 or 7. Again, Farai knew four or five of them.

Farai stood up. There was wild ululation, especially from his wife and her friends. This encouraged Farai to declare that he had come to join 'for good'. There was more clapping and ululation at this.

The sermon itself was about asking and being given, seeking and finding, knocking and the door being opened. The pastor, sweating from head to toe, beseeched his congregation to ask anything they wanted in the name of the Lord. He gave the example of the difficult times they were living, and how some people were living large because of their faith. "Nothing is impossible with God," he declared amid Haleluias and amens. "Just give yourself up to him. Surrender your life. Be good and walk in his ways!"

All in all, it was a good sermon, and the pastor did justice to the verses he read. Then it was time for gifts. The system for this church was that three children stood in front of the church, with bowls into which congregants dropped in their money. But before they did, a man stood up and said, "Ladies and gentleman of this beautiful church, you know what you want to ask from the Lord. You alone know the value of what you want, and what it is worth. When Abraham wanted a son, he gave offerings to the Lord, which was commensurate with what he wanted. He did not give coins, but what lay at his heart. What you give determines what you get. Let us close our eyes and pray........"

Farai was pleased, for he had $2. He had intended to offer $1 and keep the other one for his children's petty needs after service, or two cigarettes, but why not..? He wanted a job, a new home, peace in his house…he wanted so many things in his life…

A suitable tune was sung as people took turns to go up and give their offerings. Few people went up, and probably this was because they had coins. Farai sat down, happy and light hearted. He had given to the Lord.

However, no sooner had he sat down than that man, whom Farai understood to be Brother Talkmore, stood up again and said, "This is Construction Week. As you know, we need to worship in our own place. We cannot continue to be squatters. God's children are not squatters. So far we have identified a stand. It is right here in this location. It is big and spacious, but it costs money.

Altogether it needs, $15 000. We might never get it if we do not start collecting now. We hear that Kingdom Ablaze want it, just like Holy Trinity and Indigenous Fellow shippers. Let us be first…."

And the children were lined up again. A little was collected.

But the man stood up again. "Our pastor," he said, "needs to travel. He needs to meet with his members during the week, encourage them, talk to them and fellowship with them. This needs money……"

One or two stood up to contribute.

"Now," said Talkmore, "today is the 25th. As you know, we are renting this place, and we need to pay each and every month. By the time we meet next week, the month will be out. If we do not pay, we might find ourselves with no place to worship…" He demonstrated his commitment to guaranteeing a place of worship next week by dropping $3 into one of the bowls. This time no one stood up from the congregants.

"Giving is not about money only and always," said the pastor himself. 'People can give other things, such as property that we can sell, clothes, jewellery, anything that can be turned into money."

Encouraged, some people offered to bring tomatoes for sale, others offered clothes, pieces of furniture, and so on. Farai, feeling a huge pressure over him, offered to give his radio, plus $10.

Again the church clapped hands and ululated, Farai was pleased. However, he did not know whether that would last. He had a feeling that he was being fleeced. Time would tell.

They did not worship only on Saturday or Sunday anymore, but every day. And they met any time; in the morning, afternoon, or evening. For what other work was there to occupy them? Industries had long closed, and all hopes were dashed. Some of the worshippers met inside dilapidated factories and industrial areas. They cooked their sadza and sold it to each other in there.

To Farai's surprise, the politicians did not leave these worshippers alone, to pray in peace. They followed them high up in the mountains, begging them for support. They particularly liked the indigenous churches, which sprouted all over like mushroom.

"You are an example of our success as proponents of indigenization," said the politicians. "We all know the history of the traditional churches; how they were used by the white man to steal our land. But you, you are born of Africa, and your God is African. You have successfully indigenized God, and that is what we want. The Pope and the Bishops in Europe have no place here…. We want a God for and of Africa…"

Farai thought about indigenizing God. Of course, God had always been indigenous to African people, he thought. Somehow, it seemed, though, that there had been a disconnect between Africa's traditional God, and the modern one of churches and temples. Some were of mountains, but praised the same God. That was why Farai was going there, to try and find rhythm with the modern God, and live in him. He knew it was a tough road to take, because so many things were said about these churches.

One guy had told him: "If your pastor has ten armed bodyguards and you bought ten stickers and placed them on your door for him to protect you, "You are the reason why Jesus wept."

That was a way of discouraging the modern pastors and their followers, but his experiences were many and varied, and Farai was ready for the challenges. This was not the first time.

QUEEN LATIFA'S LONESOME QUEUE

At some point, beginning 2009, Mutare was known as the City of Diamonds. This was due to the recently discovered precious stones in one of its districts; Marange to be exact, where like the proverbial manna from heaven, the stones had just appeared. With the first sale, the villages were awash with people from across the district and beyond. Soon others from other nearby districts flocked, and then the whole country of loafers descended on Marange, jostling side by side in the pits and dust. As more and more people came, so did the diamonds appear-from anywhere, To start with, very little digging was done, as the stones were all over. The market for them grew too, in nearby Mutare, Harare, Bulawayo, Mozambique and beyond.

I remembered even me, as I waited for a kombi to take me home late one afternoon, a young man who knew me approached and asked if I wanted a match box full of the stones for a dollar. "Ah," I said, "what would I use the stuff for? I am no dealer. Besides, I could get arrested, you know."

"OK, give me 50c, blaz. I need just enough cash to take me home to Dangamvura."

I gave him the 50c and shoved the box into my jeans. Today, when I look back to that day, I feel like kicking myself. The value of the stones later grew in leaps and bounds, especially as they became more and harder to get. Later, one day when I was broke, I looked for that box of matches and sold the stones for almost $20. Had I waited another week, I would have got $100, or even more. Today, as I write this, one could buy a house worth half a million United States Dollars, with that box.

One of the people who benefitted from diamonds, among many others in the city and country at large, was Queen Tonderai. As was often the case in the locations, anyone with a celebrity name would automatically get the surname of that celebrity. This was perhaps to liven things up or a show that they were in the swing with modern trends, knew things and were not so backward.

Queen thus was known throughout as Queen Latifa, each time she was mentioned-in full. That became her official and unofficial name, forget Tonderai, he surname.

She was big, black and beautiful, and carried similar facial features as her namesake, Ms Dana Elaine Owens, the original owner of the name. So she carried the name with special pride.

A holder of a 4- year first degree in the Humanities at the local Africa University and a single mother of one, Queen Latifa had learned early that if she did not use her time wisely to earn money for herself, her life and that of her son would be doomed.

She had learned to hustle and combine it with the power of resistance and protest from her mother who'd been a 'general dealer' in the late 80s when she was in her 20s. At one time she was trading in goats, buying and selling them for braai meat, or to breeders.

One year there was an anthrax outbreak, and the government deployed armed Parks and Wildlife guards and soldiers on all major roads leading into and out of towns and cities. Queen Latifa's mother had bought one goat, and had it slaughtered and put into rolls of hessian material.

At a wildlife roadblock the bus stopped, and people were ordered to unload their baggage for inspection. When Queen Latifa's mother came up, the guards and soldiers exclaimed shock and surprise. Of course the surprise was mixed with gleeful joy.

Queen Latifa's mother humbly and patiently explained that the meat was for a customer, who'd already paid.

The guards and soldiers would not listen to her. They said they would confiscate the meat, while she would proceed with her journey. Mother, however, would not listen to them. She protested loudly, that it was her source of income, what did they want her to do?

As the quarrel heated up, Queen Latifa's mother suddenly pulled up her dress, stretched a leg over the other side of the goat meat, straddling over it, slipped a finger up her panties, and poured hot, misty urine onto the meat.

The guards scampered to all sides with their guns, shocked, but watching her. The passengers on the bus shouted and screamed words of encouragement to the mother, who continued to pour.

As soon as she was done, she hopped onto the bus, and received wild cheers from some Rasta youth who shouted "Woman Power!" And the whole bus caught up. They sang praises to her all the way to town and home in Sakubva. She established a new reputation that day, and people did not treat her the same as before, but with a lot of respect.

Though she wasn't sure if she could go that way, as she preferred using her brains, first, Queen Latifa discovered that it was possible and within her power to fight for what was hers, and what she believed.

She thought she understood the mentality of most men, and had no problems with that. To her, men were simple creatures who wanted one and the same thing, especially from women. Most of them thought with their penises and balls. It was therefore up to her to design ways of achieving what she wanted in a male dominated world, without risking her life and dignity.

One night Queen Latifa met a group of boys with rough diamonds in Sakubva, and since she often crossed the border into South Africa to buy stuff for sale back home, they asked if she might try the South Africa market for them. Without much ado, Queen accepted.

She took the stones from them, about 80 in total. They were a mix of the glass and industrial type. On her trip a few days later she took half the lot, hid them in her wooden carvings, and crossed the border without incident.

What she got from the sale of the stones shocked her. Altogether, she fetched 20 thousand Rands. When she arrived back in Mutare she got hold of the boys, gave them the money, claimed her expenses and declared that she had sold all the loot. They boys were happy and asked no further questions. A week later, Queen took the remaining 40 pieces to the same market in South Africa. She was wiser now, and bargained for 100 thousand Rands. The dealers offered her a used car, for which she found a licensed Zimbabwean driver and drove all the way home in Mutare, plus 40 000 Rands in cash.

Later, she became an official (though legally unofficial) buyer of the stones, which she bought at giveaway prices from the desperate diggers, and sold for thousands. During those early days, the diggers would buy basics like clean water, cooking oil, candles and pots and pans with the stones. The more enterprising ones bought cars and houses.

In no time at all, Queen became rich. She bought a house in one of the suburbs, sold her car, and bought a near new Isuzu KB 300D from a private seller. She entered into a deal with the guys at the Vehicle Inspection Directorate and got a licence, for $250, 00.

However, a few weeks after buying the Isuzu truck, as she drove into her garage, she saw two men by one of the windows of her house, leaning against the wall.

"Madam", one of them said, as they casually strode towards her, "whose truck is this?"

"Mine, of course", Queen said confidently as she banged the door and switched on the inter locker.

"We are from the CID Stolen Property Section. This truck was reported stolen two weeks ago, and we are looking for it."

"But that cannot be. I bought this truck from so and so…Here is the agreement of sale…"

"And the Registration Book? Where is it? You see, you don't have the Registration Book because it is still with the owners of this truck. The guy who bought it, and sold it to you did not have the book either. He would only get it after paying off the vehicle. As it is he has defaulted payment for 8 months, and the sellers want it back…."

Queen was lost for words. She did not know what to do or say, "What about my money? The amount I spent buying it?" she asked.

"That is an illegal arrangement you made between the two of you, and has nothing to do with the owners of the truck. We hope something can be worked out. As for now, we are taking the truck with us to Harare. Please, let us have your details…"

And after everything, including soothing her, they drove off, leaving her sobbing on the driveway, beside a yawning garage.

By now she had long stopped dealing in diamonds, because it was way too dangerous. More importantly, the government had driven everybody out, some in body trunks, and put in Chinese companies instead.

QUEEN LATIFA JOINS ZANU PF

“Pamberi navaMugabe!¹¹”
“Pamberi!”
“Pamberi neChimurenga chechitatu!”¹²
“Pamberi!”
‘Pasi newayawaya!”¹³
“Pasi nawo!”¹⁴

“Eh, Comrades, we have come to that time again. The time we have been waiting for. The time to elect our local leadership at Branch Level. These are crucial people, the people who will represent our problems. The people who carry our demands and expectations to the party and government, at branch level. These people are very important, because they are the eyes and ears of the party. Therefore, these people must be known cadres, people with a record of working tirelessly for the party. We don't want any sell-outs, or those who lean this way when it suits them, and that way when things are not going well.

---

9   Forward with Zanu

10   Forward

11   Forward with Cde Mugabe

12   Forward with the 3rd Revolution

13   Down with those ones (You know who)

14   Down with them

"Without wasting time, I am informed that there is no need to contest most positions, because the people occupying them have been doing a sterling job….."

"No!, no! no!. Every position has to be contested. Who said they have been doing a good job? Even if they were, let them be challenged. If they win again, then we all know they have been…."

"Time, comrade, time. I thought you people had already agreed on this…"

"Yes, we agreed. Some people just want to cause trouble. They want to show the enemy that we are not united…."

"No! The constitution says all positions must be contested, and we must follow that…"

"But we don't have time for all that."

"What time? Where is it, the time I mean, so that we can go and take it to give you….?"

"Excuse me, I think as it is we are wasting time. The enemy is not sleeping while we do that. What we need are strong candidates, people who are unflinching in the face of a formidable enemy. This is not time to experiment with newcomers."

"Yes! Yes! Yes!"

"In that case, I am leaving! You can go ahead with your imposition of candidates. This is exactly what cost us in the last election. Imposition of candidates. You will see! You will lose again. I'm going home!"

"Me too"

"Me too. I cannot stand this nonsense!"

"I'm right behind you."

"Me too!"

Queen remained seated. This was getting hopeless. She had just come to show her face only, for solidarity. Just to demonstrate that though she now lived up there in the suburbs, she was still very much part of the Sakubva people. She was one of them. She watched hopelessly as people trooped out. Then the man who had been addressing them turned to the incumbent local chairman and his team and said, "So what is the way forward, Comrade?"

"Let's proceed. There is nothing to wait for. We have enough people in here. The constitution says a quorum is necessary, and we have it. Let's proceed."

It was a walkover. The chairman and his team were retained and, surprise, surprise, Queen was slotted into the vacant position of Committee Member, much to the joy of the presiding officer, who had suggested 'a careful gender balance' in the team.

After the meeting Queen approached the presiding officer and asked him about projects for youth and women.

"Ah, that!' said the officer. 'Indeed, the party is running the coming elections on the wind of indigenization, economic empowerment, and employment creation. You are the people who should be running around with the slogan, and should be empowered. If you find time, please pass by my office tomorrow and we'll talk about it. Here's my number. You can call any time….."

QUEEN LATIFA'S PERCEPTION OF THE ZIMBABWE POLITICAL AND BUSINESS ENVIRONMENT.

Queen Latifa had never been political. However, from her lectures at university, the conversations that she heard around her and what she heard, read or saw, she formed a political mindset about the political environment in her country.

Queen Latifa saw Zanu PF as an organization, company or institution. Since that organization was made up of people, she also saw it as a person. It was all the same to her.

Queen Latifa believed Zanu PF was a party that feared death. It did not want to die, but live forever. To her, this was exemplified by its president, Robert Mugabe himself. Many times, Harare and the country were filled with rumours of Mubabe's death. Sometimes, the rumours would be so nigh and high that people would celebrate, loudly in the bars and streets, until they died. A week later, you would see Bob hoping onto an airplane stairs and jogging up, on another flight abroad. A few people would get arrested, and life would return to its hard way.

The same thing with Zanu PF, Queen Latifa thought. The party thought it would rule forever. It put structures to achieve that feat. But then, people had changed. Queen Latifa knew that the last election the party had won legitimately, was in the 90s.

The party had won power through violence in 1980, and it maintained that method for its sustenance. Violence was spewed everywhere, especially during election time. Sometimes, it banned international observers, ran the election by itself, and won.,

Mugabe was determined to have a one party state from the beginning. Queen Latifa remembered the first opposition party in the country, led by Edgar Tekere. Tekere had been Secretary General of Zanu during the struggle, but had fallen out with Mugabe, and formed his own political party. Words could not express the humiliation and deprivations he faced.

Even when they bury a party member, they believed that death had only come to that member, and not them. They would live forever and, as they live, they have to have the best, because the country was their's, and nobody else's.

The party was immensely helped by its leader. Mugabe used the law to amass and maintain power for himself. Queen Latifa had heard the term 'legalistic dictator' used several times at college and other meetings. Examples that were quick to come to mind were the Public Order and Security Act, passed in.........to deny people the right to strike and demonstrate. He used the law in his party, even to assume an invincible substantive position in his own party. He used lawyers every time. Often, however, he avoided the courts, especially with simple matters that he could deal personally with.

The party used the much needed food, to maintain its grip on people. A case in point is one in which the minister of Health, Obadiah Moyo, was ordered to supply medications and medical stuff to constituencies holding elections in Matebeleland.

State food, and international food aid was converted and given to Zanu PF members and their families only. In the face of severe droughts, a poor harvest or any threat to food, Zanu PF supporters were always at ease. They knew they would get food. DC and other opposition supporters were sure to get nothing. This did not make Zanu PF popular. It made people, even the recipients of free food and stuff, hate it and denied it their vote. Still, it continued to 'win'.

Queen Latifa remembered one year in which Mugabe campaigned heavily in a helicopter. Tractors lorries and buses ferried thousands to his rallies and the National Sports Stadium. That year, the people had declared that Mugabe should go. Very, very few people voted for him. However, when the results were announced, Mugabe had won. The entire nation was stunned. There was no celebration anywhere, even at State House.

Perhaps, thought Queen Latifa, that was when NIKUV was involved.

He also used violence, in close connection with the law. Queen Latifa heard of so many people who had died, disappeared, or tortured. She hoped the Organ on National Healing would carry out thorough investigations, when time came. When that time would come, she had no idea.

Like many people in the country, Queen Latifa did not see the difference between Zanu PF, and the government. She was sure that Zanu PF treated the two as one and the same. Resources were taken from government to fund the party. Since independence, all the party's activities were funded by government. The guys did not see any difference between the two. To Queen Latifa, that was the problem with a political party that comes from the bush, straight into office.

There should have been thorough training for those who assumed political office, she thought with the benefit of hindsight. However, she thought she remembered countless such trainings, expensive ones too, but where the benefits were was darkness. Political survival had taken over.

Villagers were forced to attend Zanu PF rallies. Political support was as crucial to life as life itself to Zanu PF, according to Queen Latifa. She knew though that if eventually the party lost power, it would die a forever death. No one would want to be associated with it again. People were going to deny having been members of Zanu PF.

As political power was threatened by the MDC, and money ran out for the party and government, new strategies had to be found, to ensure survival. The party began to chant land, land, land. It was a good point, internationally, but the party kept it under its wings for a long time, until the right one. The land issue in Zimbabwe reverberated from all corners of the world. Indeed, indigenous people have a right to their land, not foreigners, first. Whites had huge tracts of land which they were not using, while blacks tilled patchy pieces of the same with hoes and ox-drawn ploughs.

Mugabe proffered the willing buyer/willing seller option to the whites. This did not bear fruit, and so he mobilized his war veterans to demand what they had fought for. After all, the whites did not pay any one when they invaded that land during colonization.

So there was chaos on the land issue. To Queen Latifa, this chaos was caused by absence of negotiation between the two parties, including civil society and international partners. Money should have been mobilized and distributed for the project, with transparency, accountability and inclusion being key pillars.

To Queen Latifa, the worst thing about Zanu PF was that it was told the right thing to do, especially regarding money, finances and industry, but it refused those ideas and suggestions because they came from outside its party structures, and therefore would not do. Several times economists warned against following certain policies and doing certain things, but they were ignored, yet their warnings would come true. Still, Zanu PF refused them, and followed its own way, as 'the ruling party'.

As it was, Zanu PF benefited little by distributing the land haphazardly. It gained political popularity (and survival) and reserves of minerals underground, which they could not exploit. The people of Zimbabwe, also haven't. Very few outside Zanu PF benefitted, and hunger and starvation still stare them in the face. Daily. Even those in Zanu PF who benefitted are not happy. They lack the means and inputs. The Presidential Agricultural Command Scheme was helping out some, but not all.

The discovery of diamonds in Chiadzwa in Queen Latifa's Manicaland Province did nothing to help the local people, except Zanu PF. No investment was made in Mutare, the provincial capital. War veterans and Zanu PF members in the military ruled the roost.

Queen Latifa couldn't help imagining the egg in the face of Mugabe when Barack Obama became president of the United States in 2012. He had ranted and ranted, saying 'Never!" to the possibility. His mistrust and hatred of whites was clear.

But then things went well and Obama became president! Queen Latifa doubted that he sent a congratulatory message, and their relationship throughout Obama's two terms remained cloudy.

That change in America should have shown Mugabe that the world had changed. Instead, he hung onto the past, with a whole nation on his back. Now they were going further backwards, she thought with a rueful smile.

Queen Latifa's views on the MDC

Queen Latifa thought the MDC was an excellent party. First, it had allowed her to take part in the constitution making process (COPAC) as a rapporteur. She was not a known member of the party, but a secret supporter. This showed that the party catered for all Zimbabweans, regardless of who they were. Another thing was that the MDC's popularity and administration was very good. The party had new ideas, and it had a lot of well-educated young men and women. The party was the hope for millions of Zimbabweans across the country, and from her perspective, had more than two thirds support. Queen Latifa had voted for it ever since it contested elections.

The problem was that the party could not mobilise international or regional support to observe elections, or deal with Zanu PF's violence on its people. As a result many of its people were scared to come out in the open, or campaign. Some very brave people did, and succeeded. Not all of these, however, had the same mental capacity and integrity as physical muscle.

The other thing was that the MDC had stayed too long in the political race, without achieving its goals. It was soon going to be an old party, of failures and zero success.

They cannot claim ownership of the opposition politics in Zimbabwe, or the right to the political top office, when another party comes up and wins. The MDC had to constantly change tactics, especially on the use of violence by Zanu PF.

Finally, she believed that the MDC was Morgan Tsvangirai's dream. He had a vision for it. Now, he's dead and it's taken over by his followers. God forbid! The country needs heroes like Tsvangirai, not his followers. The man died with his dream and vision. These young men must have their own vision, form their own organisations and push it. Not depend on the dreams of others, in critical moments where hero ship is in dire need!

The truth she knew, however, was that the name MDC carried power and new, positive thinking. Anyone who stood for election under that name was assured of victory.

However, the party was characterized by failures. The latest attempt at shaking the Zanu PF government was the August 16 Peace March. Like others before it, including the Final Push of 2008, had ended in failure. It seemed the organisers had no Plan B up their sleeve, every time they planned mass action. She wished she could be invited in the planning of such actions.

She regarded the other opposition political parties and their leaders and followers as political opportunists who had no national interest at heart, but personal glory in mind. She wondered why these political parties did not join the MDC and form one strong opposition party to Zanu PF. But these parties had their reasons, and the MDC its own. So the nation stayed at sixes and sevens like that. Watching the country and their future rotting away, right in front of them.

The Zimbabwe National Army

Queen Latifa could not help but notice that those days, soldiers commanded a lot of respect (or was it fear?) among the youth. Each time there was a new group of recent recruits at the Brigade, local youth would flock to the bar, to meet them and make friends. The soldiers also liked to know the area and its people, so they would buy beer for these youth, and strong partnerships were formed.

Soldiers especially wanted information, and the youth provided it. Some of the information was really personal, and not national, and so conflicts often rose.

Modern soldiers were also young and wanted to live the modern life. They had wives and girlfriends, who expected money and 'things' from their men. Apparently, their men were failing to provide, just like all other men in the community. They complained that it was the chefs, the bosses, who were 'eating alone'. It could be a recipe for disaster, if soldiers teamed up with civilians to deal violently with their problem, of a directionless, inept and corrupt government. At that time in the country, any form of release was welcome, no matter how.

She hated military rule. It had 'fear' written all over it, and had no freedom. It seemed after their independence from Rhodesians, they were captured again, this time by their liberators. There was no freedom, if people lived among soldiers.

She was well aware in Zimbabwe, there was heavy politicization of the military. This started after the June 2000 violent elections, when a narrowly redefined national security strategy was adopted by Zanu PF.

Because of this redefined national security strategy, all the service chiefs, the Chief of Defence Staff and commanders of the army, air force, intelligence, police, prison service and national parks-appeared on national television and declared that they would not salute or recognize any leader who did not have 'liberation credential'. This was in clear violation of the constitution, which allowed the registration of all citizens as candidates. In addition, from that moment onwards, the security sector in Zimbabwe, led by the military, has been at the forefront of politics in support of Zanu PF.

She noticed that even soldiers themselves did not like to live among civilians. She asked one young soldier who told her, "From training, I want to stay in barracks, with other soldiers. We like to live our life there, like soldiers. In the community we just collect information, make money deals and get drunk…"

ZANU PF and Business

Queen Latifa remembered the jewel that Zimbabwe was at independence and compared it to now. Where industry was booming now was a forest. The town, and everywhere she went, she saw demolished buildings of factories and other industry. Locally, she remembered companies like Karina Textiles, Tanganda, Border Timbers, Cold Storage Commission, Dairy Board, Wattle, and others that closed down. Some Zanu PF guys had secretly registered indigenous companies and tried to continue, but failed dismally. Then others had come in, and others, until all that was going on was cooking and selling the staple sadza. Then that was it.

To Queen Latifa, Zanu PF especially disliked private businesses. Because they wanted power and control over the people, they wanted everything for themselves, or their members. Any private business owner had to have very strong political connections in the party to survive. His business survival was based on the type, nature and quantity of 'donations' he made to the party.

Queen Latifa was curious to interview one white businessman in Kadoma if he kept a record of his 'donations' to the party. But she was sure he did, because he was always invited, and his family were getting positions in the party. The other white guy she wished to interview was from Chimanimani.

However, Queen Latifa was happy and proud of the human spirit among Zimbabweans. They still struggled to do business. Many teachers established their own schools, which were doing better than government schools. Parents removed their children from government school and enrolled them into private schools. The government closed some of these schools, but others survived. Queen Latifa supposed politics was at play, as was everything else in Zimbabwe. Pharmacists and doctors also had private pharmacies, clinics and surgeries. Shops that sold everything were sprouting, thanks to the spirit to fight. And Queen Latifa was proud of that. Only that money was in short supply. There was no joyful life without money, and she was determined to work for hers.

She utterly supported the 'never die or give up' attitude of Zimbabweans. Even when they were killed and died of many different causes, the streets, growth points, churches and social centres were always full of them. That gave her hope.

A common thing she discovered about young, desperate businesspeople was that they were offered training and guidance by Zanu PF, and had to do business with Zanu PF only when they established their own businesses. Some of them complied for brief periods, but eventually folded up to re-establish elsewhere. This was so they would escape the party's long, begging and grabbing hand.

QUEEN LATIFA MARRIES THE PRESIDING OFFICER

The very next day after the presiding officer had given Queen his number, she visited his offices, in the company of a female friend. They talked about trivial things at the start, about politics and how certain people in the party were selfish and bent on destroying the party, and so on. "But you should never be fooled," said the presiding officer, "ours is a party with deep roots. Remember, this is a party that defeated the British army. You know, the British are a super power…and we defeated them. Ask Ian Smith!. I advise you to stick with us, and not with puppets and sell-outs…"

"Ah, Comrade, what do you take us for? We know where we came from, and we can never turn our backs on our parents. It is unAfrican to turn your back on your parents, just because they are old. The older the President gets the wiser he becomes, and we must listen to his advice. There is God in him, who keeps him alive and a leader of our blessed country."

"No, no, no the president is not old. If he is, then like wine he can only get better with age. Now, about women empowerment, let me see…."

He called out a name and a man in his forties came in. "This is the District Youth Chairman. Comrade, these ladies are high ranking office bearers from one of our strongest districts, Sakubva, and they need …." Turning to Queen and her friend he asked, "have you got land? Do you have a piece of land that you can call your own?"

"No, Comrade. But we were hoping for some mining claims. You know, somewhere we could carry out some mining activities and get income. Are such areas still available?"

"Oh that? So you don't want a farm?"

"We do, but in addition to a small mining claim."

"Very well. Now, Victor, bring me the map. Show me areas that have not been occupied yet. And give me Givvie's number."

More discussion followed that, and the two women got farms near Odzi, along the river. They were also advised that the area was famous for gold panning. "The soil is a rich red, a sure sign that there is gold in the area. If you come tomorrow, I will drive you there. Meanwhile, I will talk to the guys in the department of Lands. Count it all sealed, ladies. But tell me, where are you going now? Have you had any lunch?"

"No, but we don't want to bother you, seeing you are this busy…"

"No, no. It's ok. It's my time for lunch, and you ladies can join me…"

The ladies left their car at the party offices, but after a struggle. They had insisted that they drive it to the restaurant, for fear that some people who knew the car would spot it at the offices, and that would not go down very well with some of their friends, most of whom did not like Zanu Pf. But then the thought of being seen in the company of this well-known, high profile Zanu operative filled them with awry. But it was amazing who associated with who these days. The most important thing was personal survival, those days, and it did not matter how or with whom. In short, it was typically the 'Zvangu Zvaita' Generation. In the end they decided to leave the car and hop into the presiding officer's.

Thus began Queen's affair with the presiding officer. He did not lie to her that he was single. 'I have a wife and seven children," he said, "but I love you. As you can see, I am not very old, and can afford to keep you. In fact, I have been waiting for just your type for a small house…"

Queen, being from the ghetto, knew just what she wanted. She showed him her house in Greenside, and told him all about herself. She had a son, but no husband. They were simply alone…of course, with her parents in Sakubva, though her father spent most of his time in the rural areas, where he had a small plot of land that he enjoyed ploughing. This thrilled the presiding officer, who showered her with praise and presents. She got the mining claim she wanted, plus the land, her own. His family lived on a farm-only a few kilometres out of town. With time he forgot to go there altogether, deciding on spending time in town with Queen, at his flat or her house.

She introduced him to her parents, who were too spoiled by Queen and the officer to protest the relationship.

But soon, problems developed. Queen fell pregnant. She could not remember how or when, but it happened. Worse still, she kept postponing its termination until it got too late. The presiding officer went over the moon, while Queen sulked. "I will marry you! I swear, I will," he said.

And in a few weeks' time after the announcement, Queen got married. It was the traditional type, of lobola and formalities.

As the pregnancy grew, Queen's mother advised her to visit her husband's farm, 'just in case anything happens, and your baby might need security..."

So Queen began to pester her new husband about seeing his relatives and the rest of his family. He did not protest, and so one bright Saturday morning they set off, just the two of them. There was no ceremony, and when they arrived they were received by the officer's family and a few friends. Introductions were made, rather authoritatively by the officer. He introduced Queen as his little or small wife... and his other wife as the 'big wife'. Everything was quietly and calmly done, and everybody seemed happy. Food was prepared, and they ate. Each ate from his or her own plate, except for the children, who ate from big bowls.

After the meal, the Big wife said to Queen, 'Amainini, please come and I will show you around our yard."

Rather pleased, Queen stood up from where she sat, shook her shawl and wrapped it around her waist, like respectable elderly, married women do. First, they went to the cattle kraal. "You see amainini, all these cattle are ours, yours and mine, plus of course our children and the little baby you are carrying...' she giggled slightly, then proceeded, "there are 150 of them altogether, so it's going to be 75 for myself and 75 for you...."

They proceeded to the goats. "We have about 80 goats altogether on the farm. Forty for you, and forty for myself..."

Queen was beginning to marvel about this wonderfully considerate, kind woman. She nearly threw her arms around her, but just managed to hold herself. They went to the next pen.

"Here, we have 60 pigs. Again, its half-half. Thirty for you, and thirty for myself."

They proceeded to the fowl run and vegetable beds, and by now Queen was besides herself with joy. Then they came to the family cemetery, where there were four graves.

"This amainini, is the family cemetery," said the Big Wife. 'This first grave is for our mother in law, our husband's mother. You know, she was too talkative, and wanted to poke her nose into everything that our husband and I did. She did not take me long....after five days here, I had done her in, kkkkk."

They inched further, to the next grave. "In this one lies our brother in law, you know, our husband's young brother. You know what he did? After sleeping with me for only three nights, he became excited or grew cold feet at the same time, and threatened to report the affair to his brother, our husband. Ahhh, the very next morning he was cold as ice. Kkkkkkkk.

"This third one is rather interesting. You know, this husband of ours, after living with me on this farm for ten years, brought a second wife, just as he has done today. Kkkkk. Ah, she did not even spend the night. Before nightfall she had kicked the bucket…Kkkkk…"

"And the fourth one…"

The Big Wife did not even finish…for she discovered that she was talking to herself. When she turned, she saw Queen disappear in the kitchen. A few seconds later she saw her prodding the dusty road, handbag in hand and shawl in a flare behind, with her husband in hot pursuit.

She stifled an outburst of laughter, then turned to join her neighbours, with whom they would openly laugh and enjoy themselves.

QUEEN LATIFA PICKS HERSELF UP

Queen Latifa leant her mistakes with the Presiding Officer. Now she had two babies, and life was not looking rosy. She decided to adopt a completely different attitude to life; one without romantic love. A firm believer in the adage: Yesterday is in the tomb, and tomorrow is in the womb, she had always regarded regret as a useless feeling, and wanted to see how far she could go. Marc had gone away, probably back to the States, she did not know.

Like 90% of Zimbabweans, she'd grown up a Christian, and her family went to the United Methodist Church. However, because of church politics and the splits and counter splits, she'd stopped active participation, and spent time doing her things. She wondered if people ever thought of the impact of such fights and splits on the faith and spirit of congregants.

She was amazed at the close similarities between religion and politics in the country. They both had a lot of in-fighting and bickering and splits. She knew that the reason for this was money. These two were major sources of big money in the country, due to the masses of people they attracted. Talk of lazy people and easy money. Unlike many Zimbabweans who put their fate in the arms of a priest, pastor, prophet or bishop, she believed in raw, hard work as the source of freedom and happiness.

She could not go back to cross-border trading, because it was getting risky with traffic accidents. In one week, three buses had accidents and killed more than 80 people. More such fatal accidents were reported over two years, and a lot of families were thrown into deep weeping and mourning.

Besides, she'd created enemies on all roads leading out of the country. She'd had fights, quarrels and finger-pointing to and out of Zimbabwe. Unfortunately, all her quarrels and fights were with her fellow citizens, Zimbabweans. Whether she went to South Africa, Botswana, Namibia, Zambia, Dubai or Mozambique, she always had a problem with a Zimbabwean customs or immigration official, policeman or fellow passenger. It was the quest for money that led to this, following the rampant corruption across the country, from the lowest level of society to the highest, and that included cabinet ministers and their president and his wife. Zimbabweans in positions of authority pounced on fellow Zimbabweans. Queen Latifa thought she might do a program addressing that with her organization. She would set up provincial centres for education and related activities, and probably share it with the Ministry of Education and Culture. The problem, as always, was money.

She also couldn't help but notice that when a Zimbabwean got a high post, say at a company or in the region, his first move was to cut off ties with his fellows, especially the ones he grew up with. This he did to protect his reputation with the new order, and to lessen threats to his position. Who knows, his Zimbabwean kith and kin might even take his position! You never trusted a Zimbabwean. They were so fast and clever. And also desperate. Queen Latifa smiled at the thought. Perhaps, she thought that was why the political conflict was proving too difficult to resolve. There were too many intelligent minds, who depended on reason and power of thought, to be convinced easily. They argued, and spent their time arguing and sharpening their minds. Not listening to each other. She liked them a lot, however, her fellow Zimbabweans. She loved them whenever she went abroad, because they could talk openly about life, and were great company at a party, and threw the most laughable jokes.

She'd heard that **Dr. Shingi Munyeza** was coordinating talks between President Mnangagwa and Nelson Chamisa. She wished him luck in that, and hoped that he'd gone through some literature about resolving that kind of conflict, and consulted a few people.

Now that she was free of love and men in general, she put her mind and energy to her brain, and looking for money. Ever hungry for education and mental activity, now she had just completed a master degree in Peace and Governance at Africa University. She had not shined that much during the semesters, and was even threatened with a Fail in her dissertation. Luckily, she survived. But she had thoroughly enjoyed the avenues that course had opened for her, and longed for an opportunity to be practical with issues that dealt with peace in Zimbabwe, and Africa.

She was no longer involved in politics now, but simply focused on her personal, private life of herself and her two children. Her mining venture came second, and was doing very well. She had found a partner and formed the Queen Latifa Mining Syndicate with her. Queen Latifa was the claim owner, and her partner the sponsor. They shared proceeds fifty percent apiece.

With the proceeds, she soon found out that she could do a lot of things. Slowly, she began to invest in her community organization, which was now focusing on building peace in the communities.

With time, she could not understand why the government always cried about sanctions imposed by the western countries, yet Zimbabwe was rich with the very minerals that the westerners cried for, talk of gold, diamonds, platinum and all others. It was a puzzle she set out to unpuzzle.

She was sharply aware of the political tensions in her country, from her observations, television and radio reports, and interactions with people when she entered public and private offices. She longed to be involved in putting into practice, what she had learned at university.

In the entire political crisis in Zimbabwe, she strongly felt that **Father Fidelis Mukonori** ranked high up. He had mediated in the resignation of Mugabe, with **General Chiwenga**, so that Mnangagwa would take over, with a lot of skill, though no one could foretell the military nature of the incoming government. He played his part and the nation got what they wanted; the end of Mugabe,

She adored him for that, and hoped and wished he did more to resolve the entire political conflict once and for all. She longed for an opportunity to work with him, and people like **Pathisa Nyathi**. These were people she respected on the national healing subject in Zimbabwe. She also admired **Jestina Mukoko** of the Zimbabwe Peace Project. On Pathisa Nyathi especially, she still kept an article he wrote on 'Meaning of Ashes in Peace-making', published in the Lifestyle section, under Cultural Heritage in **the Sunday News Magazine** on 18 November, 2007.

During the Government of National Unity, she had designed a proposal on National Healing, and the steps to take, and submitted it to one of the three ministers in the **Organ for National Healing and Reconciliation.** Unfortunately, the minister, a female like herself, took the project proposal and formed her own organization on national healing. At that point in time, she was getting millions, but nothing was happening on the ground. That was Zimbabwe for you.

She also remembered the origins of the slogan, 'Peace begins with me, Peace begins with you, Peace begins with all of us', and how Zanu PF erroneously attributed it to the late John Nkomo, (one of the three ministers for National Healing during the GNU)at his death and after. The party used anything from anybody to build a good image of itself, without acknowledgment.

Queen Latifa had had so many furious discussions and debates during attempts at national healing meetings with lawyers as far as human rights were concerned. To these lawyers, human rights were the centre and drive of the national healing process Zimbabwe should enter, and everything that it offered.

Yet to her as a peacebuilder, human rights themselves were a source of conflict in themselves, because in Zimbabwe, they were a demand. The important thing was to have resources, first, only then can people have the power to demand their rights. Without resources, people got tired of shouting for their rights, while lawyers got rich, at the expense of the people.

There was no food and people were starving. They couldn't meet in bars, stadiums and restaurants to talk anymore, because they didn't have the money and energy. Energy to talk. Zanu PF was even killing that one. If they succeeded in that one, why couldn't they rule forever?, Yet the law was there, but there was no peace.

According to her, peace came before the law. This was simply explained by the fact that in order for people to make the law, they should be at peace, not only with each other, but within themselves. So, lawyers who were not professional peace builders had a secondary role to play. In any case, there was bound to be cases which needed the law, such as crimes against humanity, war crimes and genocide. However, even these needed to be decided on by the nation, first, as to the punishment.

Not all law promoted peace and entrenched reconciliation. Indeed, many tales were told on the African continent about how the law cut up societies, tore up families and destroyed livelihoods.

There needed to be a special law for national healing, and all sectors of society must make contribution.

Indeed, Queen Latifa agreed, lawyers had a role to play, and there must be adherence to the law by all, for peace to prevail, but then that law comes from peace, and takes peace to maintain.

Queen Latifa giggled at the idea of entrusting something as grand and national as national healing, into the hands and minds of the Gweja Generation. Some were older, but the majority were in that group

The problem with these lawyers, she thought, was that they got their message of 'human rights for all', from developed countries. Our local lawyers forgot how long it took those countries to arrive at their present human rights status. It took years, if not centuries of fights and deaths.

To catch up with these developed countries, Africans had to run, while they walked, she reflected. Yes, rights were important, and should be practiced and applauded, but she felt that Zimbabweans needed to do certain things, first.

Queen Latifa, however, liked the views of **Douglas Mwonzora** and one **Alex Magaisa**, a popular Zimbabwean academic lawyer on his Face Book Page. It was clear the man knew where lawyers began and ended. She also like Oto Saki, though she wasn't sure about **Arthur Mutambara** and **Welshman Ncube,** though the former was a robotics engineer, and not a lawyer.

Besides her idol. **Betty Makoni,** she also liked and admired **Petina Gappah**, a Zimbabwean international lawyer and prominent writer, who saw into Zanu PF's desperate propaganda of splashing state owned newspapers with congratulatory messages to Mnangagwa, after assuming a rotational regional char. This, while the space should be filled with business-related adverts and messages, and the nation was on its knees because of his incompetency, she said.

She was also sure the veteran politician, businessman and academic, **Simba Makoni**, would make insightful observations.

She had no doubt that Zimbabwe had the people to see it through a comprehensive, sustainable national healing process, and see it through a brand new, democratic phase, but it seemed the world had closed its eyes and did not care.

The country itself had colleges and institutions that produced peace experts, and such people would be used, instead of having them work in other countries like they do now.

The second group of people she had a slight problem with was the religious group, especially the predominant Christians. Some, if not most of them took it for granted that since the Bible talks about forgiveness, peace and loving our neighbours and being good Christians, it was their responsibility to take charge of the national healing process. This was far from the truth. All people in the process were equal, and had to have some form of training, first. National healing was not a religious exercise, but included all people, with their differences.

National healing and peace building was a complicated exercise which required an understanding of psychology, sociology, anthropology, history, religious studies, culture, geography, mathematics, business, International Law and a lot other things, all in one man, at the same time. Peace graduates had at least that foundation, and so should be in the lead, or facilitate training for the community leaders.

There were however a good lot of Christians who had knowledge and experience in the field, Father Fidelis Mukonori among them.

During **COPAC** she had also met and liked **Rejoice Ngwenya** and various other intelligent, sober minded people. She liked his knowledge of the Gukurahundi massacres and thought it might be helpful.

Queen Latifa also admired the courage, determination and thoroughness of **Tendai Biti**, especially his recent rant against the government for paying out US$400 million for the acquisition of Command Agriculture fertilizer to a company they did not know, and the money disappearing without trace, without the fertilizer being delivered.

As many Zimbabwean peace builders said, Zanu PF must be cleansed of the spirit of spilt blood, first. This never happened, from independence to date, and for 40 years, war veterans have been going up and down with the spirit of blood still stuck on them.

And Zanu PF encouraged that, manipulated it, and made communities fight and kill each other. They were deliberately using the war-stained guerrillas to continue killing, even in time of peace. Queen Latifa couldn't imagine the sheer cold bloodedness in that. Spoiling other people with the blood you have spilled yourself!

Queen Latifa could imagine Zimbabwe years later, free, really free again. Billions of dollars would be made out of the stories Zimbabweans experienced under the Zanu PF rule. There were so many stories to tell, pregnant wombs and bellies were cut open, lovers put asunder, families wiped out, billions made, starvation ruled while others blew money on streets and stadiums. It was a real war zone, with no police or the courts. Sometimes, the law itself was the main culprit. She imagined the horror and romantic movies that would come out.

She imagined and had secret plans of a huge compilation of the jokes Zimbabweans made about their political leaders, even videos, too, as a part of the memorialization monument, or she would do it and make money for herself. She would consult people on this, especially Professor **Vitalis Nyawaranda** at the UZ.

A Transitional justice process was inevitable for Zimbabwe, because as she understood it, it was a process that sought to address challenges that confront societies as they moved from authoritarian rule to a form of democracy. Frequently, such societies are emerging from serious conflict and violence that include widespread human rights violations, genocide and crimes against humanity. Such societies are also characterized by a breakdown in legal services, stark divisions and apportioning of blame, institutional collapse and economic downturn.

These happened in Zimbabwe, and there is video and documentary evidence.

In this light, transitional justice was not a contradiction of criminal justice but rather a deeper, richer and broader vision of justice which sought to confront perpetrators, address the needs of victims and start a process of reconciliation and transformation towards a more just and humane society.

Some of the major steps established to confront impunity had been made in the **Nuremberg Trials,** the **International Tribunal for former Yugoslavia**, and the **International Tribunal for Rwanda,** as well as the establishment of the Permanent International Criminal Court.

Zimbabwe had a lot to learn from these, including the **Truth and Reconciliation Commission (TRC) of South Africa.** These steps are also a reminder to those who commit serious criminal acts that they will face grave sanctions if and when they are brought to book. Impunity must be fought at all levels.

Realistically, however, it is impossible to prosecute all offenders during times of transition. The vexed question of selective prosecution seems to undermine the very idea of individual criminal responsibility which is fundamental to our understanding of the rule of law.

There are also other problems people face during the process, because national legal systems are in disarray and trials are often very lengthy and costly. Moreover, the almost exclusive focus by tribunals on the perpetrator(s) is often to the detriment of the victim (s). Briefly put, the aim of transitional justice is wider than prosecuting perpetrators. Punishment cannot be the last word.

Due to these shortcomings, it is impossible to deal with the true intent of justice by court procedures alone. A holistic approach to transitional justice seeks to complement retributive with restorative justice.

The holistic approach has five components:

1. Accountability.

The role of law and the fair administration of justice deserves the greatest respect. No society can claim to be free or democratic without strict adherence to the rule of law. It is of central importance that those who violate the law are punished. But there are limits to the law, and we need to embrace a multi-faceted notion of justice that is wider, deeper and richer than retributive justice.

It is not only impossible to prosecute all offenders, but an overzealous focus on punishment can make securing sustainable peace and stability more difficult.

More than justice is required, to achieve a just society. Documenting the truth about the past, restoring dignity to victims, and embarking on the process of reconciliation are all vital elements of a just society. Equally important is the need to transform society so that it does not impede the consolidation of democracy and the creation of a human rights culture. This means that the approach to societies in transition will be multi-faceted, and will incorporate consultation to realise the goal of a just society.

2.   Truth recovery

The truth and Reconciliation Commission (TRC) is one of the non-judicial mechanisms that has gained great prominence over the last few decades. A TRC is concerned first and foremost with the recovery of truth. Through truth telling, these commissions attempt to document and analyse the structures and methods used in carrying out illegal oppression, while taking into account the political, economic and social contexts in which violations occurred.

3.   Reconciliation.

Because the word 'reconciliation' has religious connotations, especially in the Christian faith, many people prefer that the word and the concept should not be used in TRCs that are seeking to recover the truth and promote the interests of victims.

At best, reconciliation involves commitment and sacrifice, at its worst, it is an excuse for passivity, for siding with the powerful against the weak and dispossessed. Religion, in many instances has given a bad name to reconciliation, representatives often having joined forces with those who exploited and impoverished entire populations, instead of being in solidarity with the oppressed.

Reconciliation is unrealistic when it calls for mere forgetting or concealing. Unless calls for reconciliation are accompanied by acknowledgement of the past and the acceptance of responsibility, they will be dismissed as cheap rhetoric. It would be interesting to learn about the experiences in Argentina and Rwanda, and Queen Latifa had videos on these.

Perhaps one of the ways in which to achieve at least a measure of reconciliation is to create common memory that can be acknowledged by those who created and implemented the unjust system, those who fought against it (like Morgan Tsvangirai), and the many more who, while in the middle, claimed not to know what was happening in the country.

Reconciliation must be understood through the lens of transitional justice. It is better understood when victims believe that their grievances are being heard and addressed, that the silence is being broken. It can begin when perpetrators are held accountable, when truth is sought openly and fearlessly, when institutional reform commences, and when the need for reparation is acknowledged and acted upon. The response by former victims to these initiatives can increase the potential for stability and increase the chances of a sustainable peace.

When leaders are prepared to speak honestly and generously about their own involvement, or at least or their government, or the previous government, then the door is open for the possibility of some reconciliation among citizens.

4. Institutional Reform

For peace and reconciliation to flourish, serious and focused attention must be given to both individuals and institutions. Institutional reform must be at the very heart of transformation. Instead of focusing only on individual hearings (like most TRCs to date), the Zimbabwean TRC will also hear institutional hearings. This brings them to the centre of our transformation. It would enable them to call to account those institutions directly responsible for the breakdown of the state and the repression of citizens.

The key question to institutional reform is Give us an account of your role in the past, how do you see your role in the future?

While dealing with the past, we must not dwell on it, but focus on the future.

In deeply divided societies where mistrust and fear still reign, there must be bridge-building and a commitment to both criminal and economic justice. For that to be a reality, institutions as well as individuals have to change.

5. Reparations

First, it is important to emphasise that to the victim, reparations occupy a special place in a transition to democracy. For them, reparations are the most tangible manifestation of the efforts of the state to remedy the harms they have suffered. Criminal justice, no matter how successful (which is impossible), is just in the end a struggle against perpetrators rather than an effort on behalf of victims.

In many ways, the dilemmas and challenges in reparations are a microcosm of the overall challenges of transitional justice. Special care must be taken to balance competing legitimate interests in addressing the harms of victims and ensuring the democratic stability and viability of the state.

Similar to other areas of transitional justice such as truth telling or institutional reform, simple judicial decisions cannot provide the comprehensive solutions demanded by such interests. Rather, solutions must be found in the exercise of judgment, and a creative combination off legal, political, social and economic approaches.

Ultimately, Zimbabwe's reconciliation had to balance two imperatives: on one hand there is the need to return to the rule of law and the prosecution of offenders, on the other, there is a need for rebuilding societies and embarking on the process of reconciliation. In helping to make states work it is important therefore to balance accountability with the shoring up of fragile, emerging democracy. The overall aim is to ensure a sustainable peace, which will encourage and make possible socio-economic development.

With the country's desperate need for a fresh start, and poor history of individual compensation since the 80s and 90s, especially regarding the war veterans being paid $50 000 each, at first, and the War Victims Compensation Fund being looted by the politically connected, Queen Latifa thought community compensation was far better and should be paid out to districts and communities, especially regarding the low level of infrastructure destruction and the need for perpetrators to rebuild and restock the structures and other victims' property they destroyed. While individual compensation could be considered for families of political murder victims, this need no necessarily be paid out in cash only but other forms. This should be spearheaded by either government or international donors.

To Queen Latifa, the methodology and strategy for national healing for Zimbabwe was there. All the structures were also there, but needed equal representation. Even the strategy was there, for it depended on specific local districts. All they needed was agreement.

There was one activity specifically for war veterans across the country, besides the national one, for all and sundry.

Queen Latifa even knew the easy step by step activities, which were heavily characterized by Zimbabwean traditional approaches.

To her, the centre of the national healing and transitional justice phases of Zimbabwe was anchored on preventing immunity. Never again should Zimbabwe fall to the levels of Zanu PF governance. There was need to prevent destroyed identities from affecting third and fourth generations.

Memory was therefore an integral part of the process, because what happens to an individual shapes not only that individual's personality but also their very brain function. Memories need to be restored after a past of conflict. Memories of victims and perpetrators alike should be shared and healed.

She also felt that there was a need to learn how to read memories, to make a distinction between what felt right and wonderful, (and the context it took place), and why it was so dismally wrong.

As far as the context was concerned, Queen Latifa thought it was best for the national healing and reconciliation exercise to consider events and cases that happened after independence, when Zimbabwe became a nation. That period covered a time span of about 40 years only, and so the exercise could be achieved.

If the nation wanted a Truth and Reconciliation Commission as what happened in South Africa, it would be good with her. She felt however that the nation should go through the minimal requirements for a TRC, to approach legitimacy and international law.

She was keenly aware of the need for Security Sector Reform (SSR), and for that she would rely on the advice of renowned Zimbabwean gurus in that field, especially **Martin Rupiya, Shari Eppel, Brian Raftopoulos** and others. She particularly liked what Rupiya said,:SSS processes are about assisting national authorities restoring and reforming the security sector for purposes of peace, security, poverty reduction, economic and social development, restoring human rights, rule of law and democratization."

Queen Latifa derived hope from the fact that all the parties to the Zimbabwe political conflict were willing to talk to each other. Although Zanu PF always used devious tricks that flew in the face of such talks, just as they did during elections. As a result, people's hopes were beginning to fade. Perhaps it was because of dishonest mediators who had their own interests, or it was because of something else, peace remained elusive. Uncleansed, blood stained people, nothing would go right.

Like many people, she believed that the people at the centre of the Zimbabwean political conflict were a tiny fraction of the Zanu PF politicians, and could be dealt with.

She also remembered that during the war, guerrillas were told to honour ancestors and traditional leadership, through the traditional leaders. They did that, and the war was successful. However, after that war, nobody went back to the ancestors to thank them and tell them the war was over. That was another crucial aspect to look into. Otherwise to the ancestors, the war was still on, and that was why there were many deaths on roads, disease outbreaks, election times and so forth.

As it was, rumours were spreading that Mnangagwa's dismal failure to govern was rooted in the blood on his hands. People said the spirits of the people he massacred during **Gukurahundi** were haunting him, just as Mugabe was haunted by the spirit of **Tongogara** and other people he killed.

To Queen Latifa, as long as those spirits were not appeased, and Zimbabwe continued to be ruled by men with blood stained hands, there would be no peace.

She thought seriously about extending the National Healing and Reconciliation activities to domestic, personal and family disputes and misunderstandings. This would make the process far reaching to allow a new, fresh beginning across the country.

She was keenly aware that a large part of the national healing and reconciliation exercise focused on finding creative ways to prevent destroyed identities from affecting third and fourth generations.

She was also aware that some of the horrific crimes committed were out of petty issues such as jealous, or revenge over a non-political but religious, social, sexual or beer issue.

As far as the continent was concerned, she reasoned that since all the countries in the region were weak militarily (except perhaps, South Africa). None of them could defeat or be defeated by the other, in the unlikely event of a war breaking out. It would not even be a war, it would drag on for endless years.

Since soldiers just ate money and did not produce anything for the people, even entertainment or toys for children, there was no need to employ such large numbers of them. Focus should be on industrial development, for each and every one of these countries. That was purposeful leadership at this age. Work on providing electricity for 24 hours, and you see what potential that alone would unleash, she thought.

She didn't understand the **SADC** region's idea of uniting with the Zimbabwe government to fight for the lifting of sanctions. These SADC nations should unite with the people of Zimbabwe to remove Zanu PF, an unwanted party and government, instead of strengthening that demon party. How could they support the same party for 40 years, while they changed their own governments every now and then? There was no sense in that.

Even before graduating, Queen Latifa longed for an opportunity to test what she'd learned from her lectures and reading, though she found the going tricky.

One example of her practical involvement in peacebuilding involved two men, who belonged to different political parties, but lived in the same neighbourhood. One day, they went up to the others house (let's call them Mr Jimalo and Mr. Mutepfa). So they went up to Mr. Mutepfa's house. Mr. Mutepfa was an ardent Zanu PF supporter, but Mr. Jimalo was MDC. At Mr. Mutepfa's house they roamed around the garden, until they came to the fowl run. There were scores of chicks, at various stages of growth. Mr. Mutepfa asked Mr. Jimalo if he liked the chicks, to which the latter replied that he actually kept some at his house, and sure, he liked them. Then Mr. Mutepfa offered Mr. Jimalo 4 healthy chicks, including one bushveldt. He said the lot would cost $US3 or 12 Bond. At least that was what Mr. Jimalo heard. He carried them in a box to his house. By the way, he had promised to pay the next Friday. When the day came, Mr Mutepfa called. Because Mr Jimalo did not want to part with US Dollars over such simple things as road runners, he offered to pay Mr. Mutepfa in Ecocash Bond.

"And how much is that?" asked Mr. Mutepfa.

"Twelve Dollars, "replied Jimalo.

"Ah twenty dollars my ass!" stormed Mr. Mutepfa. "Where have you heard of 4 by \$3 US Dollars amount to 12 Bond? I told you they were going at \$3 each, and they were 4. We agreed. That's why you took them away. Otherwise…"

Another disturbing thing was that the 4 chicks had all died. Jamalo watched almost every morning, as his maid came out of the run with a dead chick. So they had all died and he was expected to part with US\$12 for that?

When she heard the conflict, Queen Latifa adopted the various conflict resolutions that she'd learned at university, and that helped. She looked at the participants' interests, positions and history. Then proceeded to look at the iceberg model. In the end, it was decided that since Jimalo also kept chickens, he could give Mr. Mutepfa his 4, but because they had died, Mr. Mutepfa would give Jimalo 2 back. This was done to pacify Jimalo, who was complaining of his lost chicken feed, which was very costly those days. Further, when Mr. Mutepfa complained about the loss of two chicks, she suggested that Jimalo pay back one chicken to Mutepfa then, or later after two weeks. After haggling, Jimalo agree, and parted with the chicken there and then.

So this case gave her the desire for more conflicts to resolve, especially in conflict ridden Zimbabwe. But it was not easy. The nature of the conflict itself was a matter of life or death for some, and this made it difficult for Queen Latifa to develop a keen interest in resolving local conflicts. However, she kept a diary of the major ones. Others she tried to make documentaries out of, using the equipment from her Community Organization. But this too, involved a lot of people and things, and so was not easy.

What especially bothered her was the fact that Mugabe told everyone in the world, from Unite Nations, African Union and SADC platforms that was peace in Zimbabwe. From her studies, she learned that this was negative peace, and was worse than physical violence because it affected every part of the body, including the mind. There was structural violence in the country, and those at the top did what they wanted with anybody, and no questions were asked.

The government ignored human rights, completely as a measurement of the peacefulness of a country. It said human rights were selfish, and promoted group rights, which it supervised.

She chuckled to herself when Mugabe addressed international guests and emphasized that Zimbabwe was a country at peace, so they must come in and invest. Queen Latifa wondered what kind of peace? People were dying in hospital queues, road accidents, and disease, hunger and so forth, and there was no war. Typically, Zanu PF understood peace as silence; absence of gunfire sounds. That was peace, to them.

AT THE INTERNATIONAL PEACE CONFERENCE

Because she had a registered organization and a desire to change things for the better, Queen latifa still sent out project proposals, when she was in the mood, and one day received an offer from a United States based international peace organization, to showcase the kind of life Zimbabweans were living. She knew the dangers she had to face by narrating negatively about Zimbabwe, especially from the ruling party. Because of her experience and education, she got the opportunity to participate at the conference, and got the return air tickets and accommodation, too. She tried to go away as silently as she could, and indeed, managed to.

At the heavily populated conference, when her turn came up to speak, she introduced herself as Queen Latifa, but before she said "Tonderai", the participants clapped hands so loudly, it was not heard. As she mentioned that she came from Zimbabwe, she flashed the map of Africa on a screen chart clearly showing Zimbabwe in red. There was a little more clapping. That emboldened and encouraged her

She'd had many stories to choose from, until she'd settled on this one.

"My story is based on the current political conflict in my country, where neighbours have turned against each other, almost overnight, because of politics and the political parties they belong to. It is the story of ordinary people at the grassroots." She spoke clearly, using appropriate gestures.

She told the story as if it were happening live before the audience's eyes, alternating her voice projections with the characters. The people's eyes were glued on her.

"Two close neighbours competed for the same post in the same party. These were fairly well educated people, both with families. However only one of them would win and have the post, so the post went to the other one. This did not please the loser, who felt there had been a lot of unfair irregularities, which could be true. So, instead of embracing and moving forward, these two remained locked in deep enmity.

A point to note is that a position at whatever level in a political party in Zimbabwe, carries with it power, money, fame, popularity and worth. So it was a do or die situation for the contestants.

"One Saturday afternoon, the loser, who was a peasant farmer was passing the growth point where the winner had a shop. He had a donkey which drew a cart. Inside the cart were bags of maize he was carrying from the showgrounds.

As he passed one of the shops, his eyes were caught in a flash of blinding yellowish light. He stopped, walked a step or two, and then turned it around with his toe. He bent down to pick it up, but was disappointed to see that it was a castle lager bottle top. A beer bottle top.

As he stood erect, ready to throw it away into the grass, his eyes met those of his enemy, Kanda, standing on the stairs of his shop. Kanda was watching him with a keen and amused interest. It was then that Muza, the other guy, instead of throwing the lid away, quickly shoved it into his pocket, with a fake smile of glee.

One and a half hours later, Muza was resting under a tree in his yard when two police constables came up to him, and announced that he was wanted at the station, immediately.

The police station was close to the showgrounds, so it was another hour of walking for Muza. At the station there was a crowd, who gave way to Muza and the constables as they came up. In the group Muza also spotted Kanda, though he did not give him the benefit of a full glare.

The Chief Constable accused him of picking up a diamond of the glass variety, which was very expensive and highly sought after.

Apparently some dealers, who included a deputy minister and prominent sons of ministers had lost the diamond when they had attended the agricultural show the previous day. They wanted it back, and had threatened the Chief Constable with unspecified action if the diamond was not found.

"Is this him?" asked the chief constable, looking at Kanda.

"Yes it is," replied Kanda stepping forward gleefully.

"What is it? Muza asked, perplexed.

"The glass diamond that you picked up at the growth point," replied the chief constable. "A Deputy Minister who was at the showgrounds this afternoon lost his diamonds, and Mr. Kanda here spotted you picking them up. Give us the diamonds, Muza, or you're going to spend your whole life in prison," he finished.

"Diamonds? I know nothing about diamonds, and have never seen one. I don't know what you are talking about," Muza protested innocently.

At hearing this, the people at the station door laughed, along with the chief constable. This puzzled Muza more.

"Those diamonds are worth millions of US Dollars, and you'd better hand them over," the chief constable said with emphasis. "Mr. Kanda here saw you. Can you tell us again what you saw, Mr. Kanda?'

"Sure, yes. At around 4pm this afternoon, I decided to take a breath of fresh air outside my store. I saw Mr. Muza pick up some shiny objects from the ground, just a few metres from where I stood. It was clearly a valuable thing that he picked, because as soon as he picked it up, he quickly dropped it into his trousers pocket and smiled. I demanded that he stop, but he refused, and suddenly rushed away".

Then Muza remembered the castle bottle lid he had picked, dug his hand into his trousers pocket and brought it out.

"This is what I picked!" he exclaimed, looking into people's eyes.

At that, they laughed. Even the constable laughed.

"Search him!, the chief constables ordered his deputies. Rough hands seized the old man's body. They turned and shook him, but found nothing. He ordered that Muza be put into the single cell there, and a party was sent to search his house.

"For a whole week Muza was detained at the police station, until, fearing for the human rights issue and the incarceration of a person without trial for a period of time, they released him, with a stern warning that they would be watching his step every time.

"Muza, now frail, worn, hurt and humiliated, felt deeply embarrassed. People jeered at him and whispered nasty things wherever he went, which was not many places. Children shouted abuse at him from behind corners of buildings and bushes.

No one wanted to be seen in his company, and his friends now shunned him. He had tried to explain what had happened, but no one had listed. Groups of people would disperse when he tried to join them. In the end he grew tired, hopeless and broken. His health deteriorated and he walked with difficulty.

"After 4 weeks of picking up the bottle top, he was found dead in his hut. On the day he was buried, a goat herder found the diamonds wrapped in a plastic paper, on a toilet windowsill."

At this, all the people in the conference hall said "Haaa!" together, and clapped hands.

After that there was a deep silence, their minds hung on the story, a tear dropping here and there, faces hung. They had difficulty believing what they had just seen and heard before their eyes.

"This is just one of the many conflicts that are in my country. There are many and varied, and at different levels of society. People do not live normal lives any more. One has to always check over one's shoulder as one goes about one's business or talks to a friend. You don't know who the enemy is, or what he will do.

Many of the conflicts are now perpetuated by jealousy, when one family has goodies such as bread, margarine, drinks, even electricity, and the other does not. The conflicts emerge from very ordinary, everyday things, but could end up involving whole families, neighbourhood and entire community.

I ask the world to keep an eye on my country. Zimbabweans are known to be hardworking and educated, the world over, please help them regain their suitable place in the world", she finished, to another round of applause.

FARAI'S DREAM

The much awaited 16 August peace march had come and gone, bringing nothing in the wind. The police left it until the last hour to ban the march, and the High Court followed thereafter. Very legalistic.

And again, the MDC Alliance and the people were left with nothing else to do. Fatso knew Queen Latifa's new qualification and what she was doing, and wondered if she would love to be consulted. He was sure she would come in handy.

As it was, ZBCTv interviewed people who said they'd been disturbed by the stupid call, as many customers stayed home, as per call. As a result, they couldn't get what they wanted, and the business also couldn't. Everyone interviewed on Tv, and those who met in streets and places, said it was a stupid call.

However, news soon spread that Zanu PF had used their Border Gezi Youth brigades and ghost workers to beat up any people they met on streets. They gave them police uniforms, instructions and cash, then released them. Many people, even those traveling to hospitals and long distances, were beaten up, and told to go home.

Zanu PF used these youth because it knew that the police would never beat up people, even for marching.

Anyway, for the MDC Alliance and the people of Zimbabwe, that was another failure.

However, at least their voice was heard. What about Zanu PF? Farai thought. With their record of failures, couldn't they have taken this call as an opportunity to work with the MDC, and chart the way forward for Zimbabwe and her Zimbabweans?

Did Zanu PF believe that it could save this country alone? After forty years of failure?

If, and when that happened, they would begin to kill each other again, Farai thought. It had happened before, a period which popularized their favourite song, "Zimbabwe Ndeyeropa (Zimbabwe is about Blood).

As it was, people were beginning to say that if things remained as tough as they were, they might call for Mugabe's return, and they would vote for him, rather than keep Mnangagwa. Of course, to Farai and his ghetto crew, that was nonsense. But it could happen. A lot of nonsense was happening in Zimbabwe.

The social scene was dead. People criss crossed roads looking for the day's meal. Farai couldn't help but notice that there was no meaningful music being produced anymore. Whatever meaningless rhymes the younger generations were crazy about, they couldn't dance to it. In fact, when these youth listened to 'Madhebhura'. They love and dance to it well enough. This means we're in the past, with them. If a Zimbabwean who died in the 80s should resurrect today, he would miss nothing, except maybe the now obsolete cell phone.

Anyway, enough of the 16th August Peace March.

Farai's left lower eyelid had been twitching for three days. One night during this period, he had a strange dream. He dreamt the whole Mutare City in darkness. This was 2019. There was no electricity for days, and at night people wandered around in darkness. People on WhatsApp groups reported that the whole country was in the same situation; electricity was finished, and there was nothing the government could do, except wait for international relief.

There was also no fuel and cars, combis and buses did not move. The news was that the country had run out of fuel. In other words, the government had run out of foreign currency to buy electricity and fuel from outside suppliers.

In that dream, shops and supermarkets were full of food items such as maize meal, sugar, cooking oil and a variety of other goodies, but people had no money to buy the food. Because of the government's stringent cash flow control systems, very little cash was circulating, and it circulated among the rich people, with the ordinary people having very little or none of it. They would get into a shop, find the prices too high and just walked out.

At first, people had tried to break into these shops and loot, but several had been shot dead and no one attempted to break in any more. People just stayed away, because soldiers were roaming streets and corners, guns at the ready to shoot at anyone who misbehaved.

In the dream Fatso and his friends still met in the local council bar as before. Just to talk and commiserate in numbers. During such meetings people would fight over such little change money as 50c. On one occasion in the dream, Farai saw a man he knew well being killed over a 25c coin. It was a dangerous dream.

When Farai looked around himself during the day, he saw the reality in his dream. Indeed, people were hungry, but they had no money in their pockets. In the bar and bottle stores he visited, the same song was repeated over and over again, by everyone he met, Can you do a little for me?" That was the song, although it came in different words, it was the same begging song.

Most people, including women and children, stayed in their homes, 24 hours. It was rumoured that there were gangs of people who went around, especially at night, with the intention of stripping people they met of their clothes, for sale elsewhere, far away. Such bandits and robbers were the talk of town, and it seemed there was nothing the government or anyone could do about them.

On top of these problems, there was also a disease outbreak, in the dream, and clinics and hospitals were jammed by people who needed care and attention. This made Farai think of the cholera and HIV/AIDS diseases of the past real life, which had wiped out whole families and left just the young people. Again, in the dream, as in real life, doctors and nurses were on strike, and no services were being offered.

In his dream, Farai foresaw Zimbabweans eventually killing each other for meals; pure cannibalism. Schools had been closed because teachers were no longer coming to work, and children spent their time in homes with their parents. These were eaten, first.

In one family he knew, Farai dreamt of the father one day saying,: "We start with the toes and fingers, first, then move on to the next parts." The family did not argue, but appeared to agree with what the father was saying. The father produced a long, sharp knife and began to cut off the toes of the last born girl child that Faarai knew so well. She did not scream, but smiled as she was cut. The father deposited the toes and fingers into the bowl on a wooden fire for cooking.

They began to eat, as Farai watched from a distance in his dream.

As people ate each other in their homes, and continued to mingle and mix outside, they discovered that their flesh was beginning to fall off. Even as two people stood and verbally greeted each other, their flesh was falling off. Often, an ear would fall off, or an eye, lower lip, finger, and so on. It was normal to see a person with bare teeth, no lips, or another without a leg, arm or any other part. Still, the people continued to interact as they do today, in a normal way.

It was as if they were rotting as they walked. And indeed they were. They still died, however, but quicker and faster now. Everywhere you went in the country, you saw dead bodies strewn, lying unburied. Soldiers, however, were not affected, and marched around in immaculate uniform. All around, it was perfectly normal to see completely pink people, sometimes with blood droppings.

Men especially walked naked, to prevent their skin being pulled off by clothes when contact was made with skin. Women still wore their clothes, and died faster and in larger numbers.

Even as they met and greeted each other, the word 'bho' continued to be used in greeting exchanges. They said 'bho' with a jerking of the right thumb, accompanied with a smile, even as flesh, teeth, and other parts of the body rotted and fell off, littering streets and causing falls and other accidents on pavements.

There was no sign of the politicians, in the dream. Perhaps they had fled to other parts of the world, enjoying life on their looted wealth.

In the dream, Farai remembered the phrase 'no head' repeatedly used. He had had discussions with his peers, about Zimbabwean currency being almost the only one, globally, without a human head imprinted on it. Some said that was why it was tossed about. It had no value, because it did not carry a sign of human life on it.

Farai wondered what he could do about that.

Still in the dream, Farai saw a few years later the world sit down to discuss Zimbabwe's hellish tragedy.

"They appeared normal. Y' know, now Zimbabweans were always smiling, happy people, but that was only on the surface."

"It's their culture.' somebody replied. "Zimbabweans smiled a lot, and did lots of wonderful stuff with their minds. How could they let this happen to themselves?"

"It's called African politics. It's a do or die game. It's also an opium. You can't feel anything…"

A few people at the conference, however, blamed it on cowardice. "Zimbabweans were cowards! How could they not stand up against all that nonsense we heard?"

"It's the entire world that is cowardly, not Zimbabweans. We shouldn't have let that party rule for that long…Things have to change from now on."

"But Mugabe himself called for more African representation at the UN, and we denied him…many times even."

"Yes, we denied him. More African representation is democracy. How could we give Mugabe what he was denying his own people? That's impossible!

If we did, we would not be democratic to the people of Zimbabwe, or Africa, but to Mugabe himself!"

Farai had this dream for three nights. It was the same dream, but it had different phases or episodes and characters. On the fourth day, he went to see a prophet he'd heard about, in the same Sakubva location. The prophet asked Farai if he was injured or harmed in any way in the dream, and he said nay.

"In that case," said the prophet, holding his bible in one hand and extending some fetishes to Fatso, "You are safe. However, your dream is a warning of terrible times ahead, so I advise you to change your life style and do something honourable." With that, he made a sign of a cross across Farai's front belly, and was finished.

Farai knew just what he would do. He had looked at himself for a long time, and wondered how he could make his big voice and frame work for him. He could not get into politics, because he'd had enough of that. Besides, there were too many parties already, and he wouldn't know where to start. At least from politics, he'd learnt such things as democracy, human rights, etc; words a technical guy like him would never know. That, plus the injuries, was enough.

After visiting the prophet, he knew what he would do. Yes, he would form a church, his own, and call it the Zimbabwe End Time Salvation Church.

He would preach about his dream, and ask those who did not want to meet it in their lives join him. Of course, there would be money involved. Farai would cleanse the congregants of their sins, then pray with and for them for several days until they were saved. He would also learn how to caste demons and save tortured and tormented souls.

For that, he knew he had to go to Nigeria, but he thought he should visit some Zimbabwean pastors and Evangelists, first. He would not fail. He saw mental pictures of his highly successful and popular church. Many people were forming churches these days of hardships, and he saw no reason why his own church would not prosper. People needed salvation, and he saw himself going international. The beginning was the problem, but he was ready for that

MEETING PRESIDENT OBAMA

The last day of the conference, one of the officials came up to Queen Latifa and said, "There's a representative from one of the big organizations in the States who wants to see you." He pointed at the door, where a man stood. Queen Latifa went to meet him.

"My name is George Staple, and I'm from the **Obama Foundation**. If you can find time, President Obama would like to have a word with you, please."

Queen Latifa was baffled. She'd always wanted to meet **President Obama.** A few tears dropped as she stood there and said, "Yes. Yes, please.

"Let's go. I will bring you back in 30 minutes."

President Obama himself came to her as she sat in a lounge. As she stood up, he flashed a wide smile and took her hand, but she nearly fell down at his sight.

He sat them down.

"I heard your story at the conference. Very pitiful. And I've heard many stories about Zimbabwe, your country. We don't want, or are allowed to interfere. This is an issue about you and your people. All we can do is help. Tell me, how can we help your organization and people?"

This was the question Queen Latifa had been waiting for, for years. Now composed (she soon found out that the Ex-President was heart-warming and set her at a comfortable ease). She told him about her proposal, in which she wanted to build the Chikanga Peace Project in her neighbourhood.

The project involved more than 300 000 residents of Chikanga and Sakubva suburbs.

She told him the Chikanga Peace Project was a project that aimed to pool the resources of the residents of Chikanga and Sakubva high density suburbs together, to bring about change to their lives.

This change was mostly in the area of development for the self and community. The project aimed to bring about this change through combining modern creative, innovative technical ideas to traditional ones. The project aimed to ultimately end up an industrial hub of music productions, videos, documentaries, films, fine arts, African attire, potteries, carving, weaving and other products. All age groups were included in the project, from the youths to those beyond 65.

She told him what he knew already, and that was, ever since independence in 1980, Zimbabwe had been plunged in a political conflict, with the same ZANU PF party still in power since then. There was no telling the impact of that political conflict, but the long and short of it was that the nation had retrogressed, while others had progressed. Many dreams had been shattered, especially during Mugabe's 38 -year rule. Neighbours had been made to turn against each other overnight. There was no trust between family members, neighbours and relatives, let alone citizens.

She added that generally, Zimbabwean youth felt excluded from community and family life—such as household and community decision-making processes or engagement in community events – and were organizing new movements inspired by a narrative of intergenerational oppression and divides that kept youth excluded and vulnerable to recruitment by political elites.

Indeed, many of the grievances that helped politicians recruit youth to engage in violence remained unaddressed. Zimbabwe's Human Development Index was only then slowly recovering to early 1990s levels: 72% of Zimbabweans were below the poverty line, and only 47% were in secondary school.

Youth felt they were the first generation to be worse off for their parents, and blamed the repressive formal state structure for stagnating progress and their potential. While the constitution said one thing, the government and people in general, did another. Marginalization was especially pronounced for girls and women who were less than half as frequently as boys and men to be consulted by their families in decisions affecting them.

Queen Latifa told the president that her organization adopted a two-pronged approach towards resolving the scenario described above. First, the organization sought to work to promote non-violent social change in order to help scale down without inciting violence. Second, given the past direct correlation between economics and violence in Zimbabwe and the current economic crisis, the organization sought to start cash-for-work programs in conflict hot spots that could help reduce youth vulnerability to mobilization.

The Chikanga Peace Project had two main objectives:

1. To create space for the people of the community to freely express their minds and opinions about any subject that affected them. The same space would be used for community public announcements and to express what was happening within the community that affected peace and or development.
2. To create a Chikanga Peace Park, where youth engaged in various forms of art, music, video filming. Documentary making, photography. Internet access, dramas and other products for sale within the country and across the world. The park would also be a bridge for youth and others to connect and link up with other youths across cities and the world.

The total budget for the project would be US$55 000.

President Obama liked the idea and proposal, and expressed that to Queen Latifa. He asked her if the amount would be enough, and she said yes. He then asked for her account details, and promised that the money might get to Zimbabwe before she did.

But as soon as she arrived at the Harare International Airport, however, she was called into a security office, where four men and a woman sat. They asked her to tell them where she'd been, and what had happened.

Queen Latifa knew that these people might already have information about her trip, so she stuck to the main points as much as possible. When she mentioned the US$55 000, however, she noticed that they were surprised, and wished she hadn't.

"What you said in America is a typical example of selling away your country. Why betray your country with lies? Where did that story you told them happen?"

Before Queen Latifa answered she was hurled forwards and upwards.

"Come here. Follow me." Said the head of the security agents. As Queen Latifa stood up, she was told, "We are taking you to a secure place. Then release you for your journey to Mutare, soon. But we need to talk a little bit,"

But she was not released so soon. When they got into a bakkie, everything appeared changed to her. The streets they moved in were strange, until there was darkness all around her. She knew then that they'd left Harare.

Her head was covered in a large woolen hat, so that she could not see. She was pushed to the ground, where electrodes were connected to her feet and switched on. She could not believe the pain that went through her body. The same was repeated on the other leg.

She cried and moaned but knew that no one would hear her. Then she was raised to her feet, and suddenly a rush of cold water was thrown at her. She fell down.

Many other things were done to her; beatings, kicks, and sometimes repugnant kisses on her numb lips. Altogether this went on for two weeks, and she grew so lean and evidently wasted. She could not walk without help.

Independent newspapers reported of her missing, and frantic efforts were made to locate her. After carefully tracing her movements at the airport, the State was accused of kidnapping her.

Voices were raised and fingers pointed at the government from international organizations like Crisis International, Human Rights Watch, and others across the world. That was when she was released.

She was driven to her Sakubva home one night and left at the door, after a harsh warning to her never to go to America again, or communicate with any one there. They were watching her.

She did not want to give interviews, but found that she could not avoid that. She told the world about her trip to the United States, and her capture at the airport. She had no idea who captured her, she said, though she knew. People could make their own guesses.

When she checked her bank account four days later, she found that the money from the Obama Foundation had actually arrived. A friend at the bank told her that the money had been tampered with slightly, but all back in her account.

She wondered what to do. Emboldened by the ordeal she had gone through with the State security agents, and the money she was getting from her mining activities, she set about organizing her project. This time she feared no one, and nothing would stand in the way of her dreams.

At first many people opposed the project, and called her names for her efforts. However, when she mentioned money for work done, and a work schedule put into place, many soon joined her.

Huge masses of youths came to work on it, at a small fee per day. She discovered that all the young men and women knew each other, and that was an advantage. She also discovered that though she did not know these youth, they knew her.

Later she discovered that she knew most of the houses from which these youth came. Years back, somebody she knew had stayed in that house, a friend, schoolmate, a boy she exchanged novels with, and so forth. That meant they all knew each other, and because they stayed in the same neighbourhood, they were one.

A strong bond was formed by these youth, and they loved each other and their work. Violence, drunkenness, and drug abuse were frowned upon, and reduced drastically.

The only talk among the youth was money, for starters. They needed it, and worked their backs off for it. And they got it!

Queen Latifa was especially happy to see well known members of the Gweja and Hwindi communities working shoulder to shoulder with everybody else. Some elderly men, including war veterans, joined in too> The whole community of Chikanga Phase 1 was at last united.

They paved the entire Spar or Chikangaz shopping centre, such that drainage of water was efficient, and people were free to walk around as they shopped. It grew so popular that it became the talk of town and beyond. At the centre they constructed a stage, and installed a pillar, onto which they attached a big speaker. Space was also made for a microphone.

Queen Latifa talked to the business owners at the place, to have the speaker connected to their radio, such that the music that played in their shop also played on the speaker, to audiences around and beyond. The business owners would rotate, each for a week, and would be the patron of the Chikanga Peace Project that week. They would offer special services and goods to the public, and customers were encouraged to buy from them.

The stage was also used to make announcements, especially of activities or events that threatened peace in the community. People who were affected by domestic violence, starvation, attacks, harassments, abuse, and any violation would go to the stage, pick up the microphone, and say it.

Queen Latifa had no doubt that soon, the stage would be used to host modelling competitions, dramas and other activities. It was theirs, to use as they wished.

As the project grew, many people brought business plans to Queen Latifa, and she sat down and discussed with them. Some wanted to build electrical shops, food cafeterias, boutiques, hair salons, cell phone repair shops, and a variety of other goodies.

However, she suggested that the project would build these for them, in a unified, up to standard fashion, and they would rent. Meantime, they had to submit applications showing their capacity and ability in their chosen area.

She negotiated with the City authorities for space in a disused section of the Chikanga Bar, and established the Chikanga Peace Park. There was established music recording equipment, music practice, filming and recording studios, a large room for computer access and training in computer skill, as well as wifi,. A fashion house, drama recordings. Stone and wood carvings, tie and dye, and others. The Peace Park had a lot of latest communication gadgets, and was making a lot of progress.

Soon, the Zimbabwe Broadcasting Cooperation was their biggest customer for music videos, films and dramas, but they soon extended their clients and customers to other Tv and radio stations across the region, and world.

The Chikanga Peace Project became an international site for peace; many important gurus in the world of peace visited, and ordinary folks around the world competed to be there, send live videos from there, take part in discussions on international and global issues, and seek refuge, advice and guidance.

It became an excellent example of a peaceful, warm and world family in one place for joyful surrender to life and what it brings.

Queen Latifa now believed in the power of community mobilization for change, and the opportunity to appreciate it.

At about that same time, Queen Latifa saw herself extending her hand to victims of the 16 August Peace March. Thousands had been beaten up in Harare on the day, but the ZTv announced and carried interviews to the effect that the march had been a failure, and nobody had taken part. Yet thousands of people had been butchered. Some said 25 had been killed, and 37 injured. Statistics were still coming in.

This was likely to happen in every town across the country, starting with the capital, Harare. According to sources, the MDC Alliance had planned that the marches would take place in every major city, on a day to be announced. That would definitely mean more deaths. Who in Zimbabwe was prepared to face that? That was the question that was answered and ended at independence in 1980. Was it the gun, or the people?

To Queen Latifa, the difference didn't make any difference, so she helped many such victims of the Peace March with blankets, transport, clothes and food. The money came from her gold mining company, Queen Latifa Mining Syndicate.

She now had three mines, and they were all doing very well, thanks to her discipline. Again, she could not understand why the government was always complaining about sanctions, especially when she looked at the potential in mining, and what she herself, a woman, was getting out of it.

But she could not tell this to anybody, lest she be declared a sellout. She thought how amazing it was that America and her allies said they had imposed 'targeted sanctions' on Mugabe and his cronies, but the government turned around and said those sanctions were on the entire country and nation.

While individuals on the target list of sanctions could not go to America, for example, ordinary citizens could. Queen Latifa could not see how that affected national economics, despite how much and often it was hollered about on radio and tv.

OBAMA VISITS QUEEN LATIFA

Queen Latifa was in constant communication with President Obama and the Obama Foundation regarding the Chikanga Peace Project. At the bottom of her heart, there was nothing she wanted more than for the President to visit Zimbabwe, and her town of Mutare. She had hinted at this with the President, but he had laughed slightly and said, "Sure. I'd love to. Let's see how that goes."

Now she was ready for him to visit. The thing that excited her the most about the Chikanga Peace Project was what was happening outside the Chikanga Peace Park, at the stage. Women and girls, especially felt free about announcing the abuse they suffered at the hands of men. Most of these men were known in the community, and they felt very embarrassed when they were reported at the Peace Project. Robberies, thefts, bullying and any other things which threatened peaceful living in the suburb were also announced.

Also, the business owners wanted to extend their time to four weeks, as patrons.

In the project, she involved the local war veterans, who had liberated the nation, but had stuck with Mugabe for so long, defending him and fighting people who were against him.

Queen Latifa felt that in order for them to regain their stature and position in the community, war veterans had to apologize and be with the people. She talked to some of the war veterans, with the intention of involving them in the project. She felt that the war veterans had to be closer to the people they liberated, and not a single individual, though he was president.

Most of them agreed to be patrons of the project, and announced it after heated exchanges with the few others who remained outside.

This was a dream come true for Queen Latifa, and she wanted to share it with President Obama and the world. So she wrote him. She expressed her fear over the distance from Harare to Mutare.

The aerodrome was in disrepair and she needed money to repair it, so that the President would travel with speed. After wide consultations with the relevant authorities, and President Obama, the money came. It wasn't much, and Queen had to add to it from her gold earnings and savings.

When the aerodrome was completed, she constructed a road from the aerodrome to Chikanga Shopping Centre that went through Sakubva, high up. The road, which she proposed to be called Freedom Way, was not for cars, but pedestrians only. Along it were beautifully constructed shops of various wares: clothes, food, beer, ice cream, baths, fish, traditional handy tools, you name it. Everything was well constructed and arranged. Along the Freedom Way were stairs, which people used when they got near their destination.

News had spread fast in the country that President Obama would be visiting, and the whole nation was abuzz with expectation. Every newspaper was keen to interview this ghetto woman who was bringing one of the most powerful men in the world to rural Mutare.

Queen Latifa appeared four times on TV.

She herself went up to Harare to meet Obama, and travelled with him and his entourage to Mutare by a hired small viscount plane. They left Harare in one of the rarest scenes many would capture for a century to come.

She was afraid the President would find the walk from the aerodrome to Chikanga Shopping Centre, where the Peace Project was, rather too long so, for this one time only in the history of the Freedom Way, they rode in two cars. And the crowds…. It seemed they wanted to swallow them.

But the atmosphere was ethereal. There was warmth and camaraderie everywhere, including across the city and the suburbs. For once the entire city and country stood as one, in respect and love for each other. Everyone was a friend, brother, sister…No more 'Comrade' The word 'Comrade' was buried forever on that day. People just became who they were…people. To love, live, enjoy, be fair, grow, and develop, together.

Queen Latifa led President Obama straight to the stage of the Peace Project and picked up the mike. She saw colourful, beautiful people all around her, and her heart was filled with emotion. She looked at President Obama (whom she held by the hand) and said into the mike, "Mr. President, I didn't know that dreams come true. Have they, in your life?"

As a matter of fact, Obama was about to snatch the mike from Queen Latifa's hand when she spoke into it. This time, he snapped the mike right out of her hand, and said, "Indeed, Queen Latifa...."

At the mention of "Queen Latifa" the crowds at the Peace Project, and those around the city and country exploded into a loud hoorah.

Apparently someone had connected the activity at the Peace Project to as many channels of communication in the world as possible, and the occasion was live to more than half the world.

Then somebody played a video of **Westlife's Life's song, Don't You that Dreams Come True.**

Obama turned to Queen Latifa, swung her into his hands and began a slow, tasty dance. The whole world danced with them, right to the end of the song.

But then somebody came up and whispered into Obama's ear, and he had to leave.

Years later, the joke that went round was that Obama had been told that there were Zanu supporters also looking at him, and it was not safe...

The Westlife song became so popular in the country that everywhere you went, it was played. Children sang it everywhere. It became a song of hope for the nation, especially looking at what they had gone through.

A year later, people and opposition parties demanded that there be elections. Because they were supported by international pressure, the government complied. Civic society heavily demanded that Queen Latifa be included as a presidential candidate, much against her will.

The government responded by stopping her mining operations. The entire nation campaigned heavily for her and she won, becoming the first female and second president of the country.

She had a huge job ahead of her, but had country-wide support, a strong cabinet and the entire world at their beck and calling.

Lyrics of the song 'Dreams Come True' were used to compose a new national anthem, which had the 'Ishe Komborera Africa' tune to it.

The celebrations that followed Queen Latifa's victory spanned across the nation, and everybody, including Zanu PF supporters, were in wild jubilation, similar to or better than 1980. There were no enemies, but a job to be done. First, she thought the word 'comrade' had been used and abused for too long, and preferred just to be called President or Ms. She would not give herself executive powers, but shared with her cabinet and national council.

After only a few months in her job, she was surprised to find that nobody wanted to be associated with Zanu PF anymore. Even the hardest opponents of the west, and proponents of Zanu agendas and missions, fell silent. Zanu cabinet ministers spent time in their homes, quietly living their lives, as they should have thirty years before.

A point to note was that a few years before the emergence of Queen Latifa as a leader, there had been talk in certain circles around the country about change never coming to Zimbabwe without bloodshed. People had vehemently said that since independence had come through bloodshed, change would not come without people dying. But that was proved wrong, as indeed, peace was achieved by peaceful means, just like the Zanu PF internal coup in 2017. Many people, organizations and other groups left the country in a huff when there was no genocide. Indeed Zimbabwe was a country for and of a patient and peaceful people.

THE CASE FOR DEMILITARIZATION IN ZIMBABWE

Ever since independence in 1980, Zimbabweans have been living under military rule, dominance and governance. When the war ended, war vets were unleashed into communities without any training in relations building, and persisted on what they'd been doing in the war, with freedom and licence from their government. War vets could enter school premises and disrupt the education process, clinics, hospitals and other public and private spaces at their will. This made people live in fear of them. Growing up youth, however, admired their lack of fear and respect, and wanted to be like them. The government aggravated the situation by its huge recruitment of soldiers, especially as they killed industry. Soldiers therefore, are second to war vets in social prestige and power in Zimbabwe. The same goes for the secretive and much feared Central Intelligence Organization (CIO)). Thus, Zimbabwe has been heavily militarized ever since its existence about 40 year ago, with disastrous consequences, and needs to demilitarize.

Demilitarization is a process of working towards a society which emphasizes the nonviolent resolution of conflicts, and personal and social justice. According to Harris (2006), for a society to be described as militarized, it has to have one or more of the following characteristics:

- the military controls or strongly influences government policies or action.
- there is a strong military ethos or strong ideals are dominant

Security is viewed as fundamentally a military matter and military imperatives dominate the security agenda

- the use of force or the threat to use force is high on the list of possible responses to any disputes which may arise.

All these characteristics have been present in Zimbabwe since independence. Demilitarization and significant and sustained reduction in the power and influence of the military personnel and force projection of the military can be indicated by reduction in military expenditures.

Most countries in Sub-Saharan Africa have significantly demilitarized, they have reduced their military sizes and expenses. However, the bulk of the militarization has happened in South Africa, Angola and Ethiopia.

It is surprising that while other countries are demilitarizing, considering the rate at which Zimbabwe has been increasing is military makes one wonder for what other purpose except to threaten its own people and crush them when they seek a living through illegal trading that support their lives. This is what has been happening over the years. Otherwise, which country do they want to fight? So, actually Zimbabwe is becoming a super power against its own people. This is untenable, and should not be accepted by the international community.

Hariss (ibid) also offers 7 reasons for demilitarizing.

The first is that globally, the nature of wars has changed. Almost all armed conflicts now occur within countries rather than between them. This is normally between government and groups which want power. These armed conflicts involve militias, armed civilians and guerillas as well as regular soldiers; small arms are the major cause of battle deaths and as many as 90% of casualties are civilians who die mainly of hunger and disease which occur as a result of armed conflict.

Secondly, the meaning of security has changed. The traditional definition of security as protection against external military threats, has changed. These days the type and source of threats now facing developing countries are much wider and more complex. Human security is more relevant today, and it focuses on economic, food, health, environmental, personal, community and political security. The UN estimates that a person in a developing country (such as Zimbabwe), is 33 times more likely to die as a result of structural violence or 'social neglect' than as a result of inter-country war. This means that our way of thinking about security needs to move from an emphasis on territorial security based on a strong military towards broader human security based on improving levels of human development.

Third, military expenditure retards economic development. In economic terms, it has no value. According to Dumas (2000) military activity does not grow food, it does not produce clothing, it does not build housing, and it does not keep people amused. Nor does it create the kind of machinery, equipment and facilities that can be used to (produce such services). Military activity may have other kinds of value, but it has no economic value because it does not directly contribute to material wellbeing.

In addition, military expenditure does not provide a stream of returns in the future, as does government expenditure on education, health and infrastructure.

Wheraas some high military expenditure countries may encourage both domestic and foreign investors due to stabilizing or growth enhancing influence on the economy, this has not happened in the case of Zimbabwe, because the military is clearly a destabilizing influence and likely to engage in coups. Military expenditure also has opportunity costs and may constrain more productive government expenditures. It also accrues a lot of debt.

Poverty reduction is achieved by encouraging economic growth by minimizing government involvement in the economy and maximizing the role of the private sector. While the initial beneficiaries will be business people, benefits are expected throughout society and thus reduce absolute poverty. In Zimbabwe as things stand, even rapid growth may make little or no no difference to the lives of the people.

The military also uses both human and physical resources which would have positive social rates of return in other uses. These include skilled labour, and land.

The fourth reason why Zimbabwe should demilitarize is that the military negatively affects human rights. People are denied their economic rights by expenditures on the military. People have also been abused by the military, especially in Zimbabwe and other African countries. Cases are widespread of the military attacking rioters, demonstrators, so-called illegal miners, cross border traders and other groups of people doing things that are constitutionally allowed.

Fifth, the military is ineffective in resolving conflicts. Whereas it can be effective in the short term in winning a war, this normally doesn't do anything to the underlying causes of the conflict, thus leading to renewed warfare. The military focuses on stopping the fighting only, and not the underlying causes.

Six, there are ethical, moral and spiritual reasons not to deal with disputes by force. At the level of the heart, humankind knows that the use of force or the threat to use force is not the appropriate way of dealing with disputes. Religion also rejects the demonization of the enemy to make them appear more evil, less human and therefore psychologically easier to kill. Moral means must be used to achieve moral ends. If violence is used to achieve peace, its use will corrupt the victor as to make meaningful peace unattainable. In terms of international status among African countries, there is an incompatibility between being regarded as a peacemaker and maintaining a high level of militarization.

The seventh and last reason is that there are cost-effective alternatives to the military. The military is not the only way of achieving security, and it is no longer a cost-effective way of doing so, if it ever was. To achieve socio-economic development for its millions of people in poverty, alternative approaches to achieving security should be found and implemented. As things stand, the military do not help anybody, but protect corrupt politicians and help them loot the economy without question from the people.

The good thing is that soldiers in the military themselves know it, and morale is very low. This is unsustainable, and could explode any time.

After discussions and we fail to agree, we will settle for a small, well-maintained and trained crach unit, of a thousand or less.

The Definition of 'Peace' by International and Zimbabwean Standards

Unlike elsewhere the world over, in Zimbabwe, peace means silence. It means absence of gunfire sounds. It means quiet. Despite the presence of food, it should include peace of mind, and that means money, a job, a comfortable home, affording a holiday, traveling anywhere you want, associating with whoever you want and saying whatever comes to mind about anything or anybody. These definitions are enshrined in the beautifully worded and wide reaching constitution, derived from the UN itself, but none of them has ever happened in Zimbabwe since 1980, especially between the rulers and the ruled. The reason is obvious, the rulers know that they're doing a stupid job, and don't want you to spread it. They're scared to lose their position of power and money.

As they do in the Zimbabwean political scenario, once you get a chance, use it. Use it to spoil your many friends and show them that yes, you're in the money.

It's quite embarrassing the way we Zimbabweans keep taking and taking, for the self. We seem to never get satisfied, yet across the road, a family is starving. My guess is it's because of the long history of poverty: generation after generation of poverty. So they want to compensate for that. And the worse thing is that their chain of family never ends. You want to give everyone just a piece, and you want an affirmation of your 'zvangu zvaita' culture. Some invest in mansions from Harare to Dubai. They can afford it, the country is rich. But it is rich to them only, and they don't want to share, and so are called looters. So, looters are not only in government, but across the country, but with links to Zanu PF.

But things can be different. A new order can be set. One that I call the Freedom Generation. This country is rich enough, as all our neighbours and others beyond know. We can all afford to live happily at peace, as defined in this book. The people to create that space for that new generation are there in Zimbabwe, in abundance.

The potential threat to demilitarization and national healing lies in Zanu PF, which has an old, skewed understanding of security. If we consult as widely as possible, at the back of their mind always will be the fearful suspicion that the people we consult have an intention to loot our gold and other minerals, and do not do an honest job. They suspect everybody because of their past, and because they want to loot the gold themselves and share it among themselves, while the nation wallows in poverty.

The Next Step for Zimbabweans

Zanu PF has declared over and over that freedom from colonial rule and independence came for Zimbabwe by the gun. It never mentions people or negotiations, even though there was the Lancaster House Conference in 1979, which paved way for general elections in 1980. Everyone was Zanu PF, then, and they all voted for it. That did not mean Zimbabweans loved war, but they were tired of it. Even the Lancaster House talks were initiated by complaints and cries of innocent civilians being the major casualties, and Smith agreed. It took a lot of effort to convince Zanu PF, which was still busy killing civilians.

Now, if Zanu PF came by the gun, and ruled 40 years by the gun so far, doesn't it follow that it can only be removed by the gun?

Constant references to the gun by Zanu PF shows that they're afraid. They know they lost the people and can't go on, peacefully.

At the height of stealing elections in 2008, many young men were ready and prepared to take up guns and fight Zanu PF. Only it was not spread enough, and lacked leadership and coordination.

Up to now, Zimbabweans are still ready. They're even readier now than before, because of the conditions they're living in.

I'm not advocating violence. Like the late Morgan Tsvangirai, founder of the MDC, I'm all for peace, and a peaceful transition. But oftentimes in the field of peace, you meet people like in Zanu PF, who can only be silenced by violent noise, and after that, peace prevails. Yes, indeed, war can be used as a means to peace. Zanu PF did it, and we celebrated briefly, but that peace is gone under their grip. We must derive lessons from that, and never use violence as a means to achieve permanent, sustainable peace. Violence can only be used as a last resort, and extensive negotiations come soon after. This never happened in Zimbabwe. It was one-man rules throughout, up to now.

It is when we follow the steps towards successful national healing exercise as prescribed in this book, extend it to family and interpersonal levels that for the first time, most Zimbabweans feel really at peace, and for the second, to the Last Rhodesian and Independence generations.

It would be a memorable way to say goodbye to the planet, leaving it at peace.

THE AFRICAN GHETTO AND ITS CULTURE

I was shocked the other day to hear that the word 'ghetto' has pejorative and racist interpretations. Though I was born in a village, a lot of my friends, acquaintances and neighbours were born and grew up in the ghetto. Today, I live in the ghetto, and brought up my family in the ghetto. I've worked in the ghetto as a teacher for 16 years nonstop.

Let me explain my conception of an African ghetto. It is a residential area with a high concentration of people. Some people call it high density suburb, but who wants to call it that?

To us, it is a ghetto.

All the characters in the book live in the ghetto. The setting is in the ghetto. The things that end up happening in the country start in the ghetto, no matter what they are.

A point to note is that our ghettos are not squalid, lowly or dirty. We have some of the best houses in the entire city, in the ghetto. I will post a video of some of the houses in my ghetto, but you can tell from pictures in Soweto, and other ghettos.

The more important point I want to make about the African ghetto is that it was always the source of change for the better for the entire nation. Zanu PF was born in the Highfield ghetto, and so was Kenneth Kaunda's UNIP, and Nyerere's Chama Cha Mapindizi and the Tanganyika African National Union, and Kenyatta's Kenya African National Union (KANU). The ghetto has always had the highest concentration of the brightest minds to drive a national agenda.

Of course, it was also against oppressors. I remember a place for struggle against oppression (including our own Freedom Corner and the Breeze at the Chikangaz), as well as feats against an oppressive system. I remember the exploits of the Harare guy. Norman Karimanzira, who stole a Cold Storage Company vehicle, full of pork, and vanished with it. Only that he was eventually caught. Eventually, the guy became nationally known as Cold Storage

The ghetto was the place where it was all happening. It was the place for bonding with one's community. Young babies, growing young men and women, grownups, all mixed and learned from each other. You got all the news you wanted about the entire country, from the ghetto. It was the inspiration, when morale and spirit were low. It was where you learned everything, and brought back everything you learned from abroad. It was where all life and skills to survive it was learned, because it had the best, hardened and loving teachers.

So what happened to the ghetto? Why did it die after independence, to an extent that people have no source of money, are always broke, think only of politics, wait for their parents' death to be free, etc?

Zanu PF killed ghetto life. It never invested in the ghetto, where the people who drive the nation are. There are no parks, no shades, nothing to do in the stadiums, no spirit of sport in the people, and no beer to while away time drinking.

Ghetto play and social centres are full of maize fields, vegetables, beans, okra, mhunga. Tomatoes, potatoes or anything to get a living. There's no free space. And that is independence and freedom, to them.

To add to that, they installed soldiers who stay not in their barracks, but in the ghetto, monitoring and spying on the people.

As a result, the people are scared.

However, I'm hereby making a statement that the ghetto is back. We will once again develop our urban communities and empower them. I ask that people in various centres and growth points around the country, look around themselves and start finding ways of improving them. One person could start suggesting sites, activities, services and structures, and we all join in the discussion, then we implement those activities together.

Let us never forget that the ghetto was always the place with the highest concentration of open minds. All those indigenous Zimbabweans living flashy lives in leafy suburbs across the country, have their roots in the ghetto. They are ghetto graduates. Today, the ghetto, as before should drive national politics, business, education and everything else.

My aim is to revive the ghetto culture in our townships. They should be areas of fun and enjoyment, but also where it all begins; creativity, originality, skills development, personal growth and life itself. Instead of community life being activated and improved by communications inventions like WhatsApp, people are embroiled in conflicts by them. Things must change.

My campaign is therefore championed by all ghetto dwellers in Zimbabwe, from Gaza in Chipinge, to Sakubva, Vengere, Macheke, Dombotombo, Highfielf, Mufakose, Mucheke in Masvingo to Mbizo, Mkoba, Makokoba, Lupane and Jahunda in Gwanda.

This does not mean I exclude those who stay in villages and on farms. NO!!

We're together, but as it was in the beginning, the ghetto is made up of people from the rural areas and farms, too. So we're in this together, Ghetto Stylee!

Now, I'm glad that some people in the ghetto have maintained ghetto life and ghetto culture. A good example is the WhasApp group PaKurauone. These are Sakubva, Chikanga and Dangamvura guys who originated in the oldest Mutare Township, Sakubva. They mostly meet **PaMwamuka** or Uncle John Munos place, near the stadium. In those two places, the guys play their ghetto style and spread the ghetto culture. That is a good start.

What I therefore ask is for all ghetto communities to form WhatsApp groups, chat, mix and mingle. Please, be sure to include me in your group. Get my number from 'Tsano Mbuu' on +44 7931 892525, or the guys in the Pakurauone WhatsApp group. We want to revive our African, traditional ghetto culture, of course, moving with the times. Zanu PF is dead and buried. The ghetto said it long ago, but it is final now. Ghetto Style-e is back!

PAMWAMUKA, NOVEMBER, 2019

This Friday it is Farai who has the cash. He holds a Castle Lager quart in his right hand, which he swings to his mouth in slow, elaborate motions. The left is half buried in the front pocket of his faded jeans. One foot rests on a rock, and he gazes this way and that feigning deep boredom. Forgetting that he no longer carries a big belly, he belches exaggeratedly, spreading his arms sideways. I suppress a laugh.

We are at Mwamuka Shopping Centre in Sakubva. I too am drinking-a pint of cold water. I quit beer, because it didn't make any more sense. How could I buy a beer at $10 a quart? Or $5 a pint?

I need money for a lot other needs, not beer.

Tendai emerges from the Maonde Bar direction, ever walking fast, for no apparent reason. "Hesi Eddie", he says to me.

"How far?" I ask in the latest greeting lingo these days. It means two things: How are you, and what are you doing, mostly. It also means a lot other things, depending on the situation or as a reference point to what happened the last time you met.

"Zvakadhakwa izvi[15]", Tendai responds sitting down on a bigger rock, facing Farai and me.

"Fatso, please make me one," he says.

"Iwe, I told you. I'm not the one who told you to leave teaching, ok? Do you want me to go and steal? Who would take care of my family?"

---

[15]   It's useless, meaningless. Literally, 'drunk.'

"Ha-a-a get away! Stealing what? I know you have the money. You just don't want to buy me, you're so ungrateful…?

"Look, it's not my funeral that you are poor, ok? You father is poor, and so is your mother, sister, uncle, your team called Dynamos and your government. It's not my fault either that you have no relatives to send you money from the diaspora, neither is it my fault that you left your teaching job. Go back! Others are making a living out of it! Leave me alone, will you?"

With that, Farai thrust his hand deeper into the pocket, shifted feet on the rock, and then in a wide arch-like movement brought the bottle to his lips. He took long noisy gulps, his Adam's apple bobbing up and down and the beer trickling down the corners of his mouth.

In spite of myself, I laughed at Farai's flashes, or 'bling'. That hurt Tendai, but he bravely bore it, looking up the sky, sideways at the grinding mill, and down. Watching him there, on the bare rock with his knees up close to the chin, I'm afraid he looked very much like our newspaper logo, a baboon. I suppressed a laugh.

The guys were almost all there this Friday, including Shellaz, Sheppie and Tony. Bonono hung around the verandah, trying to organize a braai. The first and (most likely) last one of the month.

"But seriously, Farai," I said, "how can you expect him to go back to teaching? There is nothing there…"

"He's Zanu PF and he should demonstrate his patriotism. Besides, others are at it. It keeps him occupied and it's better than begging, like he's doing… Besides, I don't give money to idiots like him. There are too many of them, and if we keep feeding them, they might think everything is fine in the country. Because of their large majority, idiots vote for a wrong candidate, who is like them, always, and that candidate wins…" Fatso laughed as he finished.

"What about you?" asked Tendai with fury," Where do you work? What else do you do but live off your sister in London? And do you know how she earns that money? She's a participant in pornographic movies…?

Knowing Farai, I expected him to explode at that, (especially the part about his sister) and jump for Tendai, but he did not. That meant this story was not new to him, and was either true or Farai had grown too used to it to raise his anger.

"It is not the source of the money that counts, but the money itself, and what you do with it. Have you forgotten how your mother raised you up and sent you to teachers 'college? She fucked every man in the National Railways and brewed every illicit liquor you could imagine. I could have fucked your mother, Tindo, but I refused her." Then pointing a thick finger at Tendai he continued, "Your problem is in your pride, Tindo, mfanami. You said teaching was boring and hoped with a teaching background, the world would be yours. How you misread! And now this!!"

The guys always took an opportunity to get the better of the other. That was fun to them, and that was how they lived. It kept collective memories of the good old days, and individual hopes alive,

Honestly, though, they liked each other, a lot. They had gone through a lot in life together, from birth in the 60s, school, independence, life under Mugabe, the Gukurahundi massacres, the HIV &Aids pandemic, cholera, the birth of a first child, Operation Murambatsvina, and all the twists and turns of Zimbabwean life.

They were survivors, with a capital 's'. They had even survived Mugabe's rule. The only challenge left for them was to survive Zanu PF. That was a huge one, but possible. It had come close many times before, and it was feasible. For that, they deserved international medals. All they had to do was hang around and see. They didn't want any pressure, but care and patience.

"Eddie," said Tendai, his face suddenly brightening up.

"Yes?" I answered

"Do you want to know the truth? The real truth?"

"About what?"

"This guy (pointing at Farai) that everybody calls Mabhavha. Everybody thinks it's because he drinks quarts only."

"Of course, that is the reason," said Farai matter of factly. "What other reason could there be? Quarts are bhavhas everywhere you go."

"Yes, but not everyone who drinks quarts is called Mabhavha. Why is it you only?"

"I drink them every day...Who else can afford that?"

"No. Eddie, let me tell you. About five years ago at Christmas, this guy was invited by his sister up in Greenside. You know, she is married to a mhene, a real rich bugger. As you know, things started to get really tough last year. Most people drank Chibuku, not lager. Anyone who bought you a lager that time was a real M'vet. People like Fatso-they could not even afford vhinyu, let alone sweets and napkins for their babies..."

"I don't have babies..."

"They were happy with Kariba Mhamba. So when Fatso was invited up there, he was over the moon. As he walked the whole way up there, he kept singing to himself, "Lager! Lager! Lager! Lager!"

"There in Greenside his brother in law gave him two or three from the fridge, and then Fatso suggested they go kwaMax, the shopping centre. They drank at full throttle. Fatso's intention had been to return home around 5 or 6, but the joy kept piling up. He completely forgot about home, wife and kids. From Max they drove back home, with more beer.

"In the house, Fatso grew really excited. He thanked his in-law over and over again, saying all sorts of meaningless things that embarrassed both the in-law and his sister. And then he demanded to kiss him. The in-law said nay, but Fatso insisted."

As Tendai told his story. Farai just listened, a bored and contemptuous expression on his face.

"Time-time, after dinner they retired for bed. The couple had a young son, about 10, and Fatso shared a room with him. Soon, Fatso was snoring. Deep into the night, he felt a wetness all around him. He panicked. How could it be? He had never wetted his bed before. He felt all over the bed with his hands, and his fears were confirmed, the bed was wet all over. Luckily, he had somehow remembered to take off his clothes before falling in, and they were dry.

"So to avoid embarrassment, Fatso hatched a plan. He looked over at the other side, and saw that the boy was fast asleep. Slowly, he got out of his bed, and tip-toed to the boy's. He listened to the breathing again and, satisfied that it was the regular breathing of someone fast asleep, he gently removed the linen off the boy, lifted him up, and deposited him into his own bed. Then Fatso himself got into the boy's bed. Problem solved, he said to himself, and soon was snoring again.

"Early in the morning he woke up, wanting to visit the loo. He sat up, lifted one leg out of bed and lo, a lump of faeces was deposited onto the carpet. He was shocked! Again? How could this have happened? He lifted the other leg, and another lump fell off it. Suddenly, the whole room was full of the smell. Again, panic seized him. What was this?

"As he sat there, contemplating his next move, he heard a small voice say, "Morning, Uncle."

"He looked across to the other bed and sure enough, the boy was awake, watching him with interest. He sat hopelessly as he saw his plan fall apart. Of course, he could clean up the room and flush the stuff into the toilet, but what about the linen? In the end that was what he planned to do. Without saying a thing to the kid, he stood up, put on his trousers, and tip toed into the passage. He noticed a rag in the bathroom corner, but before he took it, he heard the sound of a door opening. He froze. There were voices all over the house, a sign that people were very much awake.

"As he turned to go back into the room, he noticed a large dish, which we call a bhavha in Shona. Without thinking, he took it into the room. The first thing he did was scoop the stuff on the floor, and deposited it into the dish. Then he lifted the blankets, sheets and all and dumped them into the dish as well. For some reason, he turned the dish upside down. All this was in the eyes of the little boy. Then hurriedly, Fatso put on his clothes-shoes and all, and was out through the side door. He ran all the way back to Sakubva," Tendai finished, laughter ringing from somewhere in his throat.

I couldn't help laughing, too; in fact tears rolled down my face, an eye on Fatso, who kept saying, "He's lying! Of course he's lying!"

Then Rex came up. Rex owns one of the shops at Mwamuka, and most of the drinking that happens there is at his place. 'Hey, what's making you laugh like so?" he asked

"All I could do was point at Farai. And that was when he snapped. He dived for Tendai at full swing, but with the alacrity of a cat, Tindo stood up and darted out of reach. Farai made an effort to follow but had no chance against Tendai's lean athletic legs, so he gave up.

"What is it?" Rex asked again.

I told him Tendai's story, skipping the minor details. Afterwards Rex said, "But do you know why Tindo himself is called Polona?"

"No", I replied, but ventured a reason I had imagined by myself, "Is it not because of his clean, polony-coloured bald head?"

"Ah, not that", said Rex. And he continued, "So you don't know about his penchant for widows? Everybody knows that his main source of income are widows. Why he comes here mostly is to find out who has died-among the men of the location, so that he goes after the widow. He wipes out everything! And he starts by making visits just to change electricity bulbs."

'That is cruel," I remarked. Of course, Farai knew about that and he readily agreed with me.

"So why is he called Polona?" I asked, still not understanding.

"Because he never uses a condom on all those women…" said Rex.

It took a while for my brain to make the link, and then again, I laughed.

"By the way," said Tendai later that day, when we were gathered in Rex's bakkie, "Are you joining Queen Latifa at her Chikanga Peace Project, this weekend?"

"Of course," replied Fatso, "that one will always be my girl. How can I leave her? We'll be together till death!"

"Liar!" bellowed Tindo, "she is no longer interested in you! What would she benefit from useless clueless people like you? Just admit it, you lost her, bum!"

"Who told you that? We are still tight, my bro. wherever, she goes, whatever she does, she will always be my girl!"

"When did she last give you money, or some piece job?"

"That is not important. The important thing is she's still my lady. You can go anywhere you want, or do anything, but I'll be here, with her."

Do you see how that girl has risen?"

"In leaps and bounce, since that arrest. She rose from the ashes to instant international stardom! And boy oh boy, did I pine to be by her side! And there was my hero, Obama, on stage with her. What a lovey night. I wanted to be in somebody's arms, but I was. Kkkkk. "In double arms!"

"That girl will go far. Mark my words. Better get closer to her now. That's your line for money, boy."

"No. You go for her. I found a new channel for my money. I have this vision and dream of forming a church."

"What? A church? Preaching the gospel? And Tindo began to laugh.

"Yes. I have this revelation. About the immediate future of this country. I want to save people."

Fuck. I see you're serious. I wish you well, man. Wish me luck."

"Fuck you ..."

"Fuck you too, man."

And those were the words they mostly parted with, accompanied with a hug, most times…To meet again, in a totally different scenario, with different actors and characters.

And I, Edward Chinhanu, your ghetto writer, will be there when they meet, to bring you their latest adventures and escapades

SPECIAL MESSAGE TO ZIMBABWEANS AT HOME AND ABROAD

However much the characters in this book, along with fellow Zimbabweans across the world might hate ZANU PF, or try to hide from their conflict in religion and other areas, it remains, and Zanu PF is ruling. Just as Mugabe declared over and over during his reign, Tsvangirai did not rule Zimbabwe. His MDC lost the last election in 2018, even though it was among many popular characters on the Zimbabwean political front.

Now, listen to Mnangagwa and his country-wide talk from Mugabe's era, up to his own inauguration: 'Muchangovukura (You shall bark), muchingovukura (and still continue to bark) isu tichingotonga (while we continue to rule).

By whatever means and ways, ZANU PF will continue to rule Zimbabwe. An investigation must be made into that statement. Is it because the opposition is poor, or it's because Zanu PF has some mysterious means to get into power, and continue ruling, whoever and whatever the opposition is?

If not, such a careless statement by a leader, to the people who will sustain his leadership, is intolerable, and prosecutable.

How can you refer to fellow citizens as dogs? Because only dogs bark.

I feel like shedding tears when I hear my fellow Zimbabweans suffer and be spoken to like this. Yet they remain quiet, and create jokes out of such insults.

Clearly, like a man possessed, Mnangagwa wants war. He wants anyone who wants him out of office to remove him by war, otherwise he won't go.

And as we go through our barking, about power cuts, lack of jobs, industry, money, stolen elections, abuse by the military and other problems, they continue to rule, whether by design or hook and crook, and continue to mess up the country, while the opposition is at sixes and sevens, with some supporting Zanu PF.

Remember, in a widely circulated video, it was Mnangagwa who restrained Mugabe from fleeing the country after he'd conceded electoral defeat to Tsvangirai and the MDC in 2008, one of the most violent years in independent Zimbabwe.

And after the coup, it was Mnangagwa who cared for Mugabe's health, paid the bills and accorded Mugabe's wife, Grace, a lot of luxuries, including hiring a jet to travel from Malaysia to bury her mother. That was during the cholera epidemic, when thousands of Zimbabweans were dying. Mnangagwa and Mugabe could be a team and not enemies. as we thought.

The question Zimbabweans must grapple with for the next decades should be: What was it about Zanu PF that made the best minds in the country fail so dismally to work? This should be closely followed by a study into how Mugabe so intricately managed to divide world opinion, manipulate it to his advantage while at the same time managing to control a delicate situation at home.

A partial answer to these questions was provided by a friend the other day," Zanu PF got this country from the bush, so if we continue to make trouble, they'll return us where they got us from. We are not stationary, in one position, as other nations move forward. We are going backwards, to the bush, and surely to the soil."

As the truth showed on the ground, Mugabe took the brains of millions of Zimbabweans, their hopes and dreams and lives, and plastered them on the walls of his State House. Mnangagwa, on the other hand, seized a hammer and gun and bludgeoned them. There was no rest. Some people dared to ask who was the better dictator between them? The answer is none.

The reality on the ground is that Zimbabwe is a nation in waiting mode. Zimbabweans are waiting for power (electricity) every day. They are also waiting in queues at hospitals, to exchange money, at a food handout occasion, at a combi or bus rank, they are waiting for a better day, a better political leadership and a new dawn. The wait seems long and distant, but the world can save it.

I am therefore suggesting that we cannot wait for Zanu PF forever, to quit power voluntarily or through elections or a court judgment. That will never happen. My suggestion, fellow Zimbabweans across the world, is that we get rid of Zanu PF and commence our National Healing and Reconciliation programme on 01 January, 2020, and move onwards. That time, called the transitional justice period, will see us purge ourselves of our political divisions and enmity, come and work together as one nation.

I am giving Zanu PF until 31 December this year, before they leave power and the country. I think that is ample time.

I suggest we enlist the services of Father Fidelis Mukonori to take the lead in that process, and I help him out, here and there. Father Mukonori and I will be the middle men to stand in between Zanu PF and the MDC. For two years he will be transitional president or chairman or whatever title you choose. As we work on the transitional government, we will pick our cabinet from any party or section of society in consultation with the parties. The transitional government has two clear objectives:

1. To start the national healing and reconciliation programme and set it in irreversible mode
2. To establish the culture for Zimbabwean presidency. We will move around our ghettoes, farms and villages talking to people about the kind of presidency we want for Zimbabwe

We will also use our term to demonstrate to Zimbabweans that they're a loving, peaceful people, and that their president doesn't have to live in barricaded mansions surrounded with soldiers, or travel in armoured motorcades, or have nightmares in sleep, but lives happily with and for the people.

That was what we expected at independence, but got guns and sjamboeks instead. Yet Mandela demonstrated it was possible. In fact, the rise of Mandela to the world should have been Mugabe's. But he dwindled with it by living in the past.

He thought he'd found a personal kingdom in Zimbabwe, and Mnangagwa think so too.

Let me show them.

After the two years, you, Zimbabweans will decide on the next step, though my feeling after seeing the efforts of the MDC at its sixes and sevens, would be to hand over to their president, Nelson Chamisa to complete our remaining 3 years. This is only fair in resolving the political conflict, because he alone hasn't had the chance to feel the seat, and Zanu PF has for 40 years. Meanwhile National Healing and Reconciliation programme may continue.

Then, we have a general election, in which everyone's eyes, even from across the world, will be open. If Zanu PF want to contest, they can do so at their embarrassment and peril, because it will be a free and fair election, in the truest sense of the expression.

I promise not to contest that election. In fact, I'm not even a politician. When I told a few close friends my plans and intentions, their first reaction was utter surprise, "You?" they asked, presidential material?" and they laughed.

To add to that, I don't even carry any bling with me. For that, read **PaMwamuka, November 2019.**

That is why I'm suggesting the name of Father Fidelis Mukonori to head the National Healing and Reconciliation operation, and I work with him on that, as well as the transitional justice and presidential culture project.

My feeling is that The National Healing and Reconciliation exercise should extend to personal, family or other disputes and longstanding misunderstandings in families, couples and acquaintances. This would give our efforts the much desired national peace and reconciliation. It will be an interesting time to look back at our past and chart the way forward.

Meanwhile, Mai Shingisai Suluma would have set us into gear with a two-night nonstop live show, for which she will be ready and willing.

Like Queen Latifa in the book, a lot of our women have Zanu PF children, from the rapes and loves during the liberation struggle, to independence. Our approach to National Healing must effect the idea that we are one family, one nation, one people. However, we all know what is right, and it must be done, for our continued survival. Impunity must be fought, at all levels of our society.

It must also teach us that we cannot accept the same dominance by one unwanted group of people or culture, especially one exhibited and maintained by violence.

We should remember, as we go through the process how difficult it was to remove the colonialist, and count the blessings we got under Zanu PF.

After all, they are a minute lot. Don't be shocked to discover that the people who've been dominating and abusing us for such a long time are a very tiny group, with strong links to another tiny group in the military. Can you be scared of such a small minority of ruthlessly greedy looters, who follow politics of the belly?

We also know there are tens of thousands of Rhodesians scattered across the globe. Zimbabwe is your home. We will give everyone an opportunity to contribute to a new Zimbabwe. That is what Tongogara and the real freedom fighters died for.

A lot of people blame Zimbabweans like you and I for our situation. They blame us for being too docile, failing to use circumstances and opportunities when they arise, lacking unity of purpose and powerlessness. I tell them 'No'.

Now, I'm asking these people watch you as you do your thing with Zanu PF, this time around. They will know who you really are, smart, intelligent, patient, loving, hardworking. The Best Laughing People on the Planet. These are the factors that stopped us from engaging in widespread violence with Mugabe and Mnangagwa during the past 40 years. And of course, it must be noted, we don't just laugh at anything or any time. We must be really tickled, first, for our laughter to show.

We ask them to watch again, from your experiences and mine, as the **Independence Generation** takes centre stage in liberating the country from misrule.

They, including you and me and the younger generations, will learn a lot about how independence came about, as Smith fell. The mission is the same, but the subject different, Zanu PF must fall.

My appeal to the world is: We cannot do anything alone, as Zimbabweans. Please don't wait until we kill each other, and then shout 'Genocide!' as was the Rwanda case in 1994.

This is very close, especially if and when you read **Farai's Dream.** That is the worst case scenario for Zimbabwe, while the Best case is cast by **Queen Latifa**.

What I'm doing is nothing extraordinarily brave or heroic. I'm just doing what any normal, healthy, concerned citizen would do. Any Zimbabwean at this time in our history, including those in Zanu PF can do it, and we support them.

Even Killer Zivhu, that recently fired well- known Zanu PF sycophant, could do it. In fact, as I write this book and accomplish my mission, I feel the same as Mugabe himself, Joshua Nkomo Tongogara, Solomon Mujuru, Sydney Malunga and many others who fought in the war must have felt as they prepared to cross over for the fight to liberate Zimbabwe. This is exactly how I feel, and it's a mixture of many feelings, chief among them, victory.

When my friends left me to join the struggle in Mozambique in 1977 (from Mutambara High School), I felt very bad. Little did I know that my turn would come. Now, it is up to Mnangagwa and his team, to be stubborn, like Ian Smith was and face global shame and embarrassment, or do what the people say and live in your motherland.

If I'd crossed over and trained as a guerrilla, my nom de guerre would have been 'Captain Sensible', or 'Ghetto Style-e'. Ghetto Style-e simply means, Ghetto Style, which is loving, neighbourly, smart, friendly, compassionate, adventurous and all-embracing. That is what I hope to be, in my mission.

Enjoy the read! I know that to most Zimbabwean men, the most familiar story is **Farai Narrowly but Briefly Escapes the Zim rot.** Those in the diaspora may also find **The Highs and Lows of Ghetto Life** interesting. There are many others, just enjoy the read!

On a parting note, let me say this: Guys, our country is rich, and we don't need to be howling about imaginary sanctions, or working three jobs for a living. Remember, Ian Smith survived real world sanctions, with the same wealth. At that time, there were no advanced communication systems like we have now, there were no diamonds or high education, and oil was fully imported. Things have changed now, to our advantage, mostly, but the guys in Zanu PF don't see it. They live in the past, in the bush.

My message to them is: They must go back to the bush alone. The Zimbabweans they liberated want progress, development, civilisation and a better, longer life.

Ndatenda.

HOW TO EAT SADZA

G uys, this is who we are. This is where we came from. This is what makes us who we are: smart, strong, patient, and hardworking without giving up. I know that things have changed and we eat everything and anything these days, but I'm taking you back to good old sadza, jembe, jest, lumo, tsima, mukonde, etc. The names for this food are endless. Enjoy the meal!

Sadza should be eaten hot, served straight from the fire without slicing it like a wedding cake.

Eating it with a spoon or fork is an insult to the maize meal itself. It is a taboo, and is sure to distort the real taste

You should feel your fingers burn when you dig them into the edible mountain and reflexively pull them back at first, a confirmation that the sadza is steaming at the right temperature.

You can't wait for it to cool down, because its flavour wanes as it cools. You pinch a piece of the sadza and mould it to your preferred consistency before carving a small crate into it and dipping it into your usavi. It is common knowledge that the size of the sadza should always be greater than the amount of usavi, but you should finish them both at the same time.

The meal is eaten continuously and in silence as there's no joy in eating while doing something else or having a conversation. You can't even watch something while eating sadza. The only thing that goes with sadza is a radio tuned to a channel playing old African songs.

In fact, sadza eaten while sitting on the floor like a witchdoctor is tastier than sadza eaten on the dining table. Without interruptions, you eat, and eat, and eat, only pausing to lick the greens off your fingers.

As a rule, the last piece of sadza is for wiping the usavi plate and scooping every remaining trace of stew to conclude your dish. Drink two jugs of water and rip out a loud, satisfied belch. A thin line of sweat should form around your hairline by the time you're done

AUTHOR'S NOTE

I had a discussion with my wife about the subtitle of the book: 'A Peacebuilder's Quest to End Zimbabwe's Political Conflict'. She suggested 'Resolve' in place of 'End', because, to her, 'ending the conflict gave the impression that I was so sure the conflict would be terminated, and 'resolving' it gave the impression of attempting to end that conflict.

But I said nay, 'resolving' the conflict gave the impression of a high tower attempt, using tricky things like theories and sophisticated creations, yet the message and effort was simple and straight forward. The good thing is that in my context, both terms mean the same. We should mend the fissures, gorges and ravens that have divided us for so long, as a nation. The time is now, or never!

In any case 'resolving' a conflict and 'ending' are the same, just like Zanu PF and the MDC. For more of that, please read **The Meeting**, and **Queen Latifa's Views on the MDC** under the topic **Queen Latifa's Perceptions of the Zimbabwe Political and Business Environment**

AUTHOR BACKGROUND

A teacher, writer, peacebuilder and Transitional Justice Fellow, Edward Chinhanu has lived and worked the bulk of his life in the high density suburbs of Sakubva, Dangamvura and Chikanga in Mutare, Zimbabwe's fourth city. He is passionate about ghetto life and its vibrancy, creativity and unity of purpose. He believes, with evidence, that traditionally, the African ghetto has contained the highest concentration of creative minds in every country. To his surprise, however, the ghetto has died at independence. For seven consecutive years Edward maintained a column in the *Manica Post* newspaper, **Letter from the Ghetto.** Edward has added ghetto life and culture to his research interests, besides narratives and their contribution to peace and conflict.

Edward is passionate about writing, and among his achievements is a Commonwealth Award in 1999-2000, for his story, 'A Christmas Present for Monica', which is about the aftermaths of Zimbabwe's violent conflict. After the publication of this book, he plans to start a weekly or monthly column on how Zimbabweans cope with their political conflict, especially those from the ghetto. It will follow the lives of Farai and Shupi in the book, as well as Queen Latifa as the new president of a new, free Zimbabwe. Be sure not to miss it!

As Zimbabwe's Local Peace Expert for Peace Direct, a British international peace organisation, Edward wrote several articles and stories on the conflict in Zimbabwe, and promoting peace, between 2015vand 2018. His work can be found on www.peaceinsight.authors

Edward plans to use some of the proceeds from his book sales to fund his organisation, Africa Centre for Peacebuilding and Conflict Transformation (ACPC, email: www.acpc.org.zw).